Bless you dear read

Love Alison

#ReluctantlyPsych.

#StandUpBePsychicBeProud!

Reluctantly Psychic

Concept created by Alison Ward

Reluctantly Psychic

Copyright 2020 © Alison Ward with permission of all contributors

www.reluctantlypsychic.co.uk

ISBN 978-1-913713-01-0

First published in Great Britain by Compass-Publishing

A catalogue record of this book is available from the British Library

Set and designed by The Book Refinery Ltd

All rights reserved. No part of this publication may be reproduced, stored in a retrieval system, or transmitted in any form or by any means, electronic, mechanical, photocopying, recording or otherwise without the prior permission of the publishers.

This book is sold subject to the condition that it shall not, by way of trade or otherwise, be lent, resold, hired out or otherwise circulated without the publisher's prior consent in any form of binding or cover other than that in which it is published and without a similar condition including this condition being imposed upon the subsequent purchaser.

A catalogue copy of this book is available from the British library.

Printed in the UK

Dedication

To all you reluctantly psychic people, may this book inspire, inform, comfort and encourage you to come out of the spiritual closet.

In memory of Beano Ward, our Redfox lab.
19.1.2011 - 20.7.2020.

Foreword

A few years back, I had the pleasure of working with Angel Alison when she generously shared the story of her Awakening in *Spirit & Destiny* magazine.

She is most certainly a woman who speaks from the heart and feels passionately about helping others on their own spiritual journeys.

Reluctantly Psychic is a much-needed book – well done to Angel Alison for making this happen! I have no doubt that it will be a guiding light to those out there who want to embrace their spiritual side and gifts, but who may need a little hand-holding along the way.

This book is that hand.

It will instil courage to be the truest and best you can be, and allow you to stand up and say, *'I'm psychic and proud'*.

Tracie Couper

Features Editor, Spirit & Destiny Magazine

CONTENTS

Empaths' Journeys

In this chapter, you will read journeys from Empaths, and Highly Sensitive People (HSPs). Maybe you'll resonate with some of them and maybe they will answer questions for you. Ask yourself the question: 'Am I an Empath?' What is your answer?

Animal Connections

Empaths often have a natural deep connection with animals. They can communicate via telepathy just by looking at the animal. These three stories share the Empath's love of animals.

Miracles Abound

*An extraordinary and welcome event that is not explicable by
natural or scientific laws and is therefore attributed to a
'Divine Agency' is the definition of a miracle.
Have you experienced a miracle and not realised it?
These six stories demonstrate amazing miracles that may make
you think twice about whether you have experienced one.*

Out of Body Experiences

*Out of Body Experiences (OBEs) can be scary. Imagine being
woken up at night to see yourself hovering over your body.
This is not uncommon and actually nothing to be scared about.
Read these two stories and rest assured, 'all is well.'
You are simply evolving.*

Finding Your Soulmate

Many of us dream of meeting our soulmate but all too often it happens when we least expect it. Experiencing an abusive relationship often teaches us to let go and allow love in. That is when our soulmate experience is ready. Don't force it to happen. Forgive, let go and be open to receiving love.

Healing Journeys

These following stories share illnesses, Near Death Experiences and Awakenings, allowing the authors to start seeing the world differently. People who have overcome illness, experienced NDAs and Awakenings are much more positive and focused when they 'wake up' to their psychic gifts and abilities..

Awakenings to Soul Purpose

Many of our authors have experienced loss, abuse, and pain, yet 'we all rise'.
When you choose to look at these tumultuous times as 'lessons learnt',
chances are your gifts will surface, bringing you joy and fulfilment.

Acknowledgements

Thank you to all the beautiful souls and contributors to this book who heard the calling and got in touch to a very tight deadline. I have been moved by your stories, love and openness to share them with the world.

We did this in just 16 days!

Thank you to the guidance that asked me to create *Reluctantly Psychic*, a book conceived and born in lockdown of the COVID-19 virus in 2020, and to Alexa Whitten from the Book Refinery and Nikki Finch for creating the wonderful book cover. We used Nikki's photo and Alexa's creative skills to craft this expressive metaphor for the book. You can find more of Nikki's pictures at www.nikkifinch.com so please have a look.

Thank you to Diamond Di Pegler for her constant support and encouragement, Mike Fairbrother for all his support and techie help, Bev Taylor for being our admin angel, and my son Sam Ward for creating a clean and clear social media campaign and launch. I truly appreciate you all for your love, commitment and support.

In my role as mental health advocate, I have spoken to many people who are petrified of this virus, which has exacerbated their anxiety and created catastrophic thinking, resulting in not being able to leave the house and reintegrate into society, and developing a cleaning addiction.

The rise in mental illness caused during this pandemic might create focus on mental illness itself. Yet I believe that if people owned up to their psychic abilities – their innate gifts – and developed them further, being creative more often to find their joy in their own unique way, then we would see a decline in mental ill health.

Working hours need to fit around individuals' needs and within their most active times of the day. Many more people than usual have worked from home during the virus outbreak and have found it actually suits them, resulting in greater productivity.

Sensitive people like us Empaths struggle in busy, crowded areas. This lockdown has been a gift to many of us and we have blossomed.

There is so much common sense, experience, insight and comfort in this compilation. We have births, loss, love, pain, joy and, most importantly, fulfilment at owning our gifts, finding our purpose and declaring, 'I am no longer reluctantly psychic – I AM ME'.

Thank you, dear reader, for purchasing this book. May at least one story resonate with you.

LOVE AND BLESSINGS.

Alison Ward, concept creator of *Reluctantly Psychic,* author and visionary

Introduction

Welcome, dear reader, to this wonderful miracle of a book. It was birthed, written and compiled during the Great Awakening of the COVID-19 lockdown in 2020, in just over two weeks.

Originally, it was going to be my sixth book after *Awarded By Angels, Bringing You Back To YOU, Get That Friday Feeling, Where Is The Pot Of Gold?* and, ironically, another book on making wishes and manifesting, which will be launched in 2021.

Reluctantly Psychic shares that it's ok to be psychic, sensitive and 'weird': it's our 'normal'. Since initiating this book project, I have noticed that so many Empaths are coming out of the 'spiritual closet' and owning up to their weird and wonderful gifts. 'Weird' is a word we use often.

You will find them hidden behind a corporate mask, disguised as Angels with wings (air flight attendants), nurses, dog groomers and often complementary therapists. They know they are here to make a difference and take this very seriously.

Being an Empath is a challenging journey where you are often ridiculed for being different. You never feel that you quite fit into the world or, often, into your family; you have bright and weird dreams, pick up on how people are feeling and sense the weight of the world literally on your shoulders.

We have allergies and sensitivities to foods, materials, cleaning products, skin and hair products and anything that consists of dense, heavy energy such as lies and bullshit. We are great bullshit detectors and have to overcome challenges from people who don't respect our differences and our boundaries.

We feel deep pain, often told we are 'too much', 'too sensitive', 'weird' or 'fucking nuts'. I've been called all of the above and often by my family members.

What keeps us going? Our LIGHT! It fuels us and we know it lights up the world, one tiny beacon at a time. We hear, feel, sense and often see our purpose. No matter how much we use distraction, self-sabotage, not feeling 'good enough', we still know we have to keep going. Just like the Duracell bunny.

Getting back to the Introduction... I sat down to write the first chapter of this book and my mind went blank. No matter how much I tried, I couldn't recall all the stories that I wanted to share with you. There are so many! I then started laughing and realised it was because I had poor memory recall. This was due to my Awakening back in 1994.

On 5th July, 1994, I was beaten up and stabbed by my former partner in front of my two-year-old son. I left my body in a Near Death Experience and saw my family waiting for me as my welcoming committee. They told me 'it wasn't my time to go yet, duck!', and I landed back in my body; back in the bloody scene.

Miracle after miracle followed and our lives were to be saved that day. What I didn't know was that I'd suffered slight brain damage, which affected my memory recall. Since my recovery from The Awakening and subsequent PTSD, I have learnt to flip over the negatives into positives and to always see 'lessons learnt' in every situation. And I laughed because I realised that this book was meant to be a collaborative book. The realisation coincided with the guidance I had received at the end of 2019: that the year 2020 was to be a year of slowing down, collaborations and looking at relationships with ourselves and others.

I always trust my guidance and know from experience that if you follow yours through with appropriate action, then miracles occur. I posted a thread on social media and tagged a few people who might be interested in collaborating, and left it.

As I write, that was 16 days ago. We now have 44 collaborators, including me, and have raised nearly £1000 towards the self-publishing costs.

The idea behind the book is to eradicate the stigma of being psychic. We all have the capacity; it's humans' innate gift. This book brings love and inspiration where there is fear, hope in someone's doubt and a virtual hug to the world saying, 'It's gonna be ok'.

Reluctantly Psychic is full of individual stories from men and women across the UK, USA, France, Spain and Greece, from all walks of life, including a big chunk of people working in the corporate world, hiding behind their masks: a globally successful corporate lawyer, who felt he had to use a pseudonym to remain anonymous as it may affect his career; a female pilot, nurses and even a construction supervisor. The stories are honest, open and full of inspiration.

They guide you into accepting you being you. Glorious, magnificent, fucking amazing YOU.

Start wherever you feel inclined in the book, whether that be at the beginning or wherever it opens; it's your choice.

I have sectioned the book so it flows into all the different stories of Empaths: Empaths' journeys, animal connections, miracles, OBEs (out of body experiences), finding soulmates, healing journeys and awakening to soul purpose. I have also included a glossary at the back of the book (page 348) to help you understand terms you may not be familiar with.

Help us spread the love and light of this book by sharing on social media with the hashtag #ReluctantlyPsychic and please do leave a review on the platforms, including Amazon. It will mean our message of love, support and sense of community spirit may spread far and wide.

Bless you, dear reader.

Alison Ward, concept creator of *Reluctantly Psychic*, author and visionary

Empaths' Journeys

In this chapter, you will read journeys from Empaths, and Highly Sensitive People (HSPs). Maybe you'll resonate with some of them and maybe they will answer questions for you. Ask yourself the question: 'Am I an Empath?' What is your answer?

I saw being an Empath and different to others as a flaw, until I realised it was a gift to help me and the people who would come into my life and business.

IT ALWAYS HAPPENS TO ME

Alison Ward

As the knife tore into my skin, I saw and felt my two-year-old son's fear from across the room. I knew this was the day I was going to die because that's what Graham told me.

When I left my body, the fear and pain left me. I moved at speed to be greeted by my grandad and past family members. The love was pure and deep. It enveloped me and I didn't want to leave the party. 'It's not time to go yet, duck!' I then plonked back into my body and the bloody mess of the room.

That day was not the day I/we were going to die, because a blooming great Angel flung me over my attacker's body and gave me strength to run out of the house and summon help from the nearby shop.

That was on 5th July, 1994. I share the full story of the Awakening and subsequently finding my purpose in my book, *Awarded by Angels*. Read it in full via Amazon under the author name, Angel Alison Ward.

The aftermath and following weeks, months and even years saw me become a true Empath victim. I felt so much deep, searing pain to the depth of my soul. Yet I also felt great love from my beautiful husband, sons and family.

It took me a while to realise that being an Empath all my life was a double-edged knife! One side was experiencing joy, love, psychic awareness, out of body experiences, time-travelling, channelling the most beautiful messages of love and hope, seeing energy, auras, lights, knowing what was going to happen and embracing being weird.

It wasn't until I stopped thinking, saying, feeling and believing that it 'always happened to me' that I became empowered, awake and so very grateful. True meaty gratitude is what I call it.

To get me well and whole once more, if not for the first time in my life, I was given nudges and whispers to follow from my Angels and guides. I loved it when Steve and Dave, dressed in sharp black and white 'bouncer' suits presented themselves to me as my gatekeepers. My favourite moment was when Sarah, my gorgeous, silky-blond-haired, blue-eyed Guardian Angel attended to me when I was planning my suicide. She knelt by my bedside and stroked my arm, as gentle as a whisper, telling me, 'You are safe, all is well, it will never happen to you again.'

These nudges became daily practices that now form the behavioural programme I share in my second book, *Bringing You Back To YOU*. The simple, easy-to-follow tools brought me back to a fucking amazing version of me. I say this not to boast, simply to trigger you into owning up to the fact that you too are fucking amazing. If you don't realise it yet, maybe you and I need to have a chat. I would love to work with you if you are ready to discover it.

The process is quite simply: Think it. Feel it. Believe it. Become it. This teaches you to become aware and take full responsibility for how you think, feel and believe. When you change that inner speak to love-infused, positive words and energy, then you stop becoming a victim and it does 'always happen to you', in that your life becomes blessed in truly magical, fucking amazing ways.

I often say to my husband, 'I am the most blessed person I know.' I mean it. I am. I'm not rich financially, but I have unlimited wealth in so many ways. I acknowledge that this has been created by stepping out of the negative side of being a 'poor me' Empath and embracing and owning the gifts without embarrassment or shame.

Reflecting on my Empath's journey, I totally resonate with not fitting in; with feeling anxious and different; with being able to smell and sense things that others don't. I have now embraced not fitting in. I have found my tribe who accept me for me. If I don't feel something is right, I don't do it. If I'm given guidance to do something, I do it. It's that simple.

When I'm sad, I feel it for a day or two, then get up and start finding something to smile at. Every day I find gratitude and 'lessons learnt', and then I put the day to bed so I don't retire with a heavy emotional backpack on.

There have been countless weird and wonderful psychic happenings in my 56 years on planet Earth. One I have remembered while writing this book was when I was on retreat in Georgia, USA.

After the publication of my first book, *Awarded by Angels*, it somehow reached a spiritual teacher in America. She contacted me and we formed a lovely friendship over Skype.

Just a few months later, she told me she was running a retreat in Georgia and asked if I'd like to be her guest. It was in March and happened to fall on my husband's and my wedding anniversary, so straightaway it was a 'no, thank you' from me. But Wayne insisted I go. He had a strong feeling that it was the right thing to do. We could always celebrate our anniversary on my return.

So, off I went, a tad nervous, yet excited about meeting my new friend and other people I had never met before.

It was a wonderful week, right in deepest Georgia with some of the loveliest people I have ever met. The food was cooked fresh every day and there was an outdoor hot tub that we sat in every night, looking at the stars. We laughed, we cried. I was grateful for this gift of time and love.

On our last day, we walked down to the creek. The sun was shining on a beautiful spring day. We all went and found somewhere to sit, meditate, reflect and give thanks for the retreat.

I sat on a rock and marvelled at one of the ladies, who I nicknamed 'Faery'. Watching her hop over logs and rocks, wondering at nature in its purest form, my attention was grabbed by a deep blue-purple dragonfly. It danced and twirled in front of me. Tears of remembrance fell down my cheeks. Dragonflies were always a reminder of my friend, Gail, who passed in 2005, aged 40. The tears soon turned to laughter as I realised this was Gail in her dragonfly form. She was so proud of her beauty, it felt mean not to share.

Beckoning to 'Faery', I said, 'Come over here and watch this.'

She was by my side in an instant. 'Where is it, Alison?' she asked in her southern drawl.

Thinking she was taking the mick, I pointed at this obvious dragonfly, who was hovering right in front of us. Still she didn't see it.

Gail Dragonfly loved this new game.

I didn't accept that I was the only one seeing this magical display, so I called the rest of the party over. Not one person saw the Gail dragonfly, yet she was as clear as day to me.

I guess it was my gift from Gail. No one else was meant to see it.

It made me think, how many spirits do we see in our everyday lives that we're not aware are spirits? Maybe that person walking down the street is a spirit going about his dual existence.

Here we are now in week seven of lockdown. My son, James, has had the virus. Thank God he is as fit as a flea and overcame it well. He lives in one part of London whilst Sam, my eldest, lives in another.

I miss them.

I cry sometimes and then send them love and extra Angels to keep them buoyed.

I love them more and accept I cannot control anything in life, so I stop controlling with fear and embrace the moment with love.

My mentoring business is at a standstill. Strange as I have helped so many people overcome PTSD and anxiety. But rather than question why, I allow the void to open and present something new, with excitement. Rather than fear and go into 'lack, victim mentality', I see it as a new direction, even though I don't know yet what that direction is.

I let go of the 'how?' and 'when?'.

I trust more.

My dad is in a care home with advanced dementia. Is it a blessing he cannot see us? Does he even miss us? Is his not knowing what on earth is going on the gift he has been blessed with? All I know is, the tools I have practised since my

Awakening continue to serve me well. My energy is strong, resolute and love-infused. I constantly hear, through meditation and whispers, that I have been in training for this time all my life. I believe it because I feel it deep in my core. My soul sings at the thought of being of more service to the world.

I am a pillar of light and stand tall in my stockinged feet, all five foot two and a half inches of me. Yet I don't wear stockings in the lockdown. I'm barefooted, so I touch the grass often and connect with the Earth by grounding and being present.

I believe in miracles and welcome their arrival in all their guises.

As I write this, I have just been interviewed by a journalist for two well-known spiritual magazines. She was asking me my theories and thoughts about how wishes come true. This gave me the opportunity to talk about this book. The journalist came out of nowhere! Or did she hear the nudges and intuitively look me up?

We got on well and enjoyed a good chat about wishes, old paradigms, the Great Awakening and the power of positivity. I was even able to help her with a specific problem. I knew I'd made a difference to her day and this makes me happier and ever more grateful.

She left the call saying she would love to do more articles on the work I do. Was this a miracle?

Look what happens when you hear the whispers, act upon them and then let go of the 'how's. I'm excited to see the cause and effect this book will have on all the authors and the readers. Will it be welcomed with open hearts, eager to read about others' lives, or will people shy away from the bright light that this book has become?

The nudges and whispers remind me to let go of any expectations, trust in the flow and believe we are guided every step of the way. There are 43 other contributors to this book, which means their energies and love will also create a ripple effect of love and energy into the world. We may not know the impact of some of that effect until after we die.

I kept hearing and seeing the number 44 when we started this book. It wasn't until it was completed and I counted the contributors that I realised there were 44 in total! This makes me smile; the whispers know things before we do.

Confirmation like this helps me to trust even more.

The more you trust, the more you believe…

The Impact of Lockdown

The idea of this book was born just 16 days ago in lockdown. It is now written, all 130,000 words. What an amazing achievement.

During this time, I have been given many insights into why this has happened. I believe it is a massive reset for each of us and our world. We cannot go back to the old ways of complacency and lack of care for our environments and our lives.

The world is resetting. Mother Earth is sick and tired of being abused. She has given us all the elements in force to wake us up to start taking responsibility for our actions and the massive effect they have on the world. She has sent fire (Australia and California are among just two places that have been devasted by fires), water in great floods, and now we have this air-borne virus. Whether it was created in a lab in China or arrived naturally simply doesn't matter in truth. We need to change. YOU need to change. Create a love-infused vision; be kind, connect and collaborate with people who make living more bearable but, most of all, remember you are so very loved, more than YOU know. Learn to accept this love, accept your gifts, and shine your gifts like a beacon of light in the world. We need YOU.

Love and blessings, dear reader.

www.alison-ward.com
alison@reluctantlypsychic.co.uk
FACEBOOK: @alisonwardenergyinsights
INSTAGRAM: @alisonwardenergyinsights

Hang talks about the benefits of being an Empath and how it helps her be a more effective therapist.

JOURNEY AS AN EMPATHIC THERAPIST

Hang Acharya

Being an Empath...

An Empath is not something you wake up one day and become. For me, it was a gradual thing and often after a major life setback or a big negative experience. After pulling yourself back to 'normal', you start seeing people and situations in a different light. It's like having a new pair of eyes and growing a third eye too!

I noticed that my body could physically mimic another person. As the saying goes, 'being in someone's shoes' – literally! It really was the strangest feeling. So, for example, if I noticed a person with a runny nose, my nose would run too! If I saw someone cry, I would cry automatically.

I realised that I could intentionally psyche into other people's bodies and feel what they feel, physically and emotionally, even in another country (although I don't feel the same extent/level of pain as they do). A great advantage of having this ability is that if I have a stuffy nose, I can sit next to my husband (as he has a big nose compared to mine!) and experience his nose. Bingo! Stuffy nose all cleared up. Plus my children cannot feign any ailments to get a day off school, as I will know.

NeuroScience has proven this as we have these mirror neurons in our brains. Mirror neurons allow us to learn through imitation. They enable us to reflect body language, facial expressions and emotions.

Now that I am more in control of my energy and have learnt grounding techniques, I feel totally blessed to have these gifts.

They've probably been there all along since I was born but I think when the time is right you become the light for others. However, it's not always been plain sailing.

Being an Empath could be considered a great gift to have or, for some people, it could be a curse. But once you start managing your energy then you can really put it to good use.

My Journey so far Being an Empathic Therapist

As a child and teenager growing up, I was a born worrier. I worried for everyone and everything. I just couldn't help myself! In hindsight, I know I was ultra sensitive and was probably taking on everyone else's burdens but didn't realise it. Having a mother who was constantly worrying didn't help either. It wasn't her fault as she'd lived through tough and challenging times, like the Vietnam war. Also, my father left when I was one month old to seek a better life abroad so he could send for us six years later. Times were hard for my mother bringing up my older brother and me, alone but with the help of her family.

Throughout my adult life, I have been blessed with great health and strong stamina. I put that down to growing up in Vietnam, playing in the paddy field and living in a house made from mud and straw. A lot of things were not as clean compared to the UK, so I built up a strong immune system. Sure, I'm human and I did get aches and pains when I overdid things, and caught the odd cold once in a decade. However, all that changed in 2007 when I was 28 years old.

My job as a holistic therapist is all about improving people's wellbeing. I help to Realign the body, Reset muscles and Relax the mind. I feel I have gathered all the necessary tools so far to help people on their way back to better health. With the gift of being an Empath, this has allowed me to really fine-tune the treatment and adapt accordingly.

Feeling the Pain of Others

I was first aware of being an Empath when I discovered that I could feel other people's pain while I was doing corporate massage for a company in Leamington Spa. This is when I first started being conscious of it.

While I was massaging or treating clients, I began experiencing various pains in my body, which was very unlike me! I would ask them if they had 'pain in their left hip' or whether they had a 'toothache', or if they had a 'nauseous' feeling in their belly or a 'headache' just over their right eye. When they confirmed it, I realised that the 'symptoms' I was experiencing weren't mine.

I used to carry their 'symptoms' in my body long after they had left my treatment room. I started to recognise the familiar 'foggy' headache I'd get afterwards (a classic sign for me of transference of negative energy). Every client was different; some were more draining than others – even the positive clients. I just couldn't tell until they left. And it wasn't just clients. It was the people I interacted with on a daily basis. Some days I was totally drained. Over the years, the more clients I treated and interacted with, the more my intuition grew, and this was how I later started learning and developing further other psychic abilities.

Feeling Others' Emotions

Many years later, I realised that I could feel other people's emotions too, or may have been able to long before but wasn't consciously aware of it. I remember vividly that moment when, on a beautiful sunny afternoon with blue skies, I was travelling in a car, sitting in the passenger seat, and I started feeling really depressed. My brain was trying to figure out why as it didn't make sense. I had no reason to feel depressed… Life was great! Then I asked the person driving if they were feeling depressed. They said they were. That's what confirmed everything.

I consider myself physically strong. I multi-task and will be on the go all day long, but it was having a negative impact on my energy. Five years later, I googled what I was feeling and I discovered there was a name for it!

I am a Physical and Emotional Empath

There's lots of information on this subject online and I gave such a sigh of relief when I realised that there are others out there just like me. I wasn't going crazy! Some Empaths are so sensitive that they avoid crowds altogether. I used to avoid people on purpose because of how they make me feel. I still do. However, I am now able to manage the energy better.

I've met other therapists who have empathic abilities and have given up their jobs because of it. I simply love my job too much to do that!

Benefits of Being a Therapist with Empathic Abilities

These abilities have allowed me to become a more empathic therapist and to be in tune with my clients. Here are some reasons why they are beneficial:

- Empathising with clients, 'being in a client's shoes'. What it feels like to be them, in their body. For example, one client wasn't aware that she had one nostril bigger than the other, so was breathing more through one nostril than the other.
- I can feel for misalignment. I can feel if clients have one leg longer than the other. (This helps me when I do Dorn Method as I measure leg length differences. Now I can do that psychically.)
- I can feel how a client is breathing – my breathing will mimic accordingly (I find that a lot of clients breathe very shallowly). Usually during and at the end of a treatment, I know when the breathing is better as I feel it myself. One client was so aware of the improved changes in her breathing after her alignment, she took great gulps of air!
- I feel the energy level of clients. Being aware of this allows me to compare how they are before and after the treatment. I can also change the treatment plan accordingly and use different tools and techniques so that their energy level increases.
- I feel other symptoms of clients that they are not aware of as they are focusing on the more serious symptoms. For example, one client was feeling nauseous but didn't mention it until I brought it up. They had become so used to the feeling that it was the norm for them.
- I have often been called a 'witch' as sometimes I feel things before clients do. One time I was doing Reiki and I felt something pressing down on the client's forehead (I was positioned at the feet at the time). Sure enough, the client felt it two minutes later.
- I often feel my clients' teeth for some odd reason (I should have been a dentist!). An example: I picked up on one client's teeth issues during

the session. The client had no symptoms and was not aware of the issue at the time but, days later, the pain started. The client reported back on his next visit that he was found to have an abscess after visiting the dentist. Another client had to have a filling.

- I am also aware of other sensitive clients who have empathic abilities but don't know it. Sometimes the symptoms they are experiencing are not their own. I often guide them to the right resources online and talk about my own experience, encouraging them to seek help for their own protection.

Presently, I don't intentionally psyche into clients as it's mentally and physically draining. I've learnt that what comes through during the treatment is what I am meant to know and for the Highest Good.

Embracing the Energy/Psychic Abilities

I have been doing lots of touch therapies over the years and I love doing them as touch is so powerfully healing, both as a client receiving and in the giving as a therapist. Currently I am embracing more on the energetic/psychic side.

I started seeing spirits and guides during my treatment in July of 2013. One poignant moment when I was performing Reiki on a client; through my third eye I saw the whole room filled with men in black robes with hoods, and a smaller man – who I later discovered was one of my guides. (He helps me when I'm doing healing work). They were all standing around my client with their hands over her body. (I had rented a small treatment room in a hairdresser's back then – just enough space to move around my couch, with a white cupboard and a small sink, so it was quite crowded in there.) Some spirits that came through were from the client's side. I knew they were there and was aware of them but never wanted to probe further.

Later on, I went on a short psychic development course. I learnt that I can do psychometry – a psychic skill that enables someone to pick up information from an object that's closely connected to a person.

After that, I learnt psychic surgery using Reiki energy. I am able to clear any stuck energy and allow it to flow better, and help realign the body energetically. After all, everything is made of energy.

So, whilst we are in lockdown at the moment, I have been treating clients with distant Reiki and Emmett Technique.

I know I still have lots to learn and am enjoying this wonderful journey so far, feeling incredibly blessed, with the most amazing people in my life to share it with.

My Heart to Yours

Welcome, awakened one!

You are meant to be reading this at this very moment in time. You have chosen this before you were born: the people in your life; all your life experiences so far; whether you are in a wonderful place right now or have just been through the mill.

If you are in despair and don't know where to turn, please know that you are not alone in this. Call upon the assistance of your guides/Angels/God/the Universe for help. No matter what circumstances you are in, there is help out there! You are the creator of your life. You are the director of your life stage.

Ask and have complete faith and trust that the solution shall be delivered. Believe in the magic. Believe in miracles! Then wait. You will get the nudge: random thoughts will enter your head. You will start seeing the signs. I myself see numbers everywhere… 11.11, 02.02, 3.33. You will see messages – pay attention to them. Perhaps a sentence in a book, a message on a billboard or simply a white feather! They are showing you that they are there. The right people will come into your life to assist you. Some people may appear in your life for a short while. Others will stay for the long run. Raise your vibration by thinking more positively, letting go of people who bring you down. Be around people who believe in you and lift you up.

Once you start to realise that you can be in control of your life, life will flow easily and effortlessly. Trusting your intuition is key. It's always right and will keep you safe, even if it doesn't make sense at the time.

In time, you will become the beacon for others. You don't need to be a prime minister or president to make such a big impact! Just shine your light brightly in your corner of the world, to give others hope and to dream big. Together we shall raise the vibration of the world.

For me, by giving one massage treatment I know I am impacting seven other people. For example, a client feels wonderful after her treatment and leaves my treatment room. The positive ripple effect from the treatment will flow to her partner/children/work colleague/the man walking his dog etc… just from one massage. You have the ability to change the lives of others for the better should you wish to. You don't have to massage people – just smile! Your smile will have a positive impact on so many people… Are you smiling right now?

Declutter regularly. If your environment, for example, your home or your work space, is messy, it has an effect on you mentally.

The best way to recharge your energy in my experience is to do self-healing via Reiki, meditation, burning sage, walking in nature, gardening, being around positive people or in a positive environment. And take lots of alone time to discharge and reset.

When you do meet a fellow Empath, your heart will swell with love and joy! We 'get' each other without saying a single word.

Wishing you well on your exciting journey. Namaste x

www.suttonholistics.co.uk
FACEBOOK: @hang.acharya

Jenny shares her delightful story of being a sensitive HSP/Empath and how it took her from Scotland to living in a forest in France with her soulmate, Derek.

THE DANCE FROM SCOTLAND TO FRANCE

Jenny Anne Slater

Hello, Big Person reading this.

I'm Jenny Anne Sunshine Sparkle Starlight. I'm nearly six. My adult (Jenny, almost 57) was playing up! Fretting 'bout where to start. 'Why so serious?' I told her. 'Have fun. Writing stories is play. Easy-peasy.' She thinks too much. 'She's sensitive,' say her friends. I like her silly, free, dancey bits best. And she makes THE best cakes.

I get sad, 'cos adults forget how amazing they are. It's my job to help her remember how magic she is. We all are. Very. Magic. D'you know why? It's 'cos we come from the stars. We're here to learn, then we die and go back to the stars... But we forget when we're here... Lots.

Big Jen says adults are beginning to wake up to their magic. 'Cos the 'planet is ascending and we're evolving'. We can feel it. It's happening right now. This is why we're sharing this story. Big Jen's kinda private, but we need to share. She says waking is a mixture of messy and scary. 'Specially for big people who're sensitive, 'cos you feel different. She'll explain more.

I said, 'Let's go to the stream and splash, climb a tree, skip home. Have tea with cats and cookies.'

She said, 'Yes!'

I said, 'I want to start the story.'

She smiled. 'I'll consider it.' (Sometimes, that means 'no'.) Today she said, 'Yes.' So I'm happy.

Things I like:

    Monkeys

    Books

George Cat

Painting

Water

Growing things

Climbing trees

Dancing

Asking questions

Learning

Cooking

Swings

Sparkly, twirly dresses

Rolling down hills

Dancing on my dad's feet.

Things I don't like:

My brother almost dying

People being mean

Shouty people

My dad drinking too much

Being sick

Kids fighting

Being teased

Baked beans

Itchy labels on knickers

The smell of Grandad's pipe

People who tell lies

Kids stomping on flowers

Crowds.

Big Jen still likes dancing, an' learning. She always reads lots and thinks lots. She dances by herself now. Lucky for Derek's feet! She says, 'Life's a dance.' She's helped heaps of people over the years. I dunno exactly how she does it. You just feel safe when you're beside her. I don't quite understand the grown-up words: 'Holding space,' she says. I mean, how can you hold that? But she listens and makes you feel special and listened to. Her voice gives you 'soothes'.

She told me she's ready. Yippee. I like that. She gave me a hug, tucked Jacko in beside me. We're a good team. I love her sooooo much. She's got a big, gentle heart. She's not got kids but she'd be THE best mum. Kids sense this. So do animals (she's mummy to heaps of kittens). She's special 'cos she can talk to animals. Told you she was magic. I'm off to sleep now. Byeeeee!

I was born in North East Scotland; arriving in a rush before Dad got back from calling the midwife. He galloped upstairs shouting, 'What did we get?'

Gran called back, 'Davie, I've not looked yet!'

'It's a girl!' And they danced a jig, and were told to 'pipe down' by my exhausted mum.

A 'late baby'. With two 'big' brothers. Seven and fifteen-year gaps between us. My father, a World War 2 veteran, like many soldiers, returned with unrecognised PTSD. An artistic and sensitive man. I wondered, 'How on earth did he cope with active service?' I joined the dots; realised he had invisible scars as well as deep shrapnel-craters on his arms. He numbed out by binge drinking. My mum shielded me, yet my sen-si-tive nature felt it. I read the signs, feeling the unspoken tension between them. The sticky, pervasive energy of family secrets being swept under an emotionally lumpy carpet.

One of my earliest memories is visiting my brother in hospital. His head had been shaved, so his hair stuck up. I called him 'Spiky'. I can't remember him before. He'd been in a coma. I adored him. I was four. The smell of the ward; that hot, stifling, antiseptic air. The collective imprint of illness and death.

No one explained what had happened to him. I didn't like hospitals one bit. Mum and I would walk home through the park. As an adult, I know this brought me back into balance. As I child, I couldn't quite fathom why I felt so scared; being an empathic child, soaking up emotions like a sponge, intuitively drawn back to myself in nature.

Our house was a hive of hurly-burly. Mum had a never-ending soup pot and kettle. She'd a charismatic warmth, drawing people to her. Always room for another mouth. She made time for others. Topping up her own cup last, to her cost. It was a loving and over-stimulating environment to be in. An accomplished home cook, she taught me her art. By the age of nine, I'd mastered pastry, béchamel sauce, could fillet fish and dress crab. We grew veg, the men fished, so there were seasonal delights through the year. Happy memories. The gift of a life-long passion for cooking. We were raised on traditional 'good, hearty Scottish fayre'. I stopped eating meat years ago. Now I love creating vegan, veggie and raw treats. My mission is to 'raise the vibration on Earth, one mouthful at a time'! I didn't know it back then. I'd never heard the word psychic, but I could taste and smell flavours that weren't there.

On reflection, I'd always had my 'lights switched on', sensing things at a near visceral level; my teacher smelled different the week she had her period. (I'm cringing at how feral this reads; I'm just being honest.) I saw things, felt them, knew them.

I was close to the 'unseen' world. Surrounded by illness and trauma while being such a quiet wee lass. Honing my ability to 'escape' the human world. I felt lots that no one else ever knew about. My parents had enough to do without answering the questions of their quirky, fey daughter. They gave me their best within the bounds of too much responsibility and too little rest. I learnt to watch and intuit at a much older level; I was a wise 'bairn' (Scots for 'young child'). There were times of feeling emotionally unsafe as a girl. On the surface all was well. But I frequently felt 'too much' for my family. Too full of joy, vitality, lightness. A bright spirit-cuckoo-plonked-in-the-wrong-nest somehow.

Our gran believed in 'youngsters being seen and not heard'. Exuberant expressions slapped down by a, 'Quiet, child!...' I complied. To my own cost. Toning myself down to fit in; to not shine too brightly. Now I understand why my throat chakra closed down. Why I'd so many recurrent bouts of tonsillitis.

I felt and sensed faeries and nature spirits. Darting orbs of colour and light. I thought all kids did this! I learnt PDQ that, to fit in, I had to avoid talking about faery stuff or be picked on. I felt such a misfit. I worried about things.

I'd ask unanswerable questions: 'Mummy, what would happen if the world ran out of water?'

I felt happy and free outdoors. Always drawn to water. Caravan holidays up north. Plooterin' (splashing) in wild burns (streams) and lochs. Playing for hours... with chums; human or otherwise, while trees whispered to me...

I loved infant school. I'd had little contact with other children before. On the first day, I remember being led into a class full of kids in uniforms, which swamped our five-year-old forms! The noise, the buzzy energy. It was too much. I clapped my hands over my ears to my mum's amusement, shouted: 'I'm Jenny Anne. I want to learn please. I don't like noisy places!' The teacher took me by the hand. Ushered me to 'The Quiet Corner' full of books. Heaven.

Truthfully, I felt contained and stifled within the classroom. The rules. Being herded. Primary was cosy enough. Secondary education was hell. A large, tough comp. I lasted until sixth year. By then I'd outgrown school. It was a relief to enter further education.

I've lived my life in reverse, holding responsibilities way beyond my years early on. I was 20, nursing my mother who'd lung cancer until her passing a few months later. I was grief-stricken, yet ploughed on; assisting my brother into independent living, months before Mum passed. Keeping an eye on Dad, frailer and assuaging grief with alcohol. Studying for a degree in social work at uni... Marrying my 'Rock', Derek, the following year. Buying our first home together. The excitement of him winning an academic award, landing him a job in an engineering firm, only to deal with the uncertainty of his redundancy less than a year later, during the 80s oil industry recession. Accelerated lessons in loss and change.

We met young, just before my 18th. 'Just a friend', assisting with 'boyfriend trouble'. A leather-clad lad on a Kawasaki charger! (Thirty years later on, our story makes us smile.) A mutual attraction. Each of us 'fessed up that we felt the other was 'way too attractive to ask out on a date'. Oh, the insecurities of our teenage selves. Soulmates. We'd talk for hours and walk for miles. There was a natural ease and flow. I consciously chose a man who didn't smoke or drink. Coincidentally, Derek is allergic to alcohol! He's such a kind, grounded, practical person, who carried family responsibilities way too young as well. He's musical, artistic and creative. We're real mirrors for each other. An attraction of opposites sharing watery Piscean ascendants. By now, we're pretty skilled at 'calling each other out on our stuff'.

With both of us being sensitive, we need lots of space and downtime. The secret of our success being the space. Alone time, separate interests as well as sharing. This formula works for us; we celebrate 35 years together in August. To quote D: 'We're joined at the heart, not the hip'. Wise words. We've worked lots on our respective shizz as we've awakened. We allow each other to be ourselves (not always easy!). There's a maturity of 'allowing', a contrast to the hard-edge smoothing and power struggles of our early years! We agree that we probably married too young; both of us seeking an escape from the intensity our family situations, to be honest. Given all the psychological theories studied during my social work course, statistically, we're by far a 'wild card'. It's not always flowed. There have been challenges aplenty, yet we have managed to allow each other to grow and evolve as we go.

My father died in 1999. By then, I'd clocked up years of social work practice. I yearned for less emotionally demanding work. I'd established a Young Carers' project, was caring for my brother. Was our main wage-earner while Derek returned to uni. Wow, how did I do it? On reflection, I'm amazed. We'd a desire to create a very different life for us than that of our parents.

The Fragrant Dance Years, Scotland: 1998–2012

One day, while walking, I spoke out loud: 'I want more out of life. To do something worthwhile. Help me please!' I called to the trees... I'd felt a deep sense of 'what the feck am I doing?' I needed to retrieve the lightness in my step. I felt weighed down and on autopilot. Time for a leap. A week later, I saw an ad for an Aromatherapy course, based locally. The one-weekend-a-month home-study format was a great antithesis for my work and family commitments. They were interviewing applicants. I phoned. Sailed through the selection procedure. I was in…

It wasn't until the late 1990s, when a colleague recommended a book about HSP adults (highly sensitive people), that I realised 'this is me'. I felt so deeply and all of my senses are incredibly sharp and keen. Up to 20 per cent of the world's population are HSPs. We've got very finely tuned nervous systems. What others may take in their stride, knocks us off-centre. Some of our tendencies:

- Feeling drained after being in crowds.
- Becoming overwhelmed by noise at concerts.
- Being moved to tears by art or music.
- Having an inner-knowing about how someone is really feeling beyond the surface.
- Being affected by bright light.
- Feeling overwhelmed doing lots of tasks within a short time-frame.

If you're reading this and feeling 'this is me', please be gentle with yourself and make time to honour your sensitivity. I've finally come to peace with it. HSPs have so many strengths; we connect at a deep level, so have a unique perspective. We excel in many areas like energy healing, animal communication, psychic/ intuitive guidance. The key is keeping our own tender systems in balance... Practising compassion towards ourselves, gentleness and care. As I woke up and deepened my intuitive gifts, my sensitivity deepened. I welcomed it. Like a soul GPS!

You know when you're on track in life when things flow effortlessly. It was like this with the aromatherapy course. Pleasant synchronicities unfolded. The woman I sat beside was a social worker too. We'd met briefly at work the week before. The person opposite us had moved into the house a close friend had grown up in. There were only 12 of us studying together. Lovely souls. New friendships grew with kindreds.

The world of Plant Medicine blossomed fragrantly. My senses were in a giddy delight discovering aromas, their applications, how to blend holistically. Learning massage techniques, botany, chemistry, I was so happy and on track on this new 'garden' path.

When choosing oils, intuition guided me… Backing choices with the theory studied... I followed my intuitive 'knowings' first. In social work, I kept schtum about these 'hunches'. It was frowned upon... So I applied theory during exams, followed the protocols in the practicals required. But on completion of the course, I had the freedom to weave intuitive prompts in practice organically. This was so freeing. I developed a range of skincare products, tutored adult education classes, offered freelance training for voluntary organisations, the social work and complementary therapies skillsets giving a rich blend of experience to my expanding 'medicine bag'.

Still working part-time, I hurtled out of the Carers' Centre, cannoning into a friend who'd qualified alongside me. She was renting a room in the salon above! After a speedy 'Hi', I agreed to share her flyers with colleagues. She landed three new clients. I returned, frazzled from a meeting, to a message from her, offering a free Reiki session as a 'thank you'. Feeling tired, I booked in... not knowing what Reiki was. So I read the attached info... Hmmm, my academic head was sceptical yet my heart said: 'Trust.'

Beth explained what would happen. I got on the couch, immediately feeling warmth envelop me. I saw waves of colour drifting in. Pulsing. Dissipating. A dancing rainbow disco ball! I felt my body relax and still. A belly gurgle. I felt laughter bubble up within (now knowing these are signs of energy moving). I'd not felt like this for months. Being a 'Superwoman' was taking its toll.

I floated off that couch. Beth was clairvoyant, saw the colours too. She saw golden balls of energy turn into faeries, who were dancing all around me, clapping their hands, applauding me for being kind to nature. I'd no words! Nor reason to doubt her. It felt true. She certainly didn't know anything about my childhood Faery encounters. She said my eyes were clearer, insisting I peered in the mirror. I certainly got a shock, as they shone. I felt so... well, I couldn't quite fathom it. 'I'd like to book in again,' tripped off my tongue.

We fixed another date. I spied a poster for a Reiki Level I course. The date was our wedding anniversary. A sign! I KNEW I had to be there.

That evening, Derek said, 'You look different.' He said I was glowing. I shared what had happened during the healing session and the coincidence with the training date. Without hesitation, he said, 'Let's book together to celebrate.' (He's normally cautious about the unknown.) I sent off our deposit.

During the Reiki training, we learnt so much. How to perceive subtle energies, auras, chakras, hand positions, contraindications. We received our 'attunements' (sacred energy connection process). Again, I saw, felt, sensed soooo very much at a level beyond comprehension. Colours, lights, forms, knowings, I felt invisible hands on my shoulders. I empathised with Derek, who was unable to perceive this (yet). A former engineer, studying for a clinical degree, his logical linear brain wasn't tuned to perceive subtle energies. I must admit, my experience brought up childhood feelings of 'being weird', which Beth understood. She remarked on what a strong connection Derek had to the energy. He couldn't feel it, so took it on trust. He was shown the hand positions and gave me a session. It was powerful. We swapped. I received guidance and song lyrics! We joked about tuning into 'Radio Reiki'... As I deepened my connection with the energy, all my psychic 'clair' senses (clairaudience, clairvoyance, clairsentience, claircognisance) re-opened. It felt reassuring to be reconnected. I knew that energy healing was to play an important part in our lives.

A few months later, we took our Reiki II class. I was ready to incorporate this into my practice and was eager to learn about distance healing, the symbols and how to use them. Beth had us work with photos. We'd to choose the one we were most drawn to. My hands flamed. She guided us to record everything, no matter how strange it seemed. Images, feelings and sensations flooded in. I even heard purring! I'd pages full of scribblings. We shared these in turn. Tentatively, I explained what I felt, saw, sensed, heard, knew; colours, sensations, song titles, feelings, initials, shapes, words, names. To my astonishment, Beth confirmed everything I shared. 'You're a witch,' said Derek. I giggled and felt an awkwardness rise.

I became spiritually hungry to study, practise and learn as much as I could. Derek and I completed our Reiki Mastership together, then Beth asked if I'd be a 'guinea pig' for her to practise her Karuna Reiki training on. She'd completed her course shortly before she was on hiatus. Karuna means 'compassionate action'. So timely. I'd been putting more boundaries in place with my family, and friends who relied on us. I'd no problem being compassionate towards others. Self-compassion, however, didn't come easily. I'd a history of being hard on myself. I'd still not cracked this one. I thought how my mum had developed cancer as her body's way of alerting her to something unresolved within. The connection between body, spirit, mood, mind, emotion and health. I felt intuitively that she'd buried all the grief over Mike's (my eldest brother) motorbike accident deep inside. I was darned sure that I'd not follow her example, would do my own inner-work and learn to look after myself at a deeper level. Take time out to nurture my heart and top up my emotional jug, which emptied quickly in an enabling profession. I booked Aromatherapy and Reiki sessions into my busy calendar.

We told my brothers that they'd have to make their own plans at Christmas, as we were going to have a quiet celebration, just the two of us. I hadn't realised how much we needed to do this. We'd been driving ourselves way too hard for far too long. By then, I'd given up working part-time and was self-employed. I was my most precious resource. It had taken over 40 years to learn this. Geez. I'd been at burnout working for a charity, only a few years before. The job was manageable at the start. Then, over time, responsibilities increased, funding decreased, staff levels were frozen and I picked up the slack to my cost. HSPs need to pace themselves. Have boundaries. This was something I'd finally mastered.

My passion for energy healing/holistic health continues. I'm a real seeker. Over 20 years, I've deepened my connection and trained in many modalities. They've felt like a natural progression; everything from Angelic healing, Shamanism, Crystal and Sound healing, Japanese Facial Accupressure, head massage, Chakradance, Dream Work, Animal Communication, Raw Food Chef. Inner-journeys have been ongoing, as well as travelling the world.

Around ten years ago, while meditating, I started to feel a very subtle, all-encompassing, loving energy envelop me, which felt very different, and I sensed forms close by. Over the months, I knew this to be one of my 'Star Family' or 'Galactic Team' (energy guides from other star systems/planets). It's only more recently I've felt able to talk about this.

Now, I feel guided not to use any particular named healing modality. Our Earth and levels of consciousness have changed so much. We humans have loved to label, create systems and take out copyrights to protect healing modalities, which come from the same source: from Universal Energy. Why? It feels so ego-led and 3D. I'm relieved that our world is evolving to embrace new ways.

Now I prefer the words 'energy alchemy' to describe what I do. Each person does their own healing. We're all Sovereign Beings, whole and complete. I'm merely the channel facilitating this connection with your own beautiful heart. Our bodies, our very DNA, are changing, and our ways of connecting and directing energy healing are evolving to accommodate this.

Getting Ready to Dance in France

Derek and I had been blessed to holiday in the South of France in a charming gîte belonging to our generous friends. We loved the sunshine and spaciousness. We flirted with the idea of buying our own wee place. Great in theory... but why buy somewhere we could only enjoy for a few weeks a year or tie ourselves to a mortgage?... We could rent it out... Hmmm, not sure... All those different energies in 'our' space... We started to dream... We could move there... Why not?... Well, there's my brother; we'd miss friends; we'd have to sell our house... My ego threw up its resistance.

We looked online. Life in Scotland was great. Yet we'd been in our place for over 20 years; established a healing practice in our cabin in our woodland garden (our house was an ex-Forestry Commission) and had a third of an acre of land, beautiful mature fruit trees, fragrant and medicinal herbs, a veg garden. Oh, how I loved the land... yet the rumblings of change gathered momentum...

My aunt had died the previous year (Mum's sister). We weren't close. She was very different to my mum. On the surface, brittle, shallow. Kept people at a distance. I always felt I was emotionally too much for her. I knew she loved me; she was just unable to express it openly. My uncle, well, he was the person our family 'tolerated'... just. He was challenging to love. Loud, argumentative, boorish. (Both he and my aunt were so in need of love.) They didn't have any children. They penny-pinched to the extreme. Although they were very well off, they held a deep poverty consciousness. It was sad that my aunt died without fully being able to enjoy her abundance.

I was astounded to discover that she'd gifted some of this abundance to us... I celebrated by shouting lunch to all my friends, one by one, going for curry, afternoon tea, explaining that I wanted to heal all the energy of lack surrounding the inheritance. I was extremely grateful. Another clairvoyant pal saw my aunt raising a glass and laughing at her old ways on Earth! We now had options to turn our dreams into reality... and a spirit-side blessing from Auntie Em.

Derek was now an Occupational Therapist and had taken on a demanding post, with little support. He was out of balance. Something was going to give and he wouldn't confront it.

One morning, he was up and out early. He kissed the back of my sleepy head. I felt angsty. Rushed downstairs to hug him. I called silently to the Angels, 'Please watch over Derek today. Be extra close.'

I set up the cabin for my 9.30 client. I heard a car on the gravel. Not a familiar engine noise. I saw Derek, looking grim.

He came in. 'I was in an accident. It was the other guy's fault. He didn't see me. There were witnesses. My boss told me to take the day off.' He was shaking inside.

I KNEW something was going to happen. I urged him to visit his GP for a check. His neck was sore and he was in shock. I drove him there. He returned with a doctor's note for a month.

'I've work-related stress.'

'No kidding,' I replied. 'I'm relieved he gave you a note.'

'So am I,' said D.

We hugged. We cried. My heart ached for him. My Healing Guides belted out Van Morrison's song: 'From the dark end of the street, to the bright side of the road'.

The Universe conspired that it was time for a BIG change. Derek's job was relocated to the city. He'd a rush-hour commute. I prayed for clarity. He came home one evening and said, 'I've handed in my notice'. My heart sighed in relief.

Derek healed as he crafted wood, completing a course at a local mill. He got his bounce back and at last was on track again. Yippee. Playtime!

The Dance in France 2012–2020

I received intuitive guidance about 'the trees and the water calling you'. The words 'Perigord Vert' were whispered (this area being the Dordogne, which is a well-loved region to Brits settling in France. Strange, as we fancied a spot much less travelled). That soft, still voice, was urging me to 'trust'. An intuitive friend received similar images, reinforcing the sense of anticipation.

In June, we put our house on the market, cautious estate agents urging us to 'play safe' with the asking price. My intuition said, 'Nah.' We phoned another agency. Their rep took one look and could feel the magic. It was a quirky cottage, with amazing energy. A much-tended garden and our lovely healing cabin where we worked. I must admit, I was attached to the land and cabin. Such 'light-portals', which had transformed many hearts over the years. We'd developed loving connections with our nature spirits through time.

With 19 viewings in 14 days, selling our house was intense… I took walks in the woods to regroup. I admit to singing, 'Divine love prosper us now, divine love prospers me now' to the tune of 'My love is like a red, red rose', and imagining the excited, delighted buyer coming off the phone and saying, 'It's ours!'

It worked! We were grocery shopping when the solicitor phoned to confirm the sale. I was steering through the carpark when a 444 reg drove past. At this time, I'd see recurrent numbers; wee 'winks' from the Universe, like 11:11 or 444, which means being surrounded by Angels. At the sales office, I spied a 555, then an 888 plate (no kidding – 555 means 'change', 888 means 'abundance'). It was a charmed sale.

There was a 'plot twist'. We'd fallen in love with a mill house. The owners panicked due to a dip in the euro, so took it off the market… just as we'd sold! 'Things will only get better' was sung in my ear… Source had a 'Plan B'.

We set off for France with Parsley Sparkle, Adventure Cat, late autumn, driving South as geese flew overhead. Between December 2012 and March 2014, we lived in three rental houses. Lots of change to process. My trust was tested and, yes, we'd some 'WTF' moments, yet I knew we'd to do this.

I sensed we needed just to 'be' for a while… and a rental place in the Perigord Vert showed up.

I'd been introduced to Dianne Pegler (author of the transformational *The Sacred Order of The Magi*) through a mutual friend. I booked a reading with her. It was inspiring and spot on. We became online friends. I'd not meditated much with all our moves. But Parsley got into the habit of sitting on my lap, so I began my daily practice. Her loud, rumbling purr, a soothing anchor. I received images of The Diamond Light Grid. Information flooded through. The connection with my Star Family was strong.

Aha! I suddenly recalled Di's message: Derek and I were to be guardians of a pure energy source and all that was needed would unfold – as is the way when we dance our path with Source!

Soon after, the trees and water called – loudly. We found a seven-acre forested site, with two wooden chalets and a mountain stream nearby, in the heart of The Millevaches (means thousand springs, not cows) Nature Park.

Our hearts were set on a simpler, sacred life. We could grow organically, accommodate guests on retreat, call in sensitive, connected, nature-loving people seeking soul-nourishment.

I've always been a passionate cook but I'd no wish to cook professionally. I'd witnessed my mum run herself ragged catering for others. I'd invested so much time in holistic training, developing my skills, I really felt 'I must use these'. My heart, however, guided me to 'weave my magic with what I already have'. I had to cook.

2014–15 were full tilt. Building, land-clearing, repairing the roof and running ourselves into the ground. Parsley died. We held a beautiful ceremony during her final hours under the trees. We were relieved that she was no longer in her frail cat-suit, and she gave me a sign as she promised she would after she passed, with the song 'Across the bridge where angels dwell'. We had a deep bond and many tears fell.

Two friends in the UK passed too. We got a shock as one of them was our longstanding friend who'd introduced us to France.

I became really tired and withdrawn. My 'Moontime' was irregular. I realised I was going through perimenopause (didn't see this one coming!). My bod was bang in tune and bled at Dark Moon. We were still working intensely. We'd a squad of burly builders and a tiny month-old kitten who was found in the forest (we were feeding him round the clock). I'd not had time to meet other women nor had female friends close. I craved alone-time. There was so much male energy around.

I had to make time for myself to 'be' and not 'do'. I was done with being busy. I'd to process my unfinished biz around not having children; unresolved family wounds surfaced for clearing.

It was disheartening to read so much negativity online about menopause. The stereotypes, anti-ageing, miracle regimes... Says who? It was a volatile year.

I became at peace with expressing my shadows; anger, regret, inner-child work. Loving it all without judgement. My sensitivity, on top of feeling planetary changes, 'ascension symptoms', dealing with grief...

Cue a massive life review, a crisis of confidence... Who was this woman? Meno is a gateway to a MUCH deeper level of Awakening. Smooth passage follows by coming to peace with any emotional biggies we've not already faced.

It was an intense time of learning to embrace these changes and start to radically love this woman back into balance. Source always guided me to 'love it more' and reminded me that my earthly form was not the reality of who I was.

This self-nourishment gave me space to reconnect with my soul. I created art, poetry, danced, rested, walked, drummed, meditated and discovered how to make the process as natural as possible; guided to a plant-based diet, intuitively nourishing myself at the deepest level. Each woman is different. Each woman is the expert of what works best for her. I've amassed a wealth of knowledge that I share with HSP women, who're ready to thrive at perimenopause and beyond.

Derek was incredibly patient and loving. I can't say that I always was. I allowed myself to be at peace with this. There's a rich life to be in-joyed way beyond...

... And our glorious dance-in-France continues. I'm deepening my connection with my Star Family, using Light language in my energy work, and writing my own cook book. I finally love the woman I've become and life is good.

As I write this, a tune floods in for us, dear reader:

'I love my life, I am powerful, I am beautiful, I am free, I love my life, I am wonderful, I am magical, I am me, I love my life' (Robbie Williams).

Our truth, we remember. We expand into this as we awaken. Our magnificence as Sovereign Beings, dancing on the Earth in our human bodies, learning through perceived limitations we decided at soul level before we came here for a mere fart of time, in the quantum reality!

Lessons learnt:

- To view sensitivity as a gift.
- To have strong boundaries.
- To forgive people.
- To remember.
- Not to play small to fit in.
- Self-compassion; compassion for all.
- Not to rescue others.
- To love myself.
- To 'love it all beyond judgement'.
- Life is precious.
- To dance lightly on the Earth in partnership with nature.
- That each of us is a powerful Sovereign Being.
- Sense of humour is essential when waking up; remember to laugh, a lot.

Jenny Anne Slater is an Intuitive Vegan Chef, Multidimensional Energy Alchemist and Guide for HSPs, and serves the world online and at her magical Forest of the Stars Retreat in France.

forestofthestars.com
jenny@forestofthestars.com
FACEBOOK: @forestofthestars
INSTAGRAM: @forestofthestars

Jenny's partner, Derek, was inspired to join Jenny in his submission for this book. You may relate to Derek's journey of being a Sensitive, another name for an HSP/ Empath.

THE RELUCTANT SENSITIVE

Derek Slater

"Yes! We are all individuals!"
Life of Brian

Sensitive or Syndrome?

When I finally accepted that I was 'sensitive', I found this to be very helpful; it was a relief. I was relieved to find out that I was sensitive and wasn't just some poorly-educated anti-social buffoon. I ticked enough boxes to know that this is the reason for my inability to cope with certain social situations.

Western science does not accept what it cannot prove:

"The world is round; logically."

"It is flat until you can prove otherwise; heretic."

Western medicine is the same. I cannot be categorised by the official textbook as being sensitive because there is no such ailment or condition included in *ICD-11 – The International Classification of Diseases version 11.*

However, I find it difficult to explain the benefits and restrictions of being sensitive; it varies per person and each person's *perspective* of sensitivity is unique. Should I be more open and share my perspective of how it feels to be sensitive? Will it just cloud your judgement of me? There are days when I'm immune to being sensitive and I can do the shopping quite comfortably, ignoring the stink of the saucisson inconveniently blocking the route to the checkouts; and there are days when I'm picking up on other people's feelings and hate being in the checkout queue.

The problem is that I'm mostly unaware of the origin of my discomfort. Highly Sensitive People (HSPs) differ as much as everyone else differs and it's difficult to find common traits and categories. No one wants their individuality to be removed by being clumped together with other people with coincidental characteristics...

"Yes, I went to Earth last holiday."

"Really? What did you think of the humans?"

Lesson learnt: with the right medical reference book, the general population can be diagnosed as having at least one 'abnormal' condition.

Sensitive or Shy?

One thing that family living does not prepare you for is school. The social sub-group consisting of parents and siblings is exchanged at a stroke for one teacher and 30 peers.

I don't remember my first day at school. I do, however, remember day two because I refused to go. My sister was responsible for taking me to school then, about 100 yards from our house (1960s, pre-decimalisation), and I refused to go with her. My sister, made of sterner stuff than me, carried on (but she is almost three years my senior and had been going for two years). I ran home; the natural reaction. So my mother walked me to school. I clearly remember standing in the class doorway and feeling the combined gaze of 30 five-year-old children, all attracted to just another source of stimulation (how fast they were indoctrinated – day two!).

A note about my school. It was built from granite and there were three local schools built to the same plan at the same time. The ceilings were *really* high and the doorways could have accommodated clowns on stilts (not that *that* ever happened). Classrooms were arranged on three floors, with their doorways opening onto a central rectangular atrium. They were built in this format to accommodate large numbers of people. The only other buildings that could do this in Victorian Britain, and from which the plans were taken, were prisons.

I had a school bag. From then onwards, the contents consisted of 90 per cent Teddy Edward (transitional object of choice) and 10 per cent educational material. Sometimes he was *really* uncomfortable.

P.S. I have a strong hunch that Bill Watterson, author and illustrator of the *Calvin and Hobbes* comic strips, had a similar upbringing to me.

Surviving Secondary School

The wonderful thing about Tigger, is that he was always there. I'll explain…

Cats are like a drug to me, a narcotic (nar-cat-ic). They reduce my stress level. On holiday, my wife and I crave soothing interactions with cats. We have 'temporary adoptions', such as buying cat food for strays at Brousse-le-Chateau, and feeding daddy-long-legs to some caravan kittens in Ireland (no shops for miles; plenty of daddy-long-legs).

I returned home from school every day for lunch. Tigger arrived in 1984 when I was at secondary school. Tigger would lie on my chest and I would disconnect from the education system and connect with my cat. At the time, I thought it was cute to have a cat that let me cuddle him. Boy, was I misled! The superiority complex of we humans is immense. It was Tigger's *purpose* to lie on my chest. He was connecting with my heart chakra. Tigger was literally a heart-healer. Each trauma (a relative term, I wasn't in a war zone) that I experienced was healed with Tigger's love. He's still doing it because it gives me comfort to know that he and Parsley are now inseparable in spirit. (In cat form, Parsley bristled when he visited from beyond, but he is unfazable. In spirit form they are best chums.)

Lesson learnt: just because we can record our thoughts does not make us the superior life-form on this planet.

Sensitive: A Slow Awakening

So let's fast-forward with a short résumé of my baffled life on Planet Earth.

School career guidance:
"I see that you have maths and music; you could become an accountant. Or a piano-tuner."
(You couldn't make this stuff up!)

Further education:
"I have a motorbike, which I stripped and re-assembled; I'll be an engineer."
(Ok, that one was probably on me.)

On becoming self-employed:

"My father ran his business successfully for years whilst being unwell; how hard can it be?"

(What? That was your reasoning and the extent of your research? How wrong can you be?)

Volunteering at the local day-centre for retired gentle-folk:

Think on 'my first day at school'. Got the picture?

On returning to further education following the advice of three unconnected people:

"You would make a good OT."

(Note to self: must find out what an oatie is. Answer: occupational therapist.)

OT Psychiatric student placement, first patient interview:

Well, he's telling me that his sister is going to give him money to buy a new set of shoelaces and I can see that one of his shoes is lace-less and maybe there's a shoelace shop where he's pointing and what has he to gain by lying to me and he seems such a nice chap...

(Note to self: you are not cut out for the invisible ailments of psychiatry.)

During a Clinical Patient Assessment where the esoteric collided with the ward!

"Derek, the patient was tense because you were tense."

"Ah, that makes sense because I felt tense because the patient felt tense. My Reiki Master said that I would be picking up people's feelings."

At which point, the three senior occupational therapists all started speaking at once; not very detached or professional. Seemingly, it is medically accepted that a tense therapist can transfer their tension to a patient but not the other way around.

(Note to self: sensitivities being validated by experience.)

My NHS job transfer saw me collecting/returning medical equipment across the region. Each Thursday, I was in my own company for ten hours, interspersed with the occasional pleasant interaction with (usually) grateful staff. This particular morning, Jenny had asked that Angels watch over me because she had had a feeling. At 08.30, 90 minutes later, my laden trailer absorbed the impact of a car travelling at 60mph connecting with my vehicle, which was going at about 15mph. I feel a bump like crossing a speed bump at 6mph instead of the recommended 5mph, am physically unharmed, but the parting of the ways is nigh.

Lesson learnt: the path to enlightenment has many obstacles.

Sensitive or Spaceman?

When Jenny and I figured out that I 'probably didn't come from this planet', it was a relief. It explained why I didn't fit in and why I found social rules, well, baffling. I wasn't a buffoon; I was wired differently. *Literally* 'wired differently' in one respect. If I'm doing something and bruise myself, I can imagine the pain away: "I haven't got time for this. Leave my body." (Unless I'm bleeding and then it's a different story: "Oh, God! Oh, God! Oh, God! That's supposed to be on the inside of my skin!")

We had a hunch about my origins. Jenny would come out with words like 'Starseed' and 'Pleiadian', which validated that a lot of people don't originate from this planet. There is a queue, a backlog of souls waiting to attend 'Earth-school' because this is the only planet with the particular set of characteristics capable of sustaining a particular form of life. Confirmation came when I received a healing/reading from a dear friend, who said that I had come to this planet expecting an easy time (read that twice if it helps).

So I came to this planet from I don't know what other planet, in whatever star system, in whichever galaxy, in who knows what time-frame, in an Nth parallel universe – and I came here to relax?

This anti-social condition of being sensitive, where you just don't feel like you fit in anywhere, has actually been a gift. Without my protective armour of not understanding the human condition, my sensitivity would have been exposed. It has taken 50 (of your Earth) years for me to accept myself. Actually, that's a bit misleading. It has taken 50 (of your Earth) years for me to accept that it's all right to be different. It's normal to *not* fit in. It's also normal *to* fit in but it's good to be given the option; to be given permission to choose to fit in. "You're going to the scouts because I went to the scouts" would have been kinder along the lines of, "Try it, you might like it".

Oh, and as for reincarnation… If you have ever experienced déjà vu, defined medically as a time lag between the experiencing of a stimulus by each lobe of your brain, then you have probably lived there before ("I just have this feeling"). Jenny and I have been married before; that time, I was the woman. And what's to say it stops at being human? Why do I have such an affinity with cats? Have I had a previous life as a cat? The Earth was commissioned by the mice to find out the answer to life, the Universe, and everything (Douglas Adams). But what if it was created in order that souls could experience turmoil, and thereby learn and grow? Taking that hypothesis to the next stage leads to "have I ever been a dinosaur?" – or a cockroach (they've been here longer than we have), or an amoeba, or a plant or a…?

Lesson learnt: if the world gives you lemons, make tagine.

Significantly Sensitive

Another reading reported that my Angels like my sense of humour. (With that level of support, the rest of you are going to have to live with it or leave.) This raises a question: do you believe in Angels? Do you therefore believe in a divine force which cannot be proven to exist?

"If you believe in angels, you have to believe in zombies." – Ricky Gervais.

I'm not exactly sure about the *purpose* of zombies. What do they do? However, I have known so many people who share interactions with Angels, Unicorns, dragons, faeries, goblins, gnomes, et al. What have they to gain by passing on messages from bees, trees, crystals and rocks, not to mention cats, dogs, horses…? As far as I am concerned, this all exists. Some people can perceive them at an extra-sensory level via one or more of their senses. I had a client who reported a smell of burning whilst she was receiving a healing treatment from me. I have to respect this information as a truthful account of her experience because, for the most part, healing energy flows through me and away from me and I receive very little feedback during a treatment; a bit of 'back pressure' is usually the extent. However, her experience coincided with me using the Violet Flame and I hadn't indicated in advance that I would be doing so.

So, Angels or not? I say, "Yes". I just try to stay away from religious representations. (Don't get me started.) Stay open to messages. Stay receptive to visitations. The limit to the form of any 'divine' message is the limitation of your imagination. I sometimes get a tune come into my head for no reason and it has a message.

Lesson learnt: just because I can't prove it (to your satisfaction) doesn't make it untrue.

www.forestofthestars.com
derek@forestofthestars.com
FACEBOOK: @forestofthestars
INSTAGRAM: @forestofthestars

Yoga teacher, Angelic Reiki healer and a lover of animals, here we introduce Lisa and her thoughts on how to live a balanced, spiritual life. The rebel in Lisa is now free to roam, inspire and connect whenever she chooses.

LOVING THOUGHTS. LOVING WORDS. LOVING DEEDS

Lisa O'Connell

Life is truly a wonderful blessing. Each new day presents us with challenges enabling us to grow.

Sometimes everything is perfect. On other occasions you can find yourself on your hands and knees, lost and alone; desperate for the world to stop turning so you can jump off!

Yet, whichever of these situations we may find ourselves in, they are both equally beneficial to our progress.

The world can be a challenging place, making us feel completely vulnerable. Yet, it's truly unbelievable, magnificent and magical all at the same time.

Each of us has a story to tell. Some will have you in fits of laughter whilst others will literally break you, leaving you reaching for the nearest box of tissues.

But as we each evolve on our journey through life, we grow and expand through all of life's lessons.

I am Irish and Welsh, born in Scotland and raised in England, so I guess it's safe to say I'm definitely British. I'm a yoga teacher, an Angelic Reiki healer and an avid animal lover.

I'm also an Empath and part of a sisterhood. We have each other's backs. We guide and inspire each other to always be a better person than we were yesterday. We have trust in each other and the Universe. But most of all, we have big open hearts full of love – for ourselves, for each other, for you, for the planet, for each beautiful animal and for every living thing. We are strong, loyal, independent, tree-hugging women brought together by synchronicity.

On the physical plane, the world has begun its own spiritual Awakening in force.

The Universe is going through a huge change right now and so are you! Many people would consider this a crisis, when in reality it's probably the biggest opportunity you will ever be presented with, allowing you time to unlock the level of freedom in your hearts and minds and giving you a sense of purpose you have only ever dreamed of. Now is the time to be fiercely brave!

We have begun to move from a place of fear and anxiety to a place of pure love and light. And even though things may outwardly appear quite chaotic, the worst is behind us, allowing this Awakening to happen all around us and within us. We are experiencing a complete disconnect physically with the world, and yet within us we are experiencing a total shared connection with humanity: an unprecedented state of the world, taking away our basic human rights, but at the same time giving us time to reflect on the things that truly matter.

This time of isolation is allowing us to let go of attachments and enabling us to have a deep metaphysical connection to our own being. I'm not saying we are likened to the Buddha or Jesus Christ when I talk of spiritual Awakening, but simply that we are striving to lead a pure life for the good of ourselves, for others, for the planet, and to focus on the greater good, allowing us to visualise our true humanity.

Many things can go wrong in life where we feel we could possibly lose control, but by allowing ourselves to be the master of our own thoughts, we are more equipped to deal with them head-on instead of being an emotional rollercoaster of despair, anger or frustration.

Whatever situation we find ourselves in is irrelevant. It's how we choose to deal with these situations that is the key to our true happiness.

The Universe is conspiring to allow these changes and to make all this a possibility, because we simply cannot carry on with the lives we have been programmed to live by society. The planet needs our help!

This situation is teaching us that there is a sanctuary and a stillness to which we can retreat at any time. Use it wisely.

Buddha was once asked the question, 'If you could sum up your teachings in a single word, what would that word be?'

Buddha's response was simply, 'Awareness.'

By this he didn't mean awareness of any one particular thing, but awareness in general.

To be aware and to stay focused. To remain diligent and alert and in touch with what is happening in the world and within our minds. To consider and to explore the most basic of life's questions: 'Why am I here and what is my purpose?'

By awareness, Buddha was referring to being present in the moment and to seeking liberation of the mind.

Freedom of the mind can be interpreted in many different ways. Some like to call it Samadhi, others Nirvana, yet some know it as Moksha. Buddha himself called it enlightenment. We are ultimately all after the same goal as Buddha was: to reach that place of sanctuary and be free from all life's restraints and expectations. To find peace within us and pure happiness.

Yet you are always so busy that you often forget about the most important person in your life: YOU!

The question you're thinking now is, how do I find my peace?

Well, there are just three basic steps you must follow...

The first step is to realise that life is just temporary. It's fleeting and can be gone in a second. Nobody gets out alive so please don't take it too seriously.

The next step is to understand that not only are you worthy but you're already complete and whole.

Finally, you must understand that you are your own salvation. Your sanctuary and your refuge IS within you.

I see it in my yoga classes on a regular basis. People rushing in and out of class at the last minute, all in a flutter, distracted by the traffic they've encountered on their way to class, or the rude man who cut them up and swore at them on the way there. Not wanting to switch off their phones in case an important call comes. They're angry or flustered because they're late picking the kids up from school or late for work and it isn't their fault. We like to play the victim and the blame game all too often when things don't go our way. Our minds are always full or preoccupied and we're constantly surrounded by distractions. We allow people into our energy field to alter our feelings and our sanity. But why?

I see some students lying in Savasana pretending to relax, whilst all the time they're looking at the person on the mat next to them or around the room; their minds are flitting from one thing to the next, thinking about what to make for dinner that night or wondering if they remembered to turn off the hair straighteners they left on the carpet when they rushed out, or any other one of a million thoughts coming and going on a constant basis. We call this Citta vritti.

Citta vritti is a Sanskrit saying and refers to the thoughts that clutter the mind. Citta means consciousness and vritti means waves or memory. It translates in English to 'mind chatter'. One of the goals of yoga is to take control of Citta vritti by decluttering and quietening the mind, thereby increasing self-awareness and reducing stress. By concentrating our attention on meditation and breathing exercises, we can learn to turn off this inner chatter, enabling us to reach a truer sense of self with a more peaceful awareness.

Our life begins and ends with a breath; like each great journey starts with just one step. The rest of your life begins with each new breath. So please make each one count!

Each new breath we take is a chance of a new beginning and each time we exhale is a chance to let go. To let go of restraints and restrictions, worries, ego, fear or whatever it is stopping you from being the absolute best version of yourself you can possibly be.

Freedom is already yours. All you need do is stop blocking yourself and make yourself a commitment to attend to what is going on within you.

So, now you may ponder the question: 'What is enlightenment?'

It's the process of liberation from the tyranny of the mind. It's unconditional love and bliss. It's a permanent awakening to the absolute unity of all beings. It's a freedom available only to those ready to surrender the ego to pure awareness. And as we begin to slowly peel away our layers, like peeling an onion, we start to strip away those layers of illusion we have accumulated through our lives, which eventually leaves us in our natural state of wholeness and peace.

But how do we find the entrance to this pathway of freedom? The whole Universe has been presented with this infinite possibility right now!

This is obviously easier said than done, or right now we'd all be living in a perfect world, with no famine, war, killings, sickness, animal cruelty and the likes. This isn't the case though, because we all work on different frequencies and vibrations. Some are more advanced than others in their spiritual quest. Some may go through a thousand more lifetimes to be at the place you are now in this life because, here in the matrix, we each evolve at our own pace.

And so, we shall begin on the path to find your true happiness. To do this, you must first accept the things you don't like and want to change. You are the master of your own destiny.

You're lucky as you're always changing and evolving every second that passes.

You don't have the same body or mind you had when your life began, or as a child, or in adolescence. You don't even have the same mind or body you had when you began to read this book.

In every moment there is change. Our bodies' cells die and regenerate. Our muscles atrophy when we don't use them, our gut changes constantly depending on the foods we feed our bodies. Our skin changes from our diet and sun exposure, amongst many other factors.

Some people suddenly lose a loved one, a limb, their sight or their hearing, or hear those terrifying words… 'You have cancer'. We fight and argue with those we love because we wanted a different outcome to the situation, only to make ourselves feel worse and usually regretful.

It's how we choose to deal with these moments that counts. We have to learn to respond and not react because there is a mindful difference, not just in these circumstances but in everyday life. By responding, we let reasonable emotions take control of the steering wheel of our mind, which drives us forward. Reacting just makes us emotional and so we subsequently lose control. When we react, conflict arises thus hindering our progression.

If we choose to respond, however, this takes reasoning. By responding we are being guided not by emotion but by logic. Responding is naturally more passive, enabling us to remain calmer in challenging situations.

Our thoughts are ever changing. In each moment that passes we are changing as individuals, as a race, as humanity. Some for the better and unfortunately some not, but this is fine as each of us has their own journey to focus on and their own cross to bear. Spiritually at last, we are beginning to wake up on a global scale though. Right NOW, in this moment in time, we have been presented with an opportunity to change the things we don't like and answer many questions about our own unique journey.

Like the circle of life and death, which goes on endlessly, right before our eyes, moment after moment, life changes. Nothing will ever be as it was in that moment again. Every aspect of our lives is constantly evolving and moving along different pathways to those we may have anticipated.

So, who holds the power to change your life?

Each of us individually holds our own power. You are the ultimate authority of your life. Not God, nor the Buddha, nor Jesus Christ. Not your spouse, your parents, your children or your boss.

Your life is yours and yours alone to protect and to fully cherish.

We're always searching 'out there' for the next best thing, waiting for our joy to come to us; our minds racing too fast to keep up with its ideas; thinking if we could just get that promotion at work or that better car or that bigger house, these things will make us happier. And maybe for a short while they will. But then you'll start searching again for the next new thing to bring you that fleeting happiness all over again. This cycle never ends unless YOU stop it. The reality is, there is NOTHING 'out there'. All the tools you need are already inside you.

You may not know it, or believe it, but you already have the power you need to find true happiness – by living consciously for yourself and being totally engaged in each moment.

Life isn't about waiting, wishing or hoping. It's about creating, doing and truly living. Today is that day and that's why you're currently reading this book. It's not a coincidence you're here looking for answers. Serendipity guided you here with this book in your hands because it's where you need to be at this precise moment in time. It matters not where you are on your spiritual path. As long as you make a commitment to start living with an attitude of gratitude, the Universe will answer to your hopes and dreams.

If you want to fly, first you must give up everything that weighs you down. How are you ever going to take off with all that excess baggage attached to you?

Let yourself release, relax, restore and let go of anything in life that no longer serves you or your growth purpose. With this, I mean anything or anyone that doesn't make you feel good or vibrate at your level.

Just because you liked that thing or that person five years ago is no reason to still have it or them in your life if they're no good for you. Decluttering our lives declutters our minds.

Just let that shit go!

Let it go without fear or prejudice. Without judgment or criticism. Stop making excuses or you may run out of time. Now is the time for change. This is not a dress rehearsal. Time is so precious. You can start now by becoming the change you wish to see in the world. Say what you mean and mean what you say and always speak your truth. I'm witness to this daily, people saying one thing to themselves or to others, yet acting in a completely different manner from the words they speak. I've listened to and watched my villagers literally fighting for the last ten years to stop the opening of an illegal landfill site in our village, over which people have died – to then witness those same people drive past me with their trailers full of rubbish and dump it off a cliff into the sea next to a 300-year-old monastery, or on someone else's land or at the roadside.

My yoga classes are full of people with resolutions and all good intentions after the new year: to look after themselves more, to lose weight, to go to the gym or to find more time for themselves… They're normally not to be seen again by the end of January though, because life gets in the way. We make excuses to ourselves for the promises we've recently made to ourselves, which we then break without a second thought. You see, it all starts with you. It really is that simple.

For me, through practising yoga, my goal of liberation is not to reach enlightenment but freedom. I've never met a person who claimed to be enlightened and I'm sure that if I was granted another 100 years, I'd still be searching for the 'enlightened one'. It's an extremely ambitious task. What yoga does teach us though, is not to cling to things such as want, greed and hatred, but to free our minds of such destructive elements.

As a child, I knew I'd always been different to others. Ghost stories fascinated me and I was always obsessed with tarot and clairvoyancy, messing around with ouiji boards trying to evoke spirits, whilst not really understanding any of it yet. I was an Empath from an early age and would take on other people's issues as my own, weighing myself down worrying for them and trying to find a solution to their problems. I was always obsessed with animals and dreamed of living in a place one day surrounded by rescue animals that others had been cruel to or had abandoned, and that I could just shower with love. This is exactly where I am in my life right now and I made that happen!

I've always loved life and I still do. I was spoiled with love and affection from my parents, but I was such a rebel. I was a party girl, a wild child, a bit of a hell raiser. I'd often hear my dad say, 'I'm the boss to hundreds of men who all do as I say, yet I have one teenager who never listens to me and thinks she's the boss.' To say I was testing for my parents is an understatement! But, I believe, for no other reason than curiosity. I wanted to test those boundaries; putting myself often in risky or difficult situations because of the buzz and that adrenaline rush. I did what I wanted to do when I wanted to do it and I didn't let anyone stop me. My mum would often say to me growing up, 'I hope you have a daughter just like you one day, so you can understand the hell you've put us through your whole life.' I was a madam and I knew it, but I didn't care. Funnily enough, I did end up having a daughter. My only child. She couldn't and still can't be more loveable and nice if she tried. Rebel wasn't her middle name and she's brought me absolutely nothing but pure joy for the last 26 years. My beautiful Saoscha Montana. The funniest and nicest girl I ever did meet.

I believe Saoscha has a gift she has yet to explore. She would sit for hours in her room as a child, talking to her friends that nobody else could see. One was my grandad and one was a little girl called Oliga with long, blond hair. They'd sit for ages, playing and chatting, and she would describe in detail their conversation and playtime. This stopped at around five years of age when she started school.

One of my favourite humans who ever existed was my Grandad Bill, whom Saoscha would converse with on a regular basis. He passed from cancer in 1993. I'd been to see a clairvoyant that July in Corfu and he'd told me that I was pregnant with a little girl, due on my grandad's birthday the following March. He'd only just passed away in the April and I loved him so much that I believed this was his soul coming back to me. And even though I was a party girl living my best life, I knew from that moment life had to be different as I was going to be a mum. What the hell? I could barely even look after myself still.

Immediately, my focus was on my baby. She was all that mattered now. So, imagine my surprise when I arrived back in England a few months later and had a scan at All Saints maternity hospital in Chatham, only to be told that I was having a boy with a heart defect. I would go to the hospital once a week in those last months of pregnancy, and be strapped to a heart monitor. I'd be told things like, 'Your baby has a hole in his heart, which may require surgery when he's born'. I couldn't believe what I was hearing. I was petrified!

My due date had already passed and I was starting to feel really uncomfortable. I awoke startled one night to find my grandad sitting at the end of my bed. He told me not to worry; that I was having a little girl and that everything was going to be all right. I've received many a message from my grandad since his passing, but that is still the only time my gramps ever physically appeared to me. I still remember his gentle face with that big beaming smile, that massive presence of his, and his words, like it was yesterday. I called my mum and she told me I was crazy. So I called my grandma, who confirmed my mum's thoughts. But I knew the truth! Why did nobody believe me? My grandad was there. Right there next to me, calling me sweetheart, just as he'd done all my life. And I'd suddenly felt safe, nurtured and secure.

The very next day, after drinking a whole bottle of castor oil mixed with orange juice, because I'd heard it induces labour, I finally went into hospital, and my baby arrived after a difficult labour of over 40 hours. There was a problem though. She wasn't breathing. The umbilical cord was wrapped around her neck and her face was blue. Oh God, no! My heart was in my throat. As the midwife freed her and gave her a thump on her back, she screamed and I instantly felt calm. I asked if he was ok. The midwife's exact reply was: 'He? Well, he has a fanny so I'd presume it's a girl.'

I nearly fell off the bed. I'm surprised I didn't I was so high on gas and air! It had been for over two months that I'd been monitored for my baby boy with a heart defect, and nobody had seen it was a girl with absolutely no issues, except for the clairvoyant and my grandad! How could the others have been so wrong? I'm obviously grateful they were wrong, yet I spent those months living in absolute fear for nothing. They handed my baby girl to me a few minutes later and life really would never be the same again. This tiny little person, with those tiny little fingers that were clutching my hand, was mine. I owned her lock, stock and barrel. And to top it all off, he was a she! That precise moment was the happiest I have ever felt.

She was my responsibility. Shit! Now I had the worry of her being like me. She looked like me with her red hair and chubby fingers. Oh God! Maybe my mum HAD manifested me the naughtiest child ever, but only time would tell.

Each situation we encounter teaches us more about ourselves. If we stay calm and true in spite of adversity, we'll be shown the way if we trust our instinct. When you get that feeling in the pit of your stomach, where your third chakra resides – your solar plexus – listen to it! Your body knows. The feelings in your heart originate here. It's where we find clarity, wisdom, self-confidence and our own wellbeing. It's our seat of intuition, from where arise our gut feelings. Learn to trust these feelings more by working on yourself during this time you've been gifted now. Don't look at the negative side of things but instead use this time wisely for yourself. It's an opportunity that may never come along again.

Have a Reiki session to help filter your energy though your seven main chakras, which run from the base of your spine to the crown of your head. Our chakras can be likened to vortexes that both receive and radiate energy. Our emotions, our physical health and our mental clarity all affect how well each of our chakras work. This in turn dictates how pure the energy is that's emitted from different parts of the body. They are our centres of spiritual power. We shouldn't neglect them. They are linked to our unconscious mind, where all our experiences and actions are stored.

Our first chakra is Muladahara, which is the essence of our foundation. This chakra governs the course of our future destiny and is the foundation for the development of our personality. It's our base from where we need to ground ourselves. It's our mother providing us with energy and food.

Our second major chakra is called Swadisthana. It's our sacral chakra, which governs our creativity, our morality, pleasure and control. It's our centre of pure, steady attention and knowledge, from where rises our power of concentration. If we're able to manifest the quality of flowing consciousness, we're then able to develop the positive and spiritual qualities of our sacral chakra.

Manipura is our third chakra. It's our city of jewels, situated behind the navel. After we pass through the levels of unconsciousness and subconsciousness, we reach our consciousness here at our solar plexus.

Our next and fourth chakra is situated at our heart centre. It's called Anahata and is our seat of affection, compassion and loving kindness, enabling us to live with ahimsa – non-judgement and non-criticism of ourselves and others. Remember that love and compassion are not luxuries but absolute necessities. Without these two things, humanity cannot survive! If we have a balanced heart centre, we are able to release past wounds, hurts and attachments, living our lives, full of kindness and generosity.

Our throat chakra, Visshudha comes next. It's from where we speak to be heard. It's about clear communication. Saying what you mean and meaning what you say. So, we must use our voices for only good things. Always speak your truth and always be kind.

Our third eye, Ajna chakra is next and is considered to be our eye of intuition and intellect. Here lies the gateway to our consciousness. This can be made more powerful through meditation, yoga and other spiritual practices. It gifts us in seeing both our inner and outer worlds. It's from here where our sense of ethics and justice originate.

Finally, we arrive at Sahasrara, our crown chakra, which translates to infinite. It symbolises the infinite depths of our being. It's from here that all our other chakras emanate. It gives us that sense of realisation that EVERYTHING is connected at a fundamental level. It's the meeting point of finite (the body and the ego) and infinite (the Universe and the soul). It gives us a sense of knowing that there is a deeper meaning to life.

It really does pay to work on yourself. Only you have the power to change your life. If you're not truly content with where you are right now, change it!

Be the best version of yourself you can possibly be. You must take care of your body as it's the only real place you'll have to live in this lifetime. You need to fill yourself up with nourishment: good, natural, sattvic foods. Do something good today and become a vegetarian. We're not meant to walk through life with the rotting flesh of another soul inside us. We claim to be a race of animal lovers. We let our cats and dogs sleep in our beds yet we think it's ok to kill defenceless animals to put on our plates and serve to our children. Why is a cow's life dispensable but not your pet's?

Drink lots of water, listen to inspiring music, chant mantras, meditate, keep great company, practise morning yoga. In fact, practise yoga anytime of the day! Yoga is not, as some of you are probably thinking, about being able to touch your toes. It's about what you learn on the way down there. Yoga can add years to your life and life to your years. Yoga is just like life. It's that perfect balance of holding on and letting go. It's simply about being present in the moment and at this moment, some of you have been blessed with all the time in the world to focus on you.

I have a beautiful yoga retreat opening in the summer of 2021 here in Corfu. It should have been this summer but the Universe had different plans for all of us in 2020. It's in a beautiful place called Tsilaria. Even most of the locals don't know it exists. We have sea views. We have mountain and lake views. We're surrounded by olive trees and huge towering pine trees. The sun is mostly shining and the birds are always singing. I get to practise yoga and meditate every day. I'm once again free from the things that bind me to the rat race so many of us choose to live in. Every day I wake up and I make the choice to be happy.

I have no mortgage or rent as I live off grid in a small cabin in the woods, where I never get to sit on the sofa as it's always occupied by rescue animals. I rarely ever have a good night's sleep or am comfortable in bed because of all the animals wanting love and cuddles. I do, however, have an abundance of fruit and vegetables growing on my doorstep. There's no mains electricity or water, all these things we just take for granted. I choose to live without these luxuries. These are things that certainly make life easier, but ultimately we don't need them. I have solar for my electricity and a well for my water, meaning no bills from big corporations.

What I need is to be able to wake up each morning and watch the sun rise over the sea. I want to watch the stars at night, so bright and plentiful. I need to watch the lake at the end of my front garden as it turns into dusky purple tones at sunset. I want to sit on my veranda, watching my animals enjoying their freedom all day, whilst playing amongst my giant sunflowers. I get to indulge myself in the things I need to feed my soul. It's my life. These are my choices.

And I understand my life is not for everyone. Life really is what you make it. I made mine perfect for me. Will you love yourself enough to do the things that fulfil your soul and make your life perfect for you?

Right now, in this moment as I look back on my journey and what brought me to where I am today, I'd like to thank each and every one of you who has touched my life. Good or bad. Each one of you taught me a lesson. Each one of you helped me to grow as a person. Each one of you helped with my own spiritual Awakening. To all the yogis and Rishis, past and present, thank you for your teachings and for helping me to find myself and my calling. I'm grateful for each raindrop, for each time I look at the sea and can hear the gentle waves lapping against the shore. I'm grateful for each flower I smell, for my beautiful animals and for the food I eat. I'm grateful for my child and my wonderful friends, way too many to mention all of you. I'm grateful for my good friend Michelle, who is ALWAYS grateful. To my beautiful Reya, my amazing friend of 47 years. To my pink ladies, Alison, Nicola, Gemma, Anita and Donna, my sisters for over 30 years for always having my back. I love you all a crazy amount. My precious Amalia, Andrea, Sue, Jennie, Lou, Gaye, Vicky, Luey, Lynne, Nicola, Nicki, Leane, Susie and my wonderful Lisas, without whom life would not have been the bundle of laughs it has been. You have stood by me for as long as I can remember and I love you all so very much.

I'm proud to say, I'm a woman's woman and this is how I'll stay!

But most of all, I'm grateful for my family, who taught me to love unconditionally even when I was horrible! Your love and kindness never wavered. You may not have liked me sometimes, but you always loved me. I'm sorry for my adolescent years and beyond. Oh, and all the years before that too! I love you with every fibre of my being.

I blame my rebellion on a pure lack of knowing I was different and not knowing my direction. I knew I was spiritual but I didn't really understand. I dabbled with everything from tarot to Buddhism. You could say I was jack of all trades and master of none. But now, at 49 years old, I feel content with my choices and blessed with my life.

Each day when you wake, have a good stretch, breathe some fresh air, enjoy a brisk walk, do some yoga, call your mum to tell her you love her. Smile at a stranger. Choose to be happy, choose to forgive. And don't let other people steal your energy. It's ok to give it away but stay away from energy vampires. Remember that life truly is a beautiful blessing but above all else, don't EVER leave the keys to your happiness in somebody else's pocket.

I hope to see you here at Serendipity by the Lake, for some much needed YOU time. Whether it be on the yoga mats at sunrise or in purple aerial silks suspended from olive trees overlooking an emerald-green lake, having an Angelic Reiki session, attending a retreat, or simply living in nature and getting to swim at secluded beaches, it's all here waiting for you. We're an eco-friendly site offering brand new wooden cabins and luxury tipis. It's a place to relax, rejuvenate, unwind and let go. A place to integrate your mind, body and soul. I look forward to meeting you sweet souls and to being able to open up and share my beautiful life with you.

Love is the message.

THE MESSAGE IS LOVE.

Aum shanti. Namaste. xx

Lisa O'Connell is a collaborative author of When the Goddess Calls.

www.serendipitybythelake.com
lisacorfu@hotmail.com
FACEBOOK: @serendipityyoga
INSTAGRAM: @lisacorfuyoga

Animal Connections

Empaths often have a natural deep connection with animals.
They can communicate via telepathy just by looking at the animal.
These three stories share the Empath's love of animals.

Here Faye shares what she has never shared before. Seeing spirits, knowing stuff –
'claircognizance' – a clear sense of knowing. Maybe this happens to you too.

THE RELUCTANT PSYCHIC IN ME

Faye Louise Enchanted Goddess Kirwan

This is Something I've Never Told Anyone...

When I was young, around the age of six, I could see and sense things others couldn't. I used to think I could communicate with my Golden Retrievers, Heidi and Jessica, telepathically. When we would travel in the car with them and they would be anxious, I would soothe them telepathically, telling them it would be ok, we were going somewhere they would enjoy and I was with them so everything would be fine. Then I would tell them to count to ten and, after staring into their eyes, I would close mine while counting to ten with them, and they would fall asleep. I'm still not sure if what happened on numerous occasions was me at the age of six being able to communicate with dogs telepathically, or just some strange coincidences, but either way, I always felt calmer and the animals always had a calmer presence. Over the years, I've always been drawn to animals and especially horses. I've seemed to have a calming effect around them and a fabulous connection too.

As a young child, I used to see and sense all sorts of things. I could and still can see people's auras. I could see them a lot easier when I was younger. Now

I have to concentrate harder, but that's my own fault for becoming a reluctant psychic. I'll explain more later on. I used to ask my mum (I'm sure I've freaked her out on more than one occasion) if she could also see colours around different people. Strangely, I couldn't see animals' auras, given the connection I already had.

I also had, and still do have, a strong connection with the afterlife. First and foremost, I'm a spiritualist. I don't believe in religion but I do believe in reincarnation. I feel that my soul is a very old one and I was around in ancient Egyptian times to begin with, as I've such a connection with them. I'm completely fascinated by them and have been from a very young age.

When I was around the same age (six), things all started with the afterlife. I recall, when at my parents' home, that I used to be able to see the ghost of my Great Aunt Mary, who lived in the house before I was born. I used to see a slim, dark-haired, female ghost standing at the top of the stairs. I'd also see her in the hallway. She'd never say anything, just look out in the opposite direction. As I got older, I didn't see her as often, but on some occasions I did, especially if my dad was doing work on the house.

As I was growing up, these experiences would become less. Into my teenage years, I didn't want my friends to think I was a freak. I realise now that I should have nurtured my gift. Instead, I hid it well and forced myself into becoming a reluctant psychic.

In my early teenage years, I remember a big old-fashioned mirror sitting over the real fireplace at my mum's house. I was standing looking in it, doing my hair, and I saw an old, Victorian-style woman. But she had a baby and she was crying. They were both dressed in white yet the baby was so dark. I believe it was dead, which is why she was so upset. After this experience, I wouldn't look in mirrors; just a quick glance, here and there. I'm better now I'm older, mind.

I remember at around the age of 13 being at my mum's house, which was a very old, terraced house with an old-fashioned entryway, wide enough to get a horse and trap down. At the bottom of the garden was a brick-built shed, which we later found out was the old coffin maker's and nail maker's. There was a lot of activity in that house all the time. My mum still has the photos of the living room before I was in it with the dogs, when there was nothing. But as soon as

I was in the room, there would be so many orbs. There was even one pictured sitting in between my toes that has substance to it. Then my mum would again take pictures when I'd left the room and gone to bed etc. And the activity had stopped. It never frightened me, even at that age. I just wish now I'd embraced it more. All the orbs where white or greyish in colour, and the majority were filled with substance. I believe that I still see them now: you know the feeling you get when you see something in the corner of your eye... That's an orb.

But What Exactly is an Orb?

Some so-called orbs can be just simple refractions of light as the after-result of taking a picture with the flash on. They can be specks of dust that the light bounces off, or even a tiny insect or a tiny piece of metal or lint that's caught the flash and been picked up by the camera. But these were different. True orbs have substance. If you can, imagine something perfectly circular, which has what I can only describe as a thick, cloud-like formation. You cannot see through it and it has a border around the edge of it. The border is strong and glows brighter as the inner cloud-like formation moves. All the orbs I've seen have been white but they have been seen in different colours. I believe the orbs to be a spirit present, who is maybe not strong enough to present itself or who has been there and is just leaving, or they're simply a relative who is standing guard over you, trying to protect you, similar to what some people may call a Guardian Angel.

Quite often, it will be mainly children who are looked after by orbs, and they will tend to be drawn towards them. I believe this for a couple of reasons, mainly that there is a stronger sense of protection needed over children. But children are also much more aware and open to spiritual encounters. It's only as we grow older that we start to question things and become fearful of the unknown, which is such a shame. Imagine going through life with the same wonderment and openness as a child has, without the fear and cynicism. How wonderful would that life be and how much more would we be able to do, see and understand!

I mentioned that orbs have different colours. The most commonly seen orbs have a white or slightly silvery, almost celestial tinge. These are thought to be of positive energy, but it can also indicate that a spirit may be stuck in purgatory, or can't pass for some reason. It's ok to talk to them and let them know it's all right and they're not needed here any longer; you appreciate the help and protection but you can see to it yourself. That way, they can move on and not be stuck here without purpose.

Red or orange orbs, and any that are warm-coloured pink hues etc., these are a definite protective energy. You know when you shut your eyes and look into the sun? They're that kind of colour. I've seen a few but not many. We have green orbs too now. These orbs sense the connection to the Earth and Mother Nature. They can also indicate beings that haven't lived, or at least haven't lived for long on the Earth.

And there are blue orbs. Now, if you're trying to reach a specific spirit or the spirit world, you may see these, and be glad that you do. These are truthful, healing and quite calming. They can also be an indicator that you've reached the correct spirits.

Now there are also black orbs, but please don't be scared by these, as we know that this isn't the most pleasant colour in regard to things like this. In this case, it can just mean that these orbs have a lot of baggage and are upset or sometimes angry by what has happened to them, and they're here looking for answers that they may well deserve; another reason why they can't pass over peacefully. However, having said this, they can also be a forewarning that what you are about to do or encounter may not be so nice. So please, no matter what you are doing, make sure you have the proper protection for it.

Orbs can stick within your aura. This may be where some of the colour of your aura can come from, especially if you are particularly gifted as a psychic or you're even just a very spiritual person with an open soul. These orbs can act to guide you through the other side and protect you if you're trying to reach out to spirits.

Orbs are beautiful and I am eternally grateful I get to experience them and see them too. They can also be part of that gut instinct that we know to trust.

Orbs are mainly seen at night and can be captured on film. They can be felt too. You know when you feel like someone has just brushed your skin? For me, it's normally my shoulder. Sometimes, the rude ones will tap me on the shoulder to really let me know they are there. And when you feel like 'someone has walked over your grave' and you shudder? I believe that's the orbs and any other beings trying to make contact. Try to listen at times like this if you can. Maybe try a little meditating to see if anything else comes through.

So this experience of orbs, for me, was extremely affirming, alongside other experiences. As I mentioned, at this young age, I tried to dampen down my skill set, and it worked for a short while. Then, as I was getting older and becoming more aware of the world, things started to kick off again. At around the age of 18, we went to visit some friends in Wales, who lived in a very old farmhouse. The hairs on the back of my neck were standing up on end the whole time while I was in the living room with these friends. The staircase to upstairs was behind me and my stomach was in knots. As I turned around, there was a little boy with blond hair sitting on the stairs, around the age of five. He just stared and watched us through the spindles of the staircase. I asked my mum if she could see him and the answer was no (sorry to scare you, Mum).

After talking to some locals in the area, it transpired that this little boy had died on the farm at that age around 100 years ago, when he was trampled by a horse and cart. An absolute tragedy. The house was definitely haunted and nothing good ever happened there. My friend's horse, Anton, went down in the field with colic a couple of weeks later and died after eight hours. There were so many unfortunate accidents and so much bad luck. It was devastating. Needless to say, our friends didn't stay there that long. Neither did anyone for that matter. If I'd known then what I do now, I would have done a clearing of some sort and helped the spirit to pass over.

This time in my life is when things started to reawaken in me. I had my own business at the time and was driving to a country fair where I had a stall. My mum was with me and we had to drive the same route for three days. When I got to a certain point on this road, as I was driving, I would get an awful headache and the overwhelming urge to drive straight into the side of the house that was on the roadside. For three days, every morning this happened. So, at the end of the very busy weekend, I looked it up at home and found out that six months previously, someone had been racing down that road in their car too fast, had lost control, hit the house and ultimately lost their life. May they rest in peace.

As I was getting older, and also with the invention of Google and smartphones, I was able to look more into things. I started to go to a spiritualist church.

Every time I went, the mediums would home in on me. For six weeks running, six different mediums would pick me out of a huge crowd, and afterwards say to me how much of a strong connection they had with me. Again, I regret not taking that further, but I believe that everything happens for a reason. I'm also a great believer in spirit and destiny.

When I was in my early twenties, I decided that doing a ghost hunt would be a good idea. But although I was a sceptic when I went in, I certainly wasn't when I came out! We went to the Derby Royal Infirmary, which had been shut down. We did this at 9pm and stayed until 5am the following morning. The second I walked through the doors, a large bottle of water I was carrying got flung out of my hand, like someone had taken it from me and thrown it behind me.

During the night, so many things were happening. I could see orbs and hear voices. Then some smart-arse decided that a seance would be a good idea! Well, this is how it went:

There was myself, my mum and my brother's mother-in-law. At the time, we had our fingers on top of one another's, not touching the glass on the table. The glass started to go round in a clockwise motion. Great. We were asking yes or no questions and getting our answers. Then I went stone cold and the hairs on the back of my neck stood up. The glass jerked violently and started turning in an anti-clockwise direction. The guide proceeded to panic, took the glass off us and smashed it. Outside, she later told us an evil spirit was trying to get through.

Then there was the empty psychic ward. We sat in the dark, other than our torches, and all I could hear was a blood-curdling scream over and over, which no one else was picking up. We went to the theatres, where we all stood in a circle, linking arms, while the medium who was with us was trying to reach anyone. All of a sudden, I felt sick and like I was going to pass out. It felt like someone had got a hot needle at the top of my spine and was trying to get into me. Unfortunately, I got scared and broke the chain, which stopped it apparently. That was a spirit trying to overcome me and speak through me. The only other time I've ever had that kind of feeling is when I'm meditating and in a trance-like state, and I've heard other-worldly voices.

Throughout my working life, especially the last seven or so years, I've been drawn to care work, and the last five years especially, as I've been working in the NHS. I find myself being drawn to patients who are dying, or are recently deceased, and their family members, to console and look after them as they are grieving. I'm an Empath at heart and love to look after people, so I knew this was my calling. However, I found myself looking after the recently deceased more and more, often by doing the last offices for the patients, where we would wash them and look after them as if they were still alive, and prepare them for the next stage. I always felt so calm and at peace doing this and I like to think that, with some of the traumatic deaths, I helped to put them at peace. This was always a part of my job, something I had the pleasure of doing for others, and it was such an honour that I could do this physically for people. I've also been there for patients and their families at the time when they have passed. On the whole, it always seems so peaceful.

Skipping along through the years, I've been drawn to Angel cards and meditation. I adore the Angels and my cards. They are so intuitive, and they're something I now concentrate on. I love working with my pendants and my spirit guides. My spirit animal is a Unicorn. I'm fascinated and besotted by them. The Angels are always tapping me on the shoulder and trying to guide me through life, by sending me signs and affirmations. I truly feel at one and at peace with the cards. They're fantastic and the first thing I turn to in times of trouble.

When I turned 30, my mum paid for me to have some Reiki training and I adore giving Reiki. I love the connection I get with people and the sense of release it gives me as well as the client. My soulmate loves it too. We spend a lot of time with the Angel cards and my pendants, and I try to encourage his skills as he's very intuitive. One example of this was when we were at his sister's house, decorating her living room for her. It was a warm day and we had the window open, curtains drawn back. We were just chatting away and having a laugh while decorating, and I kept feeling a female presence. As my fiancé was standing by the window, I turned to look at him, and I could see the window fogging up and clearing over and over. It looked like when someone breathes on a mirror to write a message and it happened around 20 times. It had to be his mum, who had sadly passed too early. My fiancé could see it and I could see it, but his sister couldn't. It carried on for about two minutes and then stopped. If I hadn't seen it or my fiancé hadn't witnessed it, I doubt either of us would have believed it.

Our connection is unreal. We quite often know what the other is thinking. Very often I'll think something, and then a split second later he'll say it. I'm constantly telling him to get out of my head. We can also sense when we're near each other. If he goes off without me, I can sense when he's close again and has returned. We're so in tune with one another that only the slightest impact on our mental health can be picked up. He knows the minute I start to feel a bit down or a bit off, and vice versa. We both also have premonitions in our dreams quite often and love sharing with each other about them. Sometimes, when we're sitting in the car together, one of us will say, 'I'm not going to drive down there' or, 'Don't go down there, I've got a funny feeling'. We listen to our gut constantly and I'm so glad we understand each other so well and are so in tune with each other that it just makes sense; we don't have to question it.

My son is also starting to pick up my skills. He's six and a half now and is constantly talking to people in his bedroom and saying things like, 'Mummy, did you hear the man talking to me?' etc. So I'm keeping an eye on that and will encourage it if he wants to go deeper as he gets older. As I type this, I can hear him in his bedroom talking to his 'friends'. I'm just glad I know what it is.

Like I said previously, I believe in fate and destiny. It was just over two years ago I met my now fiancé, who is my true soulmate. We have a connection like no other. We moved to Cornwall eight months ago. When I first met him, I'd never been there. He showed me Newquay and Perranporth and I completely fell in love. I just know that Cornwall is where I'm meant to be. I feel that my skills are getting stronger here and I'm allowed to be who I want to be, not what society says I should be.

The connection I hold with Perranporth is like no other. I truly feel at home and at peace there. At the moment, we're living in the beautiful little fishing village of Mevagissey, which is amazing. As I sit here writing this, we're suffering a yellow storm warning, so it's extremely windy and grey. We love the extremities of weather. We can't wait for lockdown to be over so we can go back to my spiritual home of Perranporth. I feel so much more in tune there, calm and complete.

I highly recommend meditation for becoming more in tune with yourself, and feeling a higher presence. When you can master meditating and feel that relieved sense, it's truly amazing and you really do feel one with the Universe.

I'm going to spend more time trying to practise these skills and make them greater, and I urge anyone who has had experiences like mine or similar to practise them, and to find people who are similar to yourself and into the same things; also people who can help you sharpen your skills. After a few years of using them, I'm now teaching others to read Angel cards and understand them more, and to connect with that side of things more effectively.

To be able to heighten your vibrations is also amazing (no, I don't mean the ones shaped like a bunny). Your spiritual vibration is so important to nurture and look after. Just basic meditation can kickstart it. Then I highly recommend a deck of Angel cards and to learn all they have to offer, and to listen to your Angel guides and see if you can channel any of your own messages.

If there's anyone out there who'd like more advice, or even just to talk to someone more like themselves and with similar experiences, then please don't hesitate to contact me. I'm more than happy to talk things through. Even if you feel it might be something or nothing, I may be able to help.

I offer you all so much love and light. Take care of yourselves and each other and your world will be a much happier place.

Love and light from Faye Louise Enchanted Goddess Kirwan.

Yes, that's my official name. I changed it by deed poll as I felt it was the right thing to do at the time.

enchanted.goddess.angel.readings@gmail.com
FACEBOOK: @enchanted.goddess.designs

Born with a natural gift for connecting and communicating with animals, 'Psychic Beth' decided to believe in her gifts and was soon given confirmation that she was indeed a pet psychic.

THE RELUCTANT PET PSYCHIC

Elizabeth Lee-Crowther

As far back as I can remember, I've had a passion for animals.

Being born in Birmingham meant we were never far away from the countryside (people have a misconception that it's a completely built-up area but it's rich with beautiful places to visit).

My parents tell me that as soon as I could walk and talk, my dad would have to stop the car at the end of our road so that I could stroke two horses that lived in a field there.

I drove my parents mad for a pet and my dad took me to a pet shop to choose a rabbit. I could see a tiny, black and white Dutch rabbit in the window with about 20 others (it was the 1970s). The shop assistant lifted up many rabbits until she got to the 'one' I instinctively knew was mine. It was as if I could hear his voice saying, 'Choose me'. I called him Benji and I had him for 12 years. This was the beginning of many pets coming into my life, including guinea pigs, cats, dogs, parrots, horses and ponies.

As a child, I was obsessed with horses and rode ponies at a local stables. I dearly wanted to have my own pony but my parents weren't financially able to afford that luxury.

When I was around 11 years of age, I was riding a small white pony called Toby. I remember feeling this sense of freedom and serenity, as if time had stood still and I was in the moment of ultimate happiness, being at one with my four-legged friend.

In my mind, I would talk to Toby and he would answer me – telling me about his past, previous injuries and his aches and pains. I thought this was 'normal', something that happened when you rode horses.

It wasn't until I asked my friend, who was riding with me, what her pony was saying, that I realised by her reaction that other people weren't experiencing the same thing.

Finally, at the age of 23, I purchased my first pony, Amberleigh, and many more were soon to follow. They taught me more about this skill of 'telepathically' communicating with animals but I still hadn't told anyone – it was our secret.

Due to my love of horses, I started my own saddlery business, providing tack and equipment locally and online. People would tell me about their horses and I would recommend certain items of equipment to help them.

I would ask to look at a photo of their horse and I'd find myself telling the owner all about their background, likes and dislikes, and behaviour issues and what was causing them.

Word got around and people no longer came to buy saddlery. Instead, they'd turn up with photos of their pets for me to 'read'.

I became known as a 'Pet Psychic' or 'Animal Communicator'.

Being a naturally sceptical person, I decided to test myself, and I asked people to send me pictures of their pets from all over the world so I knew, without a shadow of a doubt, I couldn't possibly know anything about them. I needed 'proof' that the only way I could possibly know this information was from the animals themselves.

Time after time, their owners validated the information I was receiving, and it was only then that I decided this was my path.

This seemed to activate some surreal events that were to quickly follow.

I was asked to track a missing dog, which led to me appearing on *Central TV News*, and then a documentary was made. I ended up in London on *The Richard & Judy Show*, and even at Russell Brand's house, talking to his cat, Morrisey.

My life completely changed when I 'accepted' this gift, and it wasn't long before I started to have people who had passed into the spirit world coming through during the animal readings, to give a message to their loved ones.

I then bought my first pack of oracle cards – and instinctively knew how to use them for people.

Even through all this excitement and enlightenment, I knew the importance of staying 'real' and 'grounded'. I've never take anything for granted and always appreciate and honour the skills I've been blessed with. Therefore, I'm committed to sharing these skills with anyone open-minded enough to give them a go. I teach Animal Communication Workshops and Psychic Development Workshops and offer readings.

I believe all our pets have something to teach us and are healers with significant lessons to share. This has been a passion of mine since 2004, to spread the word and let people know that Animal Communication is real and exists. It led to me watching a film called *The Secret*, which is about the Universe supplying you with your desires if you ask.

Once again, my sceptic mind kicked in and I decided to put it to the test. I knew if I could demonstrate my pet psychic skills on the radio to people listening in, just by them giving me their pets' names, I could spread the word and prove animals can talk.

Less than two weeks from me putting the request out to the Universe, I was contacted by a local DJ (I had coincidentally parked my car outside his house when attending a birthday party).

After appearing on his show on The Bridge Radio in Stourbridge, we were overrun with calls. This led to me having my own weekly show on the station for over five years.

Currently, I have a radio show on Pulse Talk Radio and have written a book, *Life by Numbers*, and released a pack of oracle cards, *'Live your Best Life'* Oracle Deck.

Elizabeth Lee-Crowther is an author, Reiki Master, animal communicator, psychic medium and radio presenter.

www.psychicbeth.com
FACEBOOK: @psychicbethofficial
INSTAGRAM: @elizabethleecrowther

We move to France now, where Clare Hill shares her bond with animals, nature and astrology, amongst just some areas where Empaths have natural abilities and knowing: claircognizance.

MY JOURNEY OF TUNING IN TO THE INVISIBLE

Clare Hill

The year was 1972. I'd decided to be reborn on the planet Earth. I'd spotted a lady and was drawn to choose her as my mother in this experiment we call LIFE. On 21st May, 1973, I came into the world in Melton Mowbray, Leicestershire at 12.10 pm. Not a pleasant experience for Mother or me, as I was in the breach position and got stuck for hours. I was two weeks early and only 5lbs 13 ounces in weight.

One of my earliest memories is travelling in the back of the car and gazing up at the night sky. My fascination with the stars, planets and constellations puzzled my parents. And one of my best-loved birthday presents was a book called, *What's Beyond?*. I read it and reread it. I knew every word by heart. What I didn't know until a few years later was that I was searching; searching for home.

As a child, I never felt quite right; never at home here. Yet I have fantastic parents, who couldn't have given me a more loving childhood. I had such a happy time and to this day we are very close.

Still, the planets, stars and geography fascinated me completely, alongside the animal world, and dogs and horses became my loves.

Whilst studying geography, I felt I already knew the information on how the continents were formed, and was relearning this and could probably have taken the class! I would pore over the maps on the walls of my classroom; I absorbed so much knowledge, or I relearnt it! I remember getting chills through my body when the Earth's layers and crust and mantle were taught; and the texture, the crystals that were being discovered in different parts of the world. What were the chills all about?

So, back to the animals... Horses could often understand me, and I could understand them, read them, and sometimes I could hear their emotions and thoughts. This led me to love being with horses and horse riding, mainly because I was sensitive to their emotions and just felt happy around them. I remember watching *Black Beauty*, the films on TV, and thinking, YES, the horses do talk to those who can listen! It confused me that other people didn't hear them. These days I don't have horses around me, but dogs – well, yes, I have lots of dogs!

I wasn't able to have a dog at home, but my neighbours across the road had a puppy Springer Spaniel called Ben. He spent his days at a farm, running around, and the minute I arrived home from school, I'd get changed and call for Ben to walk in the fields. We had great fun, running and playing and hugging. I loved Ben. I could tell he liked his life at the farm but his 'person' was me. I was his human. We had a bond between human and dog that was very strong.

My grandad lived with us during my teenage years. He fought in the Second World War and had stories to tell, and in me he had a willing audience. He spoke once about a fortune teller he'd met in North Africa during one of the campaigns. With some of his fellow soldiers, they queued up and paid the fee. The fortune teller was cloaked and quite mysterious looking, and he told my grandad that he'd be fine; he'd survive the war and would have three daughters. I asked, 'What about the other soldiers?' Grandad said the guy just winked at them and told them, 'Best of luck, my boy'. This affected me as, although not exactly lying, it wasn't really truthful either

By my teenage years, I'd put away *What's Beyond?* and had started telling my classmates' fortunes via astrology. I studied the stars, planets and their placement obsessively. If there had been a GCSE in astrology, I would have got at least a B grade! My friends didn't want to know the truth; they wanted a watered-down version of the truth and the future. I continued studying my books, and then palmistry and clairvoyance. But I gave up telling them what the stars revealed, unless they could actually take that some of life wasn't all sweetness and light.

Now my eyes were wide open. I was wanting to read every book ever written! I'd heard animals and knew and could see the truth in any situation so clearly. No one could lie to me. I could spot an untruth and would not put up with it!

One of my friends tried to blame me for her misdeeds against another friend, and I remember being so cross it was like a white-hot flame was inside me.

I never spoke with her again; I cut her out of my life in that moment. My other friend and I remain friends to this day.

I spent a lot of my childhood and teenage years outside. I loved collecting flowers, herbs, and made concoctions, perfumes, all in the garden shed. I had many dried flowers; pressed flowers in scrapbooks too. I had no books to learn from, or anyone to help me; I just experimented over time – a happy time in the shed. Years later, I told one of my teachers this during a workshop making potions and creams. She laughed and replied, 'You were a witch in training!'

So, around this time, I'd started hearing people's voices in my head, normally at odd times, whilst I was walking the dog or in the garden shed with my herbs. I decided to ignore them. I didn't know whose voices they were and they weren't telling me! Of course, they carried on, but I carried on ignoring them, hoping they'd go away.

I met David, my husband-to-be, and, looking at our astrology charts, I should have seen the difficult areas! Instead, I chose to see the harmonious area and decided to go with that. We moved into a home together and got married. We inherited a lot of his grandma's furniture and things. She had sadly passed away not long before David and I met.

One item was a pretty musical mandolin, made of wood, and out of tune. I used to pick it up and pretend to play. This served to put me in a meditative state where Grandma could reach me. It freaked me out, I have to be honest. I didn't know where to turn or how to make her leave me alone. I talked to David, of course, and his reaction was that he had married a mad woman and I was making it up! He eventually did believe me when I told him details from his grandma that I couldn't possibly have known, apart from via her speaking to me.

I began to shut myself down. I closed off my mind, to save my relationship. I focused on renovating the house and planting a garden. I planted hundreds of metres of hedging plants and started a vegetable and fruit garden from scratch. I was in my element. Once again, nature was my only salvation; my happy place. The icing on my cake was when, for my 21st birthday, David asked me if I'd like a puppy. Jack became my first dog and my best friend.

Jack was a sensitive black Labrador, and would often sit and bark at no one. I couldn't see or hear anyone there and I'd shut my mind down to an extent so I thought he simply needed more training. It wasn't until I began to have vivid dreams of my ancestors and unknown people that I realised I needed to listen to the dreams and try to remember them. Jack would carry on trying to tell me there were spirits and souls in the house and I began to believe him. I looked out my old books from the loft and read and read. I worked on listening to Jack and tuning in to his thoughts and emotions, and then found I could once again hear David's grandma. She was relieved. I think, if we'd met in life, we would have got on. She learnt to respect my human life and I learnt to listen, but also to close down when I didn't want a continuous dialogue! This was a huge relief to me and I could live my life more happily.

I discovered I could hear stories when I touched items, quite often small items like jewellery. A reel of pictures would play through my mind and I knew they were related to that item. I tried to talk to friends and family about this but no one was interested. 'Ok,' I thought, 'I know what I'm seeing. It's not a made-up story.' I began to feel more and more out of sync with everyone I knew. That was a lonely time in my life as I had no one I could talk to, and of course it was before the days of the internet, where reaching out to a group on Facebook may well have helped me. That wasn't an option.

My grandad died in 1994, and David and I went to the funeral on a wet March afternoon. I remember being chilled to the bone: although it was a cold day, I was unnaturally cold. I got back in the car and David remarked I looked like I'd seen a ghost. I replied, 'No, not seen. But I have a queue of spirits all around me wanting my attention.' I didn't have the patience or the information to deal with them, but I remember crying on the way home as I really didn't want all these spirits around me. It didn't scare me exactly, but it certainly unnerved me. And, again, I had no one to talk to about this; I just had to live with it.

Our marriage ended in 2001. I'd shut myself down to a huge extent to stay in it as long as I could. I knew I had to leave, but finding the physical and emotional strength took time.

Spring 2001 arrived and I'd moved to live in a house owned by a friend; an artist. I was renting the house apart from one room, my friend's art studio. I'd got myself together emotionally, which took some doing after death threats, and such levels of violence that my mind has had to blank them out. I was having a peaceful bath one evening at my house, all quiet and calm, and I was looking forward to a TV supper, then an early night.

BANG, BANG, on the back door.

I knew without leaving the bathwater who it was. My heart sank and joined my tummy doing somersaults. How had he found me? I'd gone to great pains to keep my address secret.

I felt a power greater than I was get me out of the bath and into clothes. I opened the window and looked down. There stood David. I remember feeling all powerful and not at all scared.

'Yes,' I said, 'what do you want?'

'I want to talk with my wife,' came the reply.

'No, that isn't going to happen,' I answered. 'You talk to your lawyer, then I may reply through my lawyer.' Recently he had threatened to shoot my knees. As he was currently looking after his brother-in-law's guns, I didn't take this as an idle threat.

He called me a nasty bitch and a nasty witch. 'Hmm, that's interesting,' I thought afterwards. 'He's beginning to see just how powerful the girl he married really is!'

I found a solicitor, after much delaying on my part. I found it hard admitting that our marriage had failed. Yes, it takes two and I'd given it my all, but even so, I believe when you make vows they are meant to be forever.

On the second meeting with my solicitor, I found myself talking about a few items I would like from the house, as I'd left with next to nothing, fearing for my own safety. We talked for about an hour and I remember thinking, what a kind man and how lucky his wife and children were. The divorce petition was drafted and the legal wheels started turning.

A few weeks later, I was driving home from work north on the A1, and felt someone arrive in the car with me. I slowed down a bit and got in the near side lane. A shiver went through me. I knew then without question that my solicitor was going to be very important in my life. I have no idea who that spirit was, but was grateful for the message and their presence.

You've probably guessed what happened… I sacked the solicitor and he found me a new one. We started dating and fell in love very quickly. Honestly, I was looking to get divorced not find another relationship! What was immediately evident was that I could be myself with Martin; my complete whole self. I didn't feel like I was treading on eggshells ever. And 19 years later, we are still very happily married.

So, with my newfound freedom to be myself, exactly as I chose, what did I do? Well, I didn't really know who I was or what gave me happiness. I'd had to keep myself hidden for so long that I'd become buried alongside the nasty memories and painful years. I remember saying to Martin, 'I don't know what I like to do anymore. My hobbies have all disappeared – who the heck am I?' They were dark days, surrounded by his love, fortunately. And he let me just be, to wander around and sob, for what felt like weeks. I was healing. I was healing by letting go of the past. People talk about that: letting go. In my experience, it only happens when we are really ready to choose to go forward in life.

I was working in banking, a career I fell into by luck not judgement. I was a good lending manager, hardworking and, although not naturally good with figures, I was great with people and, well, we had calculators! My manager said to me on several occasions he couldn't work out why I had the nicest and best clients.

'Really?' I would reply.

'No,' he'd say. 'There are several of you doing the same job but you're adored by all your clients!'

'Well,' I'd respond, 'I can spot a liar at 1000 paces and I can see the good in everyone. I believe what people tell me and I can tell if they're not being true to themselves or to me.'

This partly went over my manager's head but, on some levels, he understood my strong intuition was at work here, lending the bank's money.

Martin and I bought a house together. He let me choose it really, although I didn't realise that at the time. I loved it on paper and I loved it the moment I walked in the hallway. I felt it speak to me and felt right at home there. So we bought no 29. What a busy house that turned out to be as, one by one, Martin's three sons came to live with us, in the top-storey rooms of the house. I was now stepmother to three sons, aged 12, 15 and 18, and I was aged 29. Joe, the eldest, lived with us whilst home from university, and his two brothers would join us at weekends.

I remember walking in from a trip to town two days after we'd bought the house and smelling smoke. My first thought was, oh, have I left the grill on? I opened the door to the living room/dining room to see smoke swirling around the ceiling in there. Really thick, horrible-smelling cigarette smoke! Who had been in my house smoking? Well, no one. The boys were at school and Martin was at work.

I made a cup of tea. I walked back into the dining room and the smoke had largely disappeared, but the smell lingered on. I wasn't scared, just surprised mainly.

'Who are you?' I asked. Louis: the name came into my head, straight back to me. 'Oh.' I drank my tea and thought, 'Good God, what have we taken on here?'

I then recalled that, whilst in the buying process and having a cup of tea with the vendor at her house, soon to be our house, she'd said, very casually, that she sometimes saw an old man in the garden; that he did no harm, she just thought I should know. Would you really tell your buyer this information? She did. So, I wondered if the old man she saw was the smoking Louis.

Martin came home to find me unpacking boxes and the first thing I said was, 'We have a spirit called Louis and he smokes in the dining room.'

'Oh, yes?' he replied, like it was the most natural thing in the world. By now he was used to me, I think, and accepted what I said without question.

Over the years, we had to have words with Louis, in a kind way you understand. He used to like my long hair and often I would think Martin was behind me touching it. No, it was Louis. He remarked that I reminded him of his wife, Doris. We told him that we welcomed him into our home, but that he shouldn't actually touch me, please. He agreed and told us about living in the house for around 40 years until the 1960s. A few weeks later, we were all outside having a barbeque, when Tom, the youngest son, went into the house for something. He came dashing out as white as a sheet of paper saying, 'It's there, the smoke, Dad!' He had witnessed and smelled the strong cigarette smoke too. I'm glad to write that Louis did listen and never touched me again.

Tom lived with us for a couple of years later on and kind of got used to odd goings on. Whenever we did any decorating, changed furniture, and especially when we replaced the bathroom then the kitchen, we had visitors coming to have a look. Louis, mainly, and I remember once his wife, Doris. And then I looked around one mealtime and there was a cat sitting in the doorway to the hall! That was a surprise. Our dogs didn't seem too bothered by this visitor.

Martin and I had several busy years. We got married, we were both occupied with our careers and time ticked on happily. I still didn't have hobbies as such, as the garden at no 29 was too small to do much with, but I did have a shed, and a border where I planted rosemary, lavender, jasmine and honeysuckle. I made the best of what was there within budget and time really. We also bought a holiday home in France and aimed to live there in the future when the boys were all grown up.

I really felt the lack of friends. Yes, I had work friends, but none were local and we didn't see each other outside of work. I had one set of friends from my time with my previous husband, who were very kind to me, and we are still close to this day, although at a distance now. We had moved closer to my parents, and it gave me great joy to be able to have lunches together and be part of each other's lives again.

My shoulders were aching and my neck started to get more and more painful. I couldn't really explain why; tension at work maybe. Martin had trained as a hypnotherapist and past life therapist before we met and, although he was a little out of practice, I asked him to help me with my neck and shoulders, and also with my confidence and with who I really was. That sounds a bit vague, I know, but I knew for sure I wasn't on the Earth to be a banker all my life. I just didn't know who I was really here to be.

We worked together and, through hypno-healing, managed to lift a lot of the pain in my neck, but not completely. Then, one rainy Saturday afternoon, we decided to try to go back further into my previous lives. I realised at this point how fortunate I was to have such a well-trained and caring husband! He took me back within my lives to the Elizabethan era. I'd got caught up in a smuggling ring of traitorous correspondence and was executed, by axe, at Tower Hill. I had to forgive myself, the group I was caught up with and Queen Elizabeth I herself for the miscarriage of justice done to me. Imagine the emotional outpouring that came with this! Over the next few days, my neck and shoulders became pain free and, I'm glad to say, the pain has never returned.

Two more lives I glimpsed showed me information that was unknown to me, Clare. For example, I found myself as a British Infantry Soldier invading Scotland, with a huge battle raging around me. Martin asked, as he always does, if I knew where and when I was. I told him the date and the year and that I'd heard someone call this place Culloden, which Clare had never heard of before, so I spelled it out. Research after the event confirmed that I had the date exactly to the day of the last battle fought in Great Britain on Culloden Moor.

Another example was the briefest glimpse of a Russian life in the 1880s, where I had an abusive husband who would beat and insult me and accuse me unjustly of adultery. The phrase that I remembered was him shouting that he would not be 'cuckolded' by me. Cuckolding was not a word I knew so I had to look this up. Sadly, the husband killed Anastasia, following his threat. Martin explained to me what this actually meant. I think this life as Anastasia goes some way to explaining my aversion to being accused of infidelity, a theme that resonated in my present life and previous marriage.

In the most recent life before Clare, I was Isabelle. She was born in London in 1900. She married Bruce, and he presented her on their engagement with a rectangular emerald engagement ring, surrounded by diamonds. This was not a happy marriage, although their daughter, Grace brought joy to Isabelle. I was unhappy with Bruce as he was a womaniser and abandoned me in our Georgian house to look after our baby alone. I wished him dead. In 1928, Bruce died of TB and I felt such guilt as I had wished him away from me. This guilt I had carried forward to my life as Clare and I had to forgive, and release this old pain.

I found these lives fascinating and they each explained elements of my current life and struggles. I discovered that these themes had travelled through to my life as Clare and that the lessons were either not learnt, or were unresolved. Interestingly, I have always had a fascination with emeralds, and this time around found the most beautiful emerald as my engagement ring.

At last, I was beginning to know who I had been, and the story as to who I was to be was about to be revealed!

We took a short break over the August bank holiday to the Lake District in northern England. We stayed in Ambleside and looked around the shops. I remember walking into a crystal shop. Well, I got about half way in and went cold all over and started shaking. I turned on my heels and fled for the door, and outside, I bent double in pain and continued shaking. Martin followed me and sat me down. It took me a while to be able to explain that those huge, over four-foot-tall crystals had given me this awful feeling. I thought I was going to choke and had to move away quickly. 'The amethysts?' Martin said. They are known to be a gentle, loving, calming stone, so why was I having such an extreme reaction to them? Several years later, I met a crystal healer who explained to me that my body and energy field were in such discord that I was feeling everything around extremely powerfully. All the crystals in such a big shop had brought on this strong reaction.

The healer helped me work with crystals and now, thankfully, I can happily wear and have crystals around me, although we do have a large amethyst that I couldn't get near for years, but we're now friends.

My search for friends continued, and I started having a monthly massage. The therapist had started training in Reiki and needed volunteers for her case studies. I agreed and she invited me for a Reiki treatment. I immediately relaxed. Now, I'm not a person who relaxes easily. Even these days, I struggle at times to relax. This was a revelation to me. How could someone put their hands on me and make me feel calm and peaceful for an hour or two? I was so interested in this that I immediately began to read up everything I could find about Reiki. This is taught by a Reiki Master Teacher, who is trained to provide attunements to students.

I had found people who were similar to me! Four students came together for Reiki I, from all different backgrounds and stages of our lives, to learn together and take the first step on the Reiki journey. Afterwards, three of us met up and gave each other Reiki, usually once a month, and we all healed parts of our bodies, lives, souls. It was a wonderful time and connection.

In spring 2011, I was working with a terrible bully. I was trying my best to get another job, but after the recession of 2007/2008, jobs were rare. I was sent on a course for a week-long residential. It was all going well until the

Wednesday lunchtime. I came out of the dining room and, the next thing I remember, I was on the ground and in a huge amount of pain.

The tutor immediately put me in his car and took me to A & E. I was X-rayed and hadn't broken any bones but I had torn all three ligaments in my ankle. Oh, the pain – oh, the embarrassment! I couldn't get to my bedroom, which was on the third floor. The tutor went and packed my things and moved me to a ground floor room. To this day, I believe I was pushed over by someone invisible! A guide, someone with my best interests at heart. I then had eight weeks with my leg up on a footstool and strict instructions from my doctor to stay at home, rest, and only put weight on the ankle in six to eight weeks' time. I was grounded. I used Reiki on myself, I meditated, I cuddled my dogs a lot! I rested.

One morning, I woke up having dreamt I'd found another job. It was such a clear dream that I immediately phoned the person I'd dreamt about and said, 'This is going to sound odd, but do you know of any jobs going in my sector?'

'YES,' he replied, 'and I was going to email you today!'

I had the first interview on two crutches in a café, then a telephone interview. Then I had to get to Birmingham to sit a written test and meet the HR Manager. It was such a turn of events, and my dear friend, Martin Day, drove to pick me up, calmed me all the way there, and waited patiently whilst I gave the interview of my life and sat the written test. I got the job. It gave me such a boost and, for the first time in my career, it gave me a good pay rise to be able to continue my studies. I said a silent thank you to whoever had pushed me from behind!

In 2014, I found myself working many hours and wearing myself down and, in February, I could barely walk and had to admit defeat and see my doctor. My lower back had started hurting on Boxing Day 2013. I'd used Reiki on myself and had sound and colour treatments too to ease the pain.

2014 was a difficult year. I had physio weekly, could hardly drive myself, and sitting was a complete impossibility. In March, I had to admit I needed more help and, fortunately, through my work's medical insurance, I could access a rheumatologist and radiologist who injected me to provide anti-inflammatory relief.

My doctor said, 'Go to your home in France. You need a change of four walls and you can potter in the garden there.'

'How will I get there?' I replied.

He told me to have my injection two days before, then fly, as the painkiller part of the injection would still be working then. We took his advice, and I flew with just the lightest handbag into Tours, France. Martin picked me up, as he had driven from home with the dogs. I had six days of zero pain. I could sit, walk, stand and lie, all without pain. But when I got home, I was back to square one and back at my doctor's.

I decided to go back to work, building up my hours and travelling by train three days a week. I felt guilty for being off work and put myself through unnecessary weeks of trying to work. I really had to listen to my doctor when he said, 'Clare, you've tried everything else. I think it's time you think about seeing a surgeon.' Mentally, I had been putting this off, feeling I had somehow failed my body.

Meanwhile, over the summer, whilst trying to cram my work into three days, I took myself to Switzerland to join Tama Do's Academy Colour and Sound Healing two-week intensive course.

Writing this now, I look back and I don't know how I even got there, let alone kept to the demanding timetable for two weeks. I loved the work and the mountain air, and my inspiring roommate got me through the worst of the pain and out of bed in the mornings and up for Qi Gong at 7am.

I got home and made an appointment with a specialist surgeon, and Martin took me to meet him. He had my MRI scans and he booked me in for spine surgery. After the operation, I remember being back in my room and feeling no pain. I asked the nurse how much medication I had in me and she said it was nearly all out of my system. After four weeks at home, lying flat, I began to regain my strength and carry on my work and my studies.

That summer, I was introduced to a lady who ran meditation groups. I went to see her and it became clear that, as a psychic herself, she would become my teacher. She explained what my psychic gifts meant and how I could use them for the best, and told me not to be afraid of them and the spirit world. It was a revelation. Over the course of two years of weekly one-to-one sessions, we directed our energies toward healing lost souls. During these sessions, we both began to realise that the memories of previous sessions faded fairly quickly and that this is perhaps how it's supposed to be. As we were dealing with such a specific moment in a person's life, their physical death, and the spiritual confusion arising out of that, other details of that person's life rarely came up unless directly relevant.

We found that, using both our spirit guides and also Angels, we were able to help these lost souls across to the light successfully. One event that does stick in my memory was helping a large group of souls, who were involved in a crash and died very suddenly. Many of them didn't actually realise they had died in the crash. Archangel Mary came to lend her help and heal both the situation and timeline for these souls, and help them to peace.

I was without a spirit guide and was becoming a little frustrated that I couldn't hear one. Over a few weeks, we were given pieces of information that formed like a jigsaw, involving a baby, the death of a lady, and the attic room of our house. It became clear that my guide was to be a soul called Esme Harriet, who had become proficient in helping souls pass over. She had attended in the early 1900s to the birth of a baby and death of a servant girl, who had died in childbirth in our house. A very sad circumstance as neither the girl nor the baby had survived. We helped both pass peacefully to the light and Esme Harriet announced she was pleased I had finally heard her, and we would work together for the rest of my life, and probably into the future too.

To this day, Esme Harriet helps me. Sometimes she goes a little quiet on me and then arrives back with full force. I was concerned she wouldn't want to move to France with us. My friend and teacher found this very funny and explained we really are stuck with each other now, having finally found one another, and, yes, Esme would be ok in France.

I met Alison Ward when we bought her fridge-freezer! I walked into her kitchen and felt, I know you! We stayed in touch and she gave me the confidence to become a Reiki Master Teacher, and supported my development. Most importantly, she taught me to cut the self-doubt and nagging voices out of my head and gave me the power to believe in myself 100 per cent. For that, I will be forever grateful, so THANK YOU, Alison.

We made the move to France in 2017, after I felt the strongest calling in 2015 from the Earth there; the souls there. I just knew I had to be there to help France and her people evolve. France is a secular society; no religion is taught in schools. However, there is a deep root of Catholic religion here and, of course, two world wars have left energy behind too.

Here in Vienne, France, I teach and practise Reiki, I'm an instructor of Shibashi Qi Gong and I enjoy being outside every second I can be, mainly gardening, walking the dogs, and learning further about growing plants and their herbal qualities too.

Am I reluctant anymore? NO! I'm the Healing Gardener, a Psychic and Healer.

Blog: https://frencheclairblog.home.blog
Facebook: @clare.hill.52
Instagram: @frencheclair

Miracles Abound

An extraordinary and welcome event that is not explicable by natural or scientific laws and is therefore attributed to a 'Divine Agency' is the definition of a miracle. Have you experienced a miracle and not realised it? These six stories demonstrate amazing miracles that may make you think twice about whether you have experienced one.

Empaths become more connected and experience miracles. Vicky found her gifts, experienced life-saving miracles and was able to leave her former life behind, doing something she loves.

THE MAGIC OF SPIRIT

Vicky Sweetlove

All the time as a child growing up, 'magical' things would happen, or there would be 'ghostly happenings'.

My first vivid memories are of having a boxer dog called Prudence. We would go everywhere together. She would run alongside my bike and be with me all day. I was only about six years old. In those days, children went out all day with no one wondering where they were, and I would play in hedgerows with the fairy people and make dens and houses in the cornfields. I would quite often be seen in the local garage, asking to have my tyres pumped up, as I would be out all day, every day on my bike, with Prudence my boxer dog running alongside me. I wanted to make sure my bike was all good to go.

Then, one day, Prudence was run over and was taken to the vets. I cried and Prudence was 'pining' to come home. My mum and dad brought her home with the thought that she was coming home to die, but she didn't. The moment she came into the house, she started recovering as soon as she saw me.

My mother worked in those days and I would sometimes be left with the neighbours. But there was one particular time when my mother had a young girl in to babysit. I only remembered this years later, through a Theta Healing training course I was attending in my forties, when it came out I had been shut in the understairs cupboard by this girl with my dog Prudence, and I had a fear of enclosed spaces. I never liked having the door closed and would sleep with the light on for much of my teenage years, until I was about 16 years old. I also never liked any women with painted nails and I could never wear nail varnish myself. I still rarely wear it now. As the memory came back, I recalled this girl painting her nails, listening to the radio. I fully understood then the 'special relationship' I'd had with my dog Prudence. She was my protector and Earth guardian.

There were many synchronicities in those childhood days, but my mother knew that, if she wanted to know something or be guided in any way, she would ask me or someone else, and she knew the answer would come from the Universe through our spoken words.

She asked me one day, when I was 14 years old, 'What do you think we should call the boutique, Vicky?' I immediately said, 'Hobbit', and Hobbit Boutique was born. This was before the Hobbit books became popular, and there was never any hesitation once she was given the answer. She went with it. It was the same when I was born. My mother asked my brother what my name should be and he said, 'Vicky.' All those years ago, Vicky was an unusual name. Victoria was more the normal, and my grandmother thought Janey was a better choice. I'm glad my mother went with Vicky.

We would often go out, my mother, Prudence the dog and me, in her 'bubble car', as she was a 'rep' and would sell carbon paper and various other things for different companies. It would be mostly between schools when we moved house – you could say that I was 'home schooled' in those weeks/months that I had off school, as that was when I read all the books on Greek mythology and the fairy kingdom whilst sitting in the car.

She would also stop the car at brooks and small streams. We would get out and she would tell me to wade in and look for any freshwater mussels, as she always dreamed of finding 'a big pearl', preferably a black one that would make us all wealthy. And I did it willingly as I wanted her dream to be reality. But

I always told her I couldn't find the mussels, as I could sense the Faery folk around and they were playing with my mother as she already had her wealth: she knew 'the Universe would provide'.

One time, I was in the bubble car with Prudence the boxer, my mother, and a paraffin heater as it was winter. My mother would always be looking for new places, new companies where she could sell her products.

She shouted out this one day, 'Look! I haven't been there before – Asouth!' She turned the little bubble car onto the road for Asouth and, before we knew it, we were on the M1 motorway, driving towards the oncoming traffic. Lorries were coming straight towards us. She kept going very calmly and didn't panic, and because she didn't panic, I felt safe and looked after too, even though we were in this tiny little car with a paraffin heater. Her belief that we were safe, and would be safe, kept us safe until she could turn off at the next junction, which she did.

Many times as I was growing up, there would be incidences or accidents where my family would be saved from near death. It's knowing your time is not now, but learn the lesson and know all is well.

My father on the same motorway, the M1, would travel up and down every day for two hours each way, sometimes more to get home to my mother in the evenings. And he'd do the same journey again the next day as General Manager for an engineering company. This one particular day, he arrived home with a new car – a three-litre Rover. We asked, 'Where's the Westminster car you had this morning?'

Apparently, that morning as he drove on the motorway, a road maintenance truck was in front of him and a metal plate sheet fell of the truck and onto the motorway as my father reached it in his car. The metal plate sheet lifted up and sliced the whole of the top of the car off and, as my father saw it coming, he tilted his head back and only his chin was caught by the metal plate. He could have had his head chopped off. He got out of the car, very matter of fact, went to the hospital for stitches in his chin, bought a new car, carried on to work, then came home – as though nothing out of the ordinary had happened to him that day. He even took the stitches out of his chin himself when the time was right.

Growing up in this environment made me believe even more in the 'magic' of the Universe: we just carry on as normal and nothing is out of the ordinary.

It's just what happens and everything is always ok, and will be ok, as long as you believe it to be. It's your self-belief and how you have been programmed and conditioned as a child growing up. If you lose the sense of 'magic' and the 'knowing' that everything is as it should be and you can carry on as normal, then that is when 'panic' sets in. And trauma does happen in our minds and in our reality. When this happens en masse to people around us, then that begins the new real 'normal', and not the normal that I grew up with, where everything was corrected by the Universe and you were put back on your 'journey of life' again as quickly as the Universe could do it for you, to fulfil your 'life's purpose'.

One of my mother's favourite sayings was, 'the Universe will provide', and no matter what you wanted or needed in life, she said to go for it and the Universe would provide.

All my life, I have lived with those words. And I remember growing up reading books about the Greek myths of the gods and goddesses and the mythical creatures. I was enthralled by stories: Enid Blyton's fairy books, the Famous Five, Noddy and Big Ears, the Girls of St Claire's, and I believed everything to be true – to me it was all real.

As we often moved house, I went to many different schools all around the UK. I would often be the 'new girl', and every now and then, being the new girl and maybe being a little different, I was bullied. But I was always a placid child and would take everything in my stride, and never cried or told a teacher, or my parents. I just knew I would be ok. Every challenge I met, whether it was being forced to eat everyone's school dinner by the dinner monitor, or playing 'right wing' in the class hockey team placed next to the 6 foot 2 girl when I was 5 foot nothing, the Universe gave me the answer. I made myself Spam sandwiches in my bedroom for my lunch every day, so I no longer had to sit and have school dinners. I was given long legs and a shorter body, and I could run faster than the 6 foot 2 girl, and weave in and out of everyone with the hockey stick and ball. All the days out riding my bike with my dog had given me strong legs.

It seemed that, just at the point where I thought I could take no more bullying, my father would come home and say, 'We're moving,' and at that point I would say, 'Thank you, God.'

Then I would be given the next challenge in my life. There were always challenges to overcome – it seemed as though I was living the books I'd read. The magical stories where coming alive in my day-to-day life.

When I started Secretarial College in North Wales, it was my first real experience of going out with friends to the pictures, meeting 'boys', and I was very naïve. I still am in many ways and very trusting of everyone I meet. My friend Olwen decided to arrange a date for me with her ex-boyfriend. I had never met him before and we all went out together to the pub. Even though we were only 16 and 17 years old, that's where you went in those days. To my surprise, I always got served at the bar even though I was the smallest and wore no makeup. After a few dates with this boy, we became girlfriend and boyfriend; and sometimes in relationships, you quarrel.

This particular time, we were arguing just as I was about to get the last bus home, which left at 10.30pm. If I missed it, there was no way to get home, and I'd never ask my parents, like children do these days, to come and pick me up. It wasn't done then. I always knew what time I had to be home, and to be home for that time, otherwise there would 'hell to pay' from my father. Mine especially would shout. My parents were probably being very protective of me as they'd not told me about the 'birds and the bees', so I was quite naïve on this aspect of life and I trusted everyone.

The bus was just closing the door as I went to get on it. I pressed the emergency button for the door to open and put my foot on the first step, just as the bus started to pull away. I saw the driver looking at me. He closed the door and I felt the bus push my body to the ground.

The next thing I knew I was lying on the ground and I could see my new wedge shoes were broken. I could also see the tyre marks of the bus on my legs – quite clearly on my tights, the imprint of the rubber. And my elbow hurt where the bus had pushed against me. An ambulance was called but I remembered the bus driver had carried on with his journey and I thought I must be ok. He wouldn't have driven off if I was seriously hurt.

I was taken to the local hospital where I was told I had a fractured pelvis, a broken elbow and a rather large hole in my left knee. My parents were told I might not walk again – they didn't tell me.

Within a few days, I got up to find my friend who worked at the hospital in X-ray.

She asked, 'How did you get here?'

'I walked. I wanted to see you,' I said.

She couldn't believe it and took me back to the ward in a wheelchair.

I kept hearing the words to ask the nurses to change the bandage on my knee, as it hadn't been changed for a week. I was then moved to another hospital in Caernarvon, where they changed the bandage immediately and the wound was found to be gangrenous. They cleaned it and it healed and got better, and I was so grateful for hearing those words as it saved my knee.

Within a couple of weeks, I was sent home to my parents. They had decorated my bedroom with posters of Led Zeppelin, and it was painted purple and orange, which I'd never been allowed to have before. My parents felt responsible for what had happened to me. Over the next couple of weeks, I was walking more and more, out with my dog and soon out with my friends again.

It was only when I met my friends who'd seen what had happened that night when I was 'hit' by the bus, that I knew a miracle had occurred. It was as though the bus and its wheels had become as light as a feather. And although the wheels went over my legs, they weren't broken. I only had a fractured pelvis and I just 'knew' that I would walk again. I never thought any differently because no one had told me that I wouldn't be able to walk, as I'd been 'protected' from hearing those words.

One of the first nights out with my friends after I was allowed to go out again, we were in Caernarvon and again getting the last bus home. This time it was a double decker and, again, I was saying goodnight to a new boyfriend, and I could see my friends waving to me from the back of the bus on the top deck – 'Hurry up, the bus is going to go!'

Just as the bus pulled away, I thought, 'Oh no, I mustn't miss it this time.' I grabbed the pole on the lower deck and, as I grabbed it, I could feel my body swing all around the pole, and I landed on the road behind the bus. It was like something out of *Some Mothers Do 'Ave 'Em*. My friends looked on in disbelief, but they rang the bell for the bus to stop, which it did, and I jumped back on again. I couldn't believe what had happened.

It was certainly a lesson from the Universe not to repeat the pattern and not to make the same mistake again – although this time the pattern had been changed and my friends stopped the bus and I was able to get on. In the work I do these days with people working in their Akashic Records, I've discovered that when you find where the pattern begins and change it, you can change their lives in the present. I realise now, looking back at some of the 'lessons' I was given to learn, it was for me to pass them forward to others and learn about how to help people change what affects them in their lives.

When I was 18 years old living in North Wales, you needed a car to get out and about. I'd passed my driving test first time and I remember thinking, 'How did I do that?' as I'd forgotten to put my flat shoes on and was wearing platforms. So you can imagine what it was like as I couldn't feel the pedals, but it was 'wow' when the instructor signed that certificate and passed it to me.

I remember taking my friends with me in the car to a pub over in Dinorwic and then we were going to a disco in Caernarvon afterwards, but you had to be in the disco before 10.30pm to be allowed in. My car was a blue Singer Chamois and I loved it, with the engine in the back just like the beetle Volkswagens. This particular night when we came to get into the car after the pub, the car park was now full and we were blocked in. There was no way out except straight ahead of me, which was over a 6 foot drop.

I knew and believed my car could be just like 'Herbie' in the movies, and I drove forward. As we went over the edge, the nose of the car with the wheels touched the ground and, just for a few seconds, we were sitting at a 90-degree angle. Then I was able to drive the car off with everything perfectly normal, and we went on with our evening out. It was only when one of my friends asked afterwards, 'How did we get out of the car park?' that I realised magic happens.

After this event, I seemed to be more aware of everything around me and I moved into the flat above Hobbit Boutique. I would tell my mother about the people who were talking and shouting in my bedroom every night. They would argue with one another, be from different time periods, and I understand now that they were reliving their stories before they died.

My mother called in the local priest to perform an exorcism and bless the flat. He came twice and each time I would tell my mother in the morning that they were still there. In the end she said to me, 'Just tell them to bugger off, Vicky, that you don't want to see them anymore.' I did just that and I stopped seeing them. Then one day, I had a party. There were lots of people in the flat I didn't know and when everyone else had left, there was still one couple there, who asked if they could sleep on the sofa as it was late and they couldn't get home.

I thought nothing of it and went upstairs to bed. A few minutes later, I heard a scream and my name being called. I ran downstairs to be told by the couple that the door to the living room was being pushed open, even though they had shoved the coffee table against it. It shouldn't have moved as it was a heavy, old-fashioned, wooden coffee table. Then I saw the living room door handle starting to move up and down very quickly on its own, and the lights began flashing on and off all over the flat.

When this couple saw the flashing lights, they ran down the stairs out of my flat, never to be seen again. I locked the door after them and everything returned to normal. The door handle stopped moving, the lights stopped flashing and I went to bed. I just had a knowing that I was being looked after by the other side.

My next experience in the flat above the shop was after I'd married my first husband. He could become quite violent when he'd been drinking. I remember on this particular night going to bed and it was late. And I was dreading my husband coming home. Then I heard the key in the door and I knew he'd be making his way up the stairs. I was dreading him getting into bed. I started to pray and I asked, 'Please, God, don't let him get into bed,' over and over again. I kept saying the words – 'Please, God, don't let him get into bed' – until I fell asleep.

When I woke up in the morning, I couldn't believe my eyes. My husband's side of the bed was empty and my husband was lying on the floor. He'd lifted the corner of the carpet up and was fast asleep between the carpet and the floorboards. I was so grateful for being looked after by the etheric world.

I knew then that I need have no fear of the 'spirit world' as they were my protectors. It was the human world that was the world to be wary of.

When my mother died I was 26 years old and it affected my life in a way that I was broken-hearted. My best friend, my mother, had left me alone. I switched off my natural knowingness. I'd met my second husband a few months before my mother died, at the structural engineering company where I worked, and, after four years of going out together and travelling from Wales to London, it seemed to be right that when he proposed I accepted and moved to Essex. My two friends got married in the same year. We were a trio, all the same height, wearing similar clothes and liking the same music. I was blonde, one friend had dark hair and the other had fair hair. So when we were all getting married in the same year, I saw it as a sign that it was the right thing to do.

My life changed dramatically. My new husband moved me to Essex and he then took a contract in Oman for two years. I was in a new home, a new area, with no friends, no husband and a son to bring up, as well as working as a personal assistant/office manager.

Then one day, I had a call at work to say my brother had died in Los Angeles. I'd only been living in Essex a few months. He was the only part of my family left as my father had died when I was 21 years old. I felt even more alone but I 'knew' that I could cope; that I had the 'will' to do it.

My husband was still in Oman and I had a couple of visits over the two years. And I went to my local health club to keep fit, where I was told about the Spiritualist church – why did I not go along?

I decided I'd try a few different Spiritualist churches, and eventually felt comfortable in Billericay. I was made welcome and told how the service would be, with an opening prayer. The medium would then start with 'channelled' words of inspiration, we'd sing hymns, and then the medium would give messages to people in the congregation from those that had passed over.

As I sat there, I could sense my mother was there. I could smell her perfume and then, when the medium spoke her name and described what she wore, how she looked and what she said, I knew my mother had come.

I felt such gratitude to hear my mother's words; to know that she and my family in spirit were always there for me and I had 'no need to worry – everything would be all right'.

I would attend Spiritualist church every Sunday, as I liked the hymns and the medium's address, the inspirational words. I sat in 'open circle', then I joined a 'closed circle' and experienced many memories of the 'magic' of when I was connecting to the spirit world and the elementals as a child growing up and in my teens.

I learnt all the basics. It was like going back to school: how to protect your energy field; how to ground yourself; how to open up to messages from Spirit; how to close down afterwards and again protect your energy field.

The more I connected with the spirit world again, the more I knew that I had been directed to come to live in this part of the world to reconnect to them, and to follow the wisdom that they shared with me.

Eventually, I was made redundant from my local job – hurrah! I found myself a job at City University in London and this changed my world completely. I was introduced to technology and spiritual wisdom working for the Information Technology Department as a PA/office manager. In this department, the professors and students invented the latest technological systems and tried them out on the unsuspecting staff, with the internet just being born, emails and also remote meetings for people in different countries. But the other side of the technology was the invention of the auragraph machine to read your aura. I had a go with everything and wanted to learn more. And I met Gina Lazenby, who had just set up the Feng Shui Society in the UK, as her then partner was a lecturer at the university.

I went on to train as a Feng Shui Consultant, and I found I was naturally intuitive with clients and their needs. Part of the training was dowsing the energies of the land and particularly geopathic stress. I loved the dowsing work and became a professional dowser with the British Society of Dowsers, and I was made Secretary of the London and Thameside Dowsing group, of which there were six other members at the time and I was the only female.

I had to prove my worth. When I went out for the first time with them to Hackney Marshes and saw a guy on the bus also clutching a pair of dowsing rods, I assumed he would be going to the same place I was and I thought, 'I'll just follow him.' Good job I did as I wouldn't have found my way otherwise. I knew then Spirit had sent me an Earth Angel to guide me and it was meant to be.

We were all given an exercise to locate a large metal object somewhere in the vicinity on the marshes. I just 'saw' in my mind's eye where the object was and what it was, and I walked straight over to it. It was a plane that had come down in the war and I told them the date. I had passed the test and was now 'one of the lads'. The only other thing I had to do was go to the pub and have a pint and not my usual glass of wine!

At that time, there were no registered women water dowsers with the BSD, so I was an anomaly and interviewed by magazines and on TV. Most women dowsers would dowse for health and spiritual work. I loved all aspects of dowsing, from health, water, archaeology and Earth energies. Working with the elementals was my favourite.

When *Spirit and Destiny* magazine asked me to write an article about me as 'The Dowser', I then started teaching courses in Feng Shui and dowsing. I was quite shy but I knew Spirit was calling me to 'pass forward' what I'd learnt and share it with others. I went to the local adult education centre and asked if I could use their venue to teach my course and I was told, only if I did the teacher training course – which I did and became a City and Guilds teacher.

During the next few years, my life was quite traumatic. My husband didn't support my spiritual beliefs and I was often belittled or made fun of in front of my children and visitors to the house, being told '*not* to talk about what I did in front of the children or his family and friends'. I felt like an outcast in my own home.

I was eventually made redundant from the job I loved at City University, as the professor I worked for went on sabbatical. When he returned, the department no longer existed and was part of a faculty. Soon after, I began to get ill with ME/Chronic Fatigue Syndrome (CFS) and fibromyalgia. My world was falling apart. I was no longer 'wonder woman'. I struggled to be Mum, cook, housekeeper, cleaner, gardener, manager of bills and do a full-time job.

I found myself so tired I could barely walk to work and home again, even though I was a 24/7 'gym bunny', going to classes in my lunch hour, in the evenings and at weekends. I realised I couldn't sustain it and gradually only managed the lunchtime classes as I got weaker and my energy diminished.

I tried to talk to my husband, saying I needed help – with a lift to the station, with the cleaning and cooking and all the chores, as well as with our children. He ridiculed me and refused to see that I was ill. I couldn't get help from doctors either as nobody believed I was ill, until finally I was diagnosed with

ME/CFS. By this time I was divorced as I had to leave the marriage in order to survive and keep going.

My spirit helpers helped and guided me to the supportive people who came into my life at just the right time – sometimes a bit lastminute.com, but the help came and I kept believing everything would be all right; that the Universe would help me to survive. I wouldn't give up and would ask to be shown how to make myself well, what could I do and where was the answer for a cure to my illness.

I worked for three London universities over the next few years. Each time, I was made redundant due to my spiritual beliefs and the 'other work' I did, teaching and consulting in Feng Shui and dowsing, even though I was an exceptional PA/office manager. But those skills kept me in good stead as I used them to build a website and manage my course listings. I also used my managerial skills to contact the media and advertise what I did. Working in those office manager positions built my confidence to speak. I would blush easily and quite often stutter before that.

Some lecturers embraced what I did and asked me to balance the energies of the classrooms, especially when they had disruptive students. They too knew where the negative areas were. If a student sat in a particular spot, they would have trouble with that person no matter who it was. A bit like Sheldon in *The Big Bang Theory*, where he has 'his spot'. It's his energy and he knows it's where he's safe. That's what we all want: our 'spot' to be safe in the world.

In the last position I held at UCL, I worked for two professors: one 'hated' what I did, very much like my ex-husband, while the other professor embraced it and was intrigued by how my crystals on the desk worked. He would often ask if I could 'heal' his migraine.

Ever since computer technology had come in, I'd become electro-sensitive and couldn't be in a place where there was WiFi or high Electric Magnetic Field (EMF). I had told this to the professors who I worked for, and they did compromise and move the photocopier away from me. All the technology in universities then was wired computer systems and wired telephone systems.

Then one day, I had to have a tooth removed and the dentist told me I'd have to wear braces as there would be a gap otherwise. The braces were made of metal. All the healthy foods I would eat every day, such as salads and fresh fruit, I couldn't eat, and I'd eat instead from the university cafeteria – soups and soft foods that didn't catch on the braces. I put on weight and could barely get to my exercise classes, and one day travelling in to work, I felt extremely tired and wanted to lie down.

I would walk each day from Liverpool Street station to Russell Square via Leather Lane market. Just as I reached the market, I felt this overwhelming need to lie down. I wanted to close my eyes and lie down there and then. But I heard a voice say, 'Keep going, Vicky, you can lie down when you get to work. There's a sofa there, keep going.'

When I got to work, I went straight up to the kitchen where the voice had told me to go to lie down. As I lay down, I could feel my body go numb. I couldn't move and felt myself drifting away. In my unconscious mind, I was aware of someone lifting my arm and shouting, 'Vicky... Vicky!'

The people in the office where I worked must have called an ambulance. As I lay there, I found myself sitting in a long, dark hallway, like a waiting room. To my right, I could see a light, and I felt the need to go towards it. As I made my way towards the light, a big head of an American Indian appeared and told me, 'It's not your time. You need to go back. Go back now.'

With that, I felt a ping in my body, and I saw myself lying on a tropical beach with white lights dancing all around me, giving me healing energy. I started to come round and felt like a rag doll. The ambulance man was in front of me saying his equipment must be faulty as there had been no heartbeat recorded a few minutes ago.

I was taken to UCLH hospital through the back door, as I worked at UCL, where I was seen by a doctor and a team of students. The doctor asked me, 'What do you think happened to you?'

'I believe I had a Near Death Experience,' (NDE) I said and, to my surprise, she agreed with me. She told me this happens quite often to people who exercise and keep fit. When something changes in their lifestyle, they can then suffer a stroke and an NDE.

I didn't realise how serious this TIA mini-stroke was until I couldn't remember telephone numbers; I couldn't retain information. Any new information I would forget the next day. I could only remember what I already knew how to do. As I realised what was happening, I tried to cover it up by using post-it notes to write down everything, and would put them in front of me on my desk.

I was called 'stupid' by the people I worked with at the university; with courses I went on to do about the office website, I would forget the information the next day. Three times I was sent on the course. I knew I wasn't functioning as I should be. I asked to go for memory tests and brain scans; nothing showed up.

I managed to keep going with my Feng Shui consultations and teaching my courses, as Spirit and the elementals would help me and guide me to do the work. I would often ask Spirit, *'Please get me out of here now.'* Be careful of what you wish for.

One day, Spirit told me to take my EMF meter into work with me, as my health was not improving and I was being consistently bullied by the people I worked with. When I arrived, I took the reading on my meter. It was at the highest point of six volts, on the red danger scale. I couldn't understand it. My desk computer and phone and everything around me was wired.

I followed the loud sound from my meter and it took me into the office of the professor I worked for. His office was on the other side of the wall next to where I sat. On his desk was the only wireless phone in the whole building, as UCL didn't have wireless phones. What was the reason for this phone being there? Was it because they knew I was electrosensitive? I left that day.

My new life working with Spirit full time was just beginning, as I had started at the College of Psychic Studies, giving Akashic Record readings. I worked as a 'seer' for a businessman for the next four years, and for a high-profile lawyer, giving them advice on how to move forward with their businesses and make their next steps. I found this very demanding as I was on call 24/7 and still trying to solve my health problems, asking Spirit to direct me to the people who would help. My clients would tell me of people they knew. I knew this was Spirit giving me direction. Each step was a step to wellness.

A nutritionist was the most helpful in regaining my strength and energy and building my muscles and immune system. Through my own 'Dowsing for Health' courses, I found that all my life I'd been 'histamine intolerant'. That was a huge breakthrough in discovering what I could eat and couldn't eat, which helped me to become pain free. Even now, if my body hurts, I ask Spirit what was the food that affected me.

I continued with teaching my courses in Feng Shui and dowsing Earth energies. My work was now more involved with space clearing, working with the 'spirit of place'. The more I worked with the land and people's homes, the more the elementals showed themselves to me and told me what the occupants of the home needed to do.

The elementals would guide me, when I was 'map dowsing' a property remotely, as to where the Earth's energies were negative and traumatised, which showed up as geopathic stress and other misaligned negative energies. I have even been shown where EMF and WiFi are affecting the occupants of the home as negative influences.

On one occasion, a client came to me as she was desperate to sell the family home. I connected by map dowsing remotely and, when I arrived, I saw that the front door to the home that they used was an arched-shaped red door, very much like a pixie door, and the main entrance doorway had been blocked off. I was instructed by the elementals of the home that the blocked-off doorway needed to be reinstated as the main entrance and enhanced with plants and respected. The red door was to be used only as a back door. As an offering for the elementals, when I tuned in to the energy of place and dowsed to find out what it should be, I heard, 'Nik Naks'.

The client was surprised and asked what they were. I told her to look for a type of crisp and she looked through her cupboard and, at the back of the cupboard, was one bag of the asked for 'Nik Naks'. I prepared the offering for the elementals, did the Earth acupuncture outside and made the offering, and within three weeks of my visit, the house was SOLD. When you work with Mother Earth and the elemental kingdom with respect, they will help all mankind.

When dowsing, I would find that the ghosts would not always have lived in the house or on the land, but would appear through spirit gateways known as portals.

Many people feel frightened of the ghosts, but actually the ghosts would be frightened of the inhabitants, especially if they were in 'their homes' and all they needed was some love, understanding and direction as to the next journey for them in the spirit world.

I found that after the NDE, my senses and awareness were more attuned to listening again to the spirit world, like I did when I was in my teens. It was as though I'd been 'retuned' into the right station again and I was listening fully once more to Mother Earth, the elementals and Spirit.

Over the next few years, I was being guided by Spirit to learn about the cause of my health problems, and I travelled the world, gaining knowledge from shamans, Feng Shui masters, dowsers and spiritual teachers, building up my knowledge, and everything I learnt I passed forward in my courses that I taught.

I learnt more about the immune system, how to support my adrenals, gut health, the intestines, the kidneys, the liver, learning to speak to my organs and acknowledging and loving every part of my body in a daily meditation.

I continue with daily meditative practices and know to trust that 'the Universe will provide' all that I need always. And I trust in the messages and guidance I receive every day.

Today, I love to go out in nature and connect with the 'spirit of place', the energy of the land and people's homes. The land and the elementals let you know what is needed to bring the balance and the harmony back into people's lives, and they just want to help everyone who asks for assistance to bring harmony back to Mother Earth.

www.vickysweetlove.com
vickysweetlove@vickysweetlove.com
FACEBOOK: @vickysweetlove
INSTAGRAM: @vickysweetlove
YOUTUBE: vickysweetlove
PINTEREST: @Feng Shui Life

Joylina's early life showed her the impact of miracles. Suffering many losses over the years, Joylina has developed her gifts and is well known in her field.

JOYLINA GOODINGS' STORY

Joylina Goodings

Where does one begin with a story of spiritual development when it's still an ongoing process? It probably started many lifetimes ago and will probably continue through future lifetimes, but we will just begin with this lifetime. The title of this book is *Reluctantly Psychic* so I will start from that perspective and how life itself gives you the experience necessary to complete the life purpose.

As a child, I could see and hear spirits and Angels. Of course, if I mentioned it then, Mummy would say, 'Don't be silly, you're not good enough to see Angels.'

I was a lonely, asthmatic child. Mum was a teacher and worked hard. If I was ill, I was looked after by an old woman who lived round the corner.

When I was three, I woke up one night to see a bright, luminescent, gentle, loving being at the foot of my bed and I just knew it was an Angel. She told me to get up and go and wake my parents. Like most children at that time, once in bed you had to stay there, so it was with great trepidation that I did as the Angel told me. My parents weren't happy at being woken up, especially when I told them an Angel had appeared in my bedroom and had told me to wake them up. They didn't believe me obviously. Dad, however, did get up and go and have a look, and the paraffin heater in my room had caught fire. I would probably have suffocated if I hadn't woken up. Of course, at this point, the lovely, gentle, loving Angel was now believed to be me seeing the fire but being confused by sleep and misinterpreting it as an Angel. After all, only very good girls can see Angels and I wasn't one of them.

I believe our early life gives us the experiences we ask for to prepare us and enable us to become what we are meant to be. We choose the culture and family we will be born into because our cultures and our families decree the experiences we will have in our early life. Our brains, our ego personalities, are programmed from the experiences, rightly and wrongly. We make assumptions. Even as babies we learn and make assumptions. Suppose we are born into a family that already has many children and little money. We are just one more mouth to feed. We cry but there isn't time or energy left. We cry and Mum snaps angrily at us. We don't know why. We end up feeling we've done something wrong even if we haven't. At that particular moment, we simply feel unloved and ask, 'Why aren't we loved?' We make a huge assumption and jump to the conclusion we're not good enough. We have thoughts and feelings of low self-esteem, lack of confidence, not being able; others seem to do it so why can't we? Conclusion: 'I'm not good enough'. And this mis-assumption gets re-enforced over and over, teachers and parents trying so hard to help us do well with their constant, 'Well done, but if you do it this way...' or 'if you practice more...' etc. So I, as well as many others, actually end up believing we're not good enough and then spend our lives proving it to ourselves by 'giving up' when things become difficult.

I remember when I was about five years old, my parents took me to the local fair. There was a gypsy there and Mum said I could have my fortune read. She went first and came out ashen, and wouldn't let me go in at all. Cheesed off, I played up for the rest of the visit. I was a strong-willed child and liked to get my own way.

Four years later, when I was nine, the family suffered a series of losses. It started in September when the family dog died. Then my father's father died in October, my mother's father died in November and my mother died in January. She caught a cold on Tuesday and died on Saturday. I'd taken the Thursday and Friday off school to look after my younger sister. I called the doctor both on the Thursday and Friday. Dad called him when he got home from work on the Friday but the doctor said it was just a cold and he would come over later. He finally arrived on Saturday morning and rushed her to hospital, but it was too late.

I knew Jesus was a healer who cured people by touching them. I wanted to go to the hospital and touch my mum. I really believed she would get better if I could just touch her. Children under 14 years of age weren't allowed to visit relatives in hospitals in those days, so they wouldn't let me. For many years, I thought it was my fault she had died and I should have tried harder to get into the hospital.

Following her death, I used to talk to her every night and whenever I was unhappy or had a problem. Her presence was a great comfort to me but I wasn't allowed to mention her to any members of the family. In fact, my father didn't mention her name or refer to her for over 30 years. When I told my friends I could see and talk to her, they just ridiculed me, so I learnt to keep it to myself. Not being allowed to go to the funeral or mention her at home, or talk to anyone about her, led to me believing she wasn't dead. Even to this day I'll see a face in the crowd and think it's her.

Later, when I was 16, my American aunt (Mum's sister was a GI bride) told me the gypsy at the fair had told my mother she would die at the age of 30, which is exactly how old she was when she had died. This frightened me so much that I cut myself off from everything, refusing even to talk to her should she appear in my dreams. My fear of the occult and everything esoteric consumed me, and I had a secret fear that I would die young as well. I spent most of my energy burying my fears and in denial of my gifts.

One evening a few years later, when I was 19, my future husband and I were having a dinner party with friends when he suddenly went very still. He started speaking in a strange voice, saying how much he loved the flowers on the table and, looking at me, he told me not to worry: sad news was coming but everything would be ok. I slapped his hand to bring him out of it. Just 15 minutes later, I had a phone call telling me my grandmother had passed. Because it was him and not me, I think I was even more frightened than usual.

I still had a fear of dying young and didn't want to abandon any children of my own, so I didn't have children until after I was 30 and, when my daughter was nine, I was extremely careful with myself, making sure I didn't take any unnecessary risks – even to the extent of having a melanoma removed under local anaesthetic rather than a general.

Life continued with its usual ups and downs and, eventually, I totally forgot my fears and my abilities. In 1991, we had a lovely holiday in America and for the last week, we stayed with my mother's sister and her husband. My Uncle Conrad had a particularly nasty variant of motor neurone disease, which made it very difficult for him to talk and hold a conversation. He was a devout Christian and, to cut a long story short, he and my husband, Andrew, joked that Andrew would make sure Conrad got to heaven if Conrad would make sure he got in too. It was a fun evening but something we all forgot about.

As time passed, my husband started drinking very heavily. We lost the big house and the big car and moved into his parents' old house. I thought he would pick himself up and start again, but he didn't. Eventually, I took the children and left. I really believed that if he lost everything, he would stop drinking; I told him if he stopped for a year and a day, we would return. Unfortunately, that was not meant to be.

On 9th April, he called me and asked to meet. In fact, although we'd been separated nearly a year, we met almost daily when I picked up the children from his place after I got back from work. But this time he wanted a private conversation. He said he'd been told by the doctor that he had terminal cancer and only two months to live. He wanted us to go home for those last two months of his life. He'd told me so many lies over the years, so I asked for the doctor's name and I phoned the hospital to check out the story. The doctor didn't exist and there was no history of any appointments in my husband's name at the hospital. That was a horrible lie and I refused to return home again. I reiterated the terms under which we would be a family once more: he had to stop drinking for a year and a day. I wasn't even asking him to get a job; just to be sober. I was more than prepared to work and support us all as he'd done for so many years.

At 2am on 10th June, the doorbell rang. There was a policeman and a policewoman on the step. I knew something dreadful had happened. My first thought was the children but they were upstairs in bed. My next was my husband. For years I'd dreaded this visit. It was like I'd always expected it. For so long, when he was late home from work, I'd rehearsed how I would behave when I was told he'd been killed in a car crash through drinking and driving. In fact, he'd died in bed the morning before. I remember in my rehearsals I'd always poured a large brandy for myself. With the reality, I made a cup of tea. I stayed up all night wondering how I was going to tell the children when they woke up, and thinking Dad must have been feeling the same all those years ago, waiting for my sister and me to wake up to tell us about Mum having died. A pattern!

According to the police, my husband had died at 10am BST on 9th June, exactly two months after our meeting when he'd told me he had two months to live. It was as if he'd known and I hadn't believed him. I felt so guilty because I loved him so. He was 42, my daughter was 11 and my son was nine.

Around lunchtime, I went to pick up the phone to ring my aunt in the USA to tell her. As I did so, the phone rang. It was my cousin ringing to tell me Conrad had passed away at 5am EST. There's a five-hour time difference between New York and London. They had died at the same time. Apparently, that conversation over dinner some time before hadn't been a joke. Needless to say, I was shell-shocked. The coincidence was surreal. How could it have happened?

A week later as I drove past the house, I saw Andrew's face at the bedroom window. That frightened me but I stopped and went in. I knew nothing about soul retrieval, Earth-bound spirits, spirit release, or anything else at that point. I was frightened but I didn't think he would hurt me. I was confused because I knew Conrad would have helped him get to heaven, so how come I could see him at the window? I went into the bedroom and sat on the bed he'd died in, and I started to talk to him in my imagination. He seemed to respond. It was just like it had been talking to my mother all those years ago but I didn't connect the two at the time.

He told me what had happened, how he hadn't suffered and how it was all part of a greater plan. He assured me the children and I would be ok. How I cried. I was distraught and felt so guilty, especially at not having returned home for those last two months. He told me everything was all right. I asked if he'd got to heaven and he said he'd shown Conrad the way but had come back to see me one last time. It didn't make sense to me then but, as I sat on the bed, I said a little prayer asking for his Guardian Angel to come and show him the way to heaven. A bright light filled the room and he smiled and disappeared. Where that idea came from, I don't know, but I've used the same simple method many times over the years to release trapped spirits.

Even after this experience, I couldn't accept that it was real. It must have all been in my imagination. I continued to bury my fears and my abilities and got on with rebuilding a life for myself and my children. I occasionally felt my husband's energy around me but always put it down to my imagination and my longing.

I wanted to be able to afford to send the children to university when they grew up so I set about finding a new career for myself. At the time, as well as being a housewife and mother, I was also working as a PA to the marketing partner of a large international professional services firm. My previous secretarial background was mainly sales and marketing in different industries, so I thought I might start studying to become a Chartered Marketer.

When I mentioned this to a member of the team, I was laughed at. They all had master degrees from the best business schools in the country so who did I, a lowly secretary, think I was, believing I couldn't only be a member of the Institute of Marketing but also become Chartered? This was when I discovered the overwhelming, positive power of anger. All my life I'd been told I wasn't good enough. I'd wanted to be a teacher like Mum but I was told I'd never make the necessary grades in my exams to get into college, and not to bother. My father had constantly told me I'd never make much of myself but I was pretty, so all I needed to do was get married and a man would look after me.

I wanted to travel the world so I thought I'd become an air hostess. But in those days you had to be a minimum of 5 foot 4 and I was only 5 foot 3, so even then I wasn't good enough. I'd spent all my life thinking I wasn't good enough because Mum would never have left me if I had been. Anyway, I was so angry I picked up the phone and enrolled before I could be persuaded not to bother.

I was now a single working mum, raising two children and studying for the equivalent of a master's degree and I hadn't even got an A-Level to my name. After my husband's death, it had never occurred to me to claim benefits. I just assumed I needed to work and work hard if I wanted to succeed.

With all the running around working, studying and taking the children to all their after-school activities, I decided I needed an outlet; something for me. With everything that had happened, my curiosity was getting the better of me and I wanted to explore life, death and the greater Universe. I started reading Quantum Physics. It had always fascinated me ever since I was thrown out of science classes when I was 11 for arguing with the teacher. It was something I just seemed to KNOW even though I didn't know how I knew. I understood Dr Stephen Hawking and often had to explain his ideas to people who I thought were much more intelligent than I was.

As I explored the works of Stephen Hawking, Dr David Bolm and his theory of the Holotropic Universe, everything resonated with me. I was also looking at patterns. I was nine and my sister was three when Mum died. My son was nine and my daughter 11 when their father died. My mother was nine and my aunt was 11 when they were evacuated in the war. It must have been terrifying for children to be sent away like that to live with total strangers. My mother-in-law had been three when her father died and my father-in-law had been nine when his father died. Of my grandmothers-in-law, one had been three when her mother died and the other nine when her father took off with the under-parlour maid. The patterns had me intrigued but what were they about? What were they trying to tell me? What was the common theme? It's obvious when you know but it took me quite a while to work it out. Abandonment leading to self-guilt and not being good enough were the underlying emotional issues.

One of the main areas of my study in marketing was Communication, and I saw a weekend course being advertised on Communication so I decided I'd sign up. I thought it was at the College of Physic Studies. When I got there, it was actually at the College of Psychic Studies but even then I didn't notice the spelling because if I had, I would have run a mile.

When the workshop began, I wondered what on earth the tutor was talking about. The course was about the human energy field and auras. It turned out, when we were doing the initial introductions, that the lady next to me, whose name was Chrissy, worked for the same company as I did, in the same building on a different floor. She thought everyone was batty as well. We decided to leave at first break. Before the first break, however, we were asked to partner up and do an exercise to feel each other's auras. I was terrified of making a fool of myself (in those days I really worried about what people thought of me – not any more I'm pleased to say). Chrissy and I looked at each other, smiled and said, 'Fake it, copy the others.'

In our pairs, one had to stand one side of the room while the other walked towards them with their hands in front of them. They then had to stop when they felt the other person's aura. Simple. I copied everyone else and then just stopped. My, how I laughed inside when the tutor said, well done, I'd got it right. I moved a fraction of an inch and Chrissy immediately turned around.

She'd sensed me go into her energy field. That was it. We were both hooked. It made no sense whatsoever but we could both do it. We stayed the course for the whole weekend and I found it fascinating. I went on to do many different classes at the college and eventually I taught there as well.

After that weekend I became very interested in healing. My belief in healing had always been there and now I wanted to learn it for myself. It was 1998 and I signed up to learn Reiki. Over the course of 12 months, I did Reiki I, II, III and started practising and teaching it at weekends. I'd also become very interested in personal development and was looking for some classes to attend.

I was still doing weekend workshops at the college and I really wanted to meet my spirit guide. I went to many workshops trying to make that connection but nothing ever happened. It seemed as if I was never going to have any kind of spiritual experience.

One day, I got really fed up with waiting for something to happen, for my guide to appear, so I decided to make him up. I expected to imagine a native American or a Tibetan monk. What I actually imagined was Obi Wan Kenobi (Alec Guiness all glowing in white). Well, we had an imaginary chat and he said his name was Sebastian. I felt quite good about it. I now had a name and face I could connect to even if it was only in my imagination. I continued pretending I knew who my spirit guide was until five years later, Bill Harrison, a psychic artist, drew me a picture of my guide. He looked like Alec Guiness and his name was Sebastian. I finally had to accept that whatever I imagined was real. That was how Spirit was working with me. Over the years, I've had many other unaccountable experiences, all helping me realise that it doesn't really matter how it works, because it just does.

In the meantime, I was still a workshop junkie. Whenever I had the time or could afford something, I was off. Unfortunately, there wasn't much time or money for my new-found hobby so I spent a lot of evenings reading and learning to meditate. After one past life weekend, I'd imagined past lives as an Egyptian High Priestess, a Tibetan monk, and a Knights Templar during the Crusades, where I was captured by Saladin and imprisoned in an oubliette (a deep hole like a well, dark, damp and horrid, where prisoners were left to die). All these past life experiences were confirmed to me and healed at various times over the years as I visited and taught in these countries.

I was trying to meditate before going to sleep when I saw a pure white light and felt an overwhelming sense of love and compassion. Out of the light came what looked like the figure of Christ. I seemed frozen and then I just thought to myself, 'It can't be. I'm not good enough.' The image smiled and vanished. Then I knew it was real; the feeling was still there and I still felt 'not good enough'. To my regret, I hadn't had the courage to accept him and had sent him away. I've never experienced him since. Perhaps it's because I believe there are many ways to God whereas most Christians believe he is the only way.

I have experienced other overwhelming, loving energies of many Angels and Ascended Masters. In fact, after Reiki, Angel workshops and retreats were the first things I taught.

Not long after this experience with Christ and long before the experiences with Ascended Masters and Angels, I got a phone call from a lady saying she had a space on her beginners' tarot class. I wasn't interested in tarot. It smacked of the occult and still frightened me. A few months later she rang again. Still not interested. A few months after that, she rang yet again. It was a 12-week course and coincided with the 12-week wait before I found out whether I'd made the grade and passed my marketing exams, and was going to receive my Chartered status. I'd read enough by then to accept that if something happens three times you need to take notice. I agreed to do the class but I did tell her that I'd be out to prove it didn't work. After all, if you lay the cards out and do a reading then it might well be accurate, but if you shuffle them and do it again, you can't possibly get the same cards so how can it be real? Well, that's what I thought anyway.

I went to the classes and found them interesting, but however hard I tried, I couldn't prove tarot didn't work. What was worse was that I seemed to be able to do it. Slowly but surely, the fear began to subside and I went on to do the intermediate course, where I learnt a very valuable lesson in how Spirit works.

On this course, we had strangers come in for a reading and the class worked together to give them the information. On one occasion, I couldn't get any information about a particular lady at all. All I could think about was my childhood. My mother's family were Swiss and we would go to Switzerland and sit around the table having lunch, speaking four languages at once. We would ski, or walk in the mountains and every year, I had an ice cream birthday cake shaped as a ballerina. Well, at the end of the lesson when we were having coffee, I spoke to the lady and told her I was sorry I hadn't been able to give her anything because I was inundated with personal memories. When I told her about them, she went a bit pale as she looked at me and explained that my memories were her life. She lived in Switzerland and she did all those things, including having just ordered an ice cream birthday cake for her daughter.

My learning was that Spirit will use anything within us to pass on information and that the more we learn and know, the easier it is. Just because the information comes as memories and not a voice in my head or a vision, doesn't make it any less real. So, I learnt that anything you think of, or experience, such as backache during healing or a reading, is all a part of what Spirit is telling you.

I also started sitting in a circle and doing trance mediumship. Most people channel one spirit but I seemed to channel many. When I asked why, I was told that I was being used as a training ground for young guides. Apparently, even up there they have to learn and practise making connections before they get to guide anyone.

I had now transformed my life. I had passed my Chartered Institute of Marketing exams and was one of only 3000 Chartered Marketers in the world. My career was going from strength to strength. I was no longer a humble secretary but a Marketing Manager with a company car and a six-figure salary package at one of the biggest professional services firms in the world. But I wasn't happy. Still, I would be with the next promotion, I told myself.

That was my wake-up call. I'd been happy passing the exams, proving I could do it and that I was 'good enough'. With each promotion, I was glad to celebrate and I was pleased my dad was finally proud of me. But the joy was short-lived because I was still in a competitive man's world and I realised that deep down, I still didn't feel 'good enough'. Maybe it was because I was born female and my father had always drilled into my sister and me that we didn't need to worry about doing well because we would marry and a man would look after us. (That was and still is his belief. He even said the same about my daughter. She was pretty and a man would look after her, whereas my son needed to go to university and do well. I've been quick to point out that shit happens, like it did to me, and education is important for girls as well.) I did, however, notice that the times I was happiest in my life were when I was training staff at work and when I was teaching and healing.

One of the things that had come out of my research into all the patterns within the family was that I was determined that neither of my children would die young or of alcoholism, which had been a recurring pattern within both my and my husband's families. The type of help my husband needed had not been available then and I wanted to create something that would be helpful in the future. To do that, I had to break the pattern. I'd already studied NLP (Neuro Linguistic Programming) as part of my sales and marketing training and I'd found it very useful and enlightening, both in terms of communication and therapy. I was by now a fully-fledged Master NLP Practitioner and Timeline Therapist but even so, I still often didn't feel 'good enough'. If I was going to open a retreat centre to help the homeless rebuild their lives, I would need more skills and, more importantly, I would need a resident, fully qualified psychotherapist on the staff. The only way I could guarantee that the staff member wouldn't leave was if I did it myself.

I was attending an introductory day on face-reading when I came across Re.Vision and their Integrative Psychosynthesis training, which is a form of counselling and psychotherapy that focuses on the integration of all facets of the ego personality with the soul. Here was a counselling training that included the spiritual aspect, and I just knew it was the one for me. The training was due to begin in a couple of weeks. I contacted them and was told I'd have to wait until next year because I needed to do their initial introductory course first. I begged for an interview and wangled my way onto the course, embarking on four years of counselling and psychotherapy training. I must admit it was harrowing facing all my unconscious issues but well worth the time and money. The training itself fed into my own ego patterns and therefore, after three years, with a lot of regret I had to leave and never completed the course. Again, it felt like I wasn't good enough but at least by this time that particular nemesis had been healed. I knew I was enough, and I'd acquired all the skills and experience I needed for wherever life would take me next.

All my life I'd wanted to travel and teach and every job I'd ever taken had been with a view to being able to make that happen in one way or another. Yet here I was, working in a global firm but with no prospects of working abroad.

I gave a lot of consideration to my life and, maybe being a bit clairvoyant, I thought the firm would be making redundancies soon and I wanted to be one of them. I'd already started on a new path. When the redundancies came along, I decided to take the bull by the horns and put my money where my mouth was. Either I believed Spirit would look after me or I didn't. I gave myself six months to see if I could make a profession out of my hobbies. If I couldn't, then I could always get another job. I was coming up 50. That was 20 years ago.

I never saw myself as a psychic, clairvoyant, healer, and it took me many years and much personal and spiritual development before I finally let go of my fear and reluctantly allowed Spirit to lead me into this way of life.

I saw a sign for a psychic fair at the local British Legion club and I went in and asked if they needed more readers. They didn't at the time but called me a couple of weeks later. That was the beginning of my professional career as a psychic, clairvoyant, healer and teacher and it has gone from strength to strength. Spirit has watched over me and my family ever since.

The spiritual path is long and hard and starts, I believe, from the soul's conception through many lifetimes and with a soul contract for each lifetime. I would not be who I am today without having travelled this pathway because it's the journey that has given me the gifts, the experience and the knowledge to share with and help others on their individual journeys.

I had always seen myself as a traveller and teacher. I was just blinded into thinking it could never be because I hadn't had classical training in teaching and none of the international companies I'd worked for had ever posted me abroad.

In these last 20 years, not only have I been happy, I've also travelled widely leading workshops, retreats, spiritual holidays. I've given lectures and talks, as well as doing readings all around this country and the world. Countries I've travelled to and worked in include America, Australia, Egypt, Thailand, Peru, Argentina, Bolivia, Chile, Easter Island, Tibet, Bhutan, and most of Western Europe. Over the years, in many of these places, I've facilitated deeply moving spiritual experiences for many people, including myself. These experiences will need to go into another book. It seems that, as you put your feet on the earth of a country that needs healing or where you've had a past life that needs healing, then strange things happen that lead you to the next and then the next. Nothing happens by accident, or chance. There is an unseen force at work, gently guiding us and watching over us every step of the way. And there is absolutely nothing to fear except fear itself, because that is what holds us back.

I've taught many hundreds of people. I've written many articles for magazines and have done radio and television. I was President of the British Astrological and Psychic Society and responsible for updating all their training courses and for the vetting and mentoring of members. During this time, I also wrote *Your Angel Journey – A Guide to Releasing Your Inner Angel*, published by O-books and available on Amazon.co.uk, as well as two other e-books.

Now my life has changed again and my focus is more upon family and caring for my parents, but I'm still doing readings and writing. I've transformed all the workshop notes and handouts into online training courses, and there are three more books with publishers awaiting publication and there will be more to come. Many of my meditations and guided visualisations are available to download from my website for free, as are some introductory training courses. I tutor all my courses and students myself, as well as doing readings worldwide via Zoom, Skype, WhatsApp Video, Messenger and Facetime.

www.joylina.com
joylina@joylina.com
FACEBOOK: @joylinalivingwithsoul

Imagine receiving signs from the Universe that pre-empt situations. How would you feel? Would you know how to act or what to do with the information? The Universe gives us miracles if we are open to receiving them.

SIGNS FROM THE UNIVERSE

Nikki Finch

Do you ever ask yourself deep and meaningful questions? Have you ever wondered what your life purpose is, or felt alone, disconnected, or wondered what you're doing here?

I never really felt whole or complete. I was always looking externally for solutions to my questions about myself and my purpose, and wondered why I often felt stuck and depressed, unable to maintain a happy state. I asked so many questions and yet I felt trapped in a loop of never getting the answers I needed to feel free.

As a child, I was told that adults know best; children should be seen and not heard and only speak when they are spoken too. And so, I believed no one wanted to hear what I had to say, and surely, I couldn't know the answers to my questions. Life had shown me that I didn't know the way, so the answers I sought were obviously to be found in the external world. I followed this path, asking externally and believing everyone else knew what the key to my happiness was, and off I went on the not-so-merry-go-round.

Whilst I looked externally, my soul gave me nudges and clues, dreams, messages and bloody big signs. However, if you aren't in the driving seat and tuned in, you clearly miss the signposts!

Eventually, I had to take note.

Depressed and lying on the sofa I was at my lowest point. I wanted to check out. It was a beautiful sunny day; the kind of day that made my heart sing; the kind of day where I would be out in nature, looking at the beauty of it all. Yet I couldn't get off the sofa and everything was wrong.

I'm not sure how long I lay there. I just knew I felt dead inside and my whole inner world was grey. Somehow, I'd dimmed my light so much that I didn't even know where to look for it or how to turn it up again. My life had turned into a process of unhappiness as I went through the motions of dragging myself out of bed, going to work in a job that I loved, that had now become a prison simply through saying no to the advances of my ex-boss, going home, eating, sleeping and repeat. Life was meaningless.

I lived on the ground floor in a building attached to the back of an old farmhouse that was now made up of apartments. It was quiet, peaceful and no one really took any notice of you. I was very much alone on so many levels.

There were no lights on. It was dark and the middle of the night. I looked out of the bedroom door, my eyes adjusting to the darkness, and caught sight of a mass: a ball of darker-looking energy moving slowly along the corridor, about 2 feet wide hovering at head height, moving along the hallway towards the bedroom. I watched it without emotion as it came closer to where I was standing. It seemed slow and purposeful. I looked at it through my eyes and yet I could also see myself standing there looking at it. I felt detached and emotionless; there was no fear. I was an observer of the scene. It was as if something negative was encroaching into my space and suddenly, it stopped moving and I was aware there was an empty silence in the space between. As I watched, somehow my presence made it move back along the corridor and away from me, distancing itself. It moved slowly and I followed, keeping the distance between us as it moved along the corridor and into the lounge.

I opened a window and stood back. It moved out, seemingly without any conscious effort on my part. It was as if love had caught the darkness, looked it square in the eye, and it'd retreated as it had been seen. I closed the window and that's all I remember.

I awoke to the sound of birds singing and the sheep grazing on the grass in the nearby field, sunshine streaming into the bedroom. I felt really calm and I stretched in the sunlight. Today felt different. Happiness was calling.

Deciding it was time to get up and get going, I walked into the bathroom, catching my reflection in the mirror. Stopping dead in my tracks, I turned quickly to face it. A sharp intake of breath and a feeling of shock ran through my body. My face was black with soot, apart from a small patch of clear skin under each nostril. I gazed in disbelief at what was looking back at me; it seemed unreal.

Turning round, I grabbed the hand towel, wet it and rubbed it over my face quickly. Dirty, black, sooty marks were evident on the white towel. Thankfully, I wasn't going mad; the soot was real. Forget my teeth, I thought, I need a shower straightaway. OMG was it in my hair too?

Showering answered that question and I watched a black stream run off my hair down my body towards the drain. My mind started to worry: what about my lungs? What had happened? I picked up the shower head and moved the water across the walls and floor. More soot flowed away in a stream towards the drain. I began to realise that the soot was everywhere. The whole room was covered in it.

I love taking a shower. It's a great place to clear my head, for ideas to pop in or to see visual metaphors. Suddenly, I realised I'd dreamt about the dark energy in the corridor. I was surprised and still a little shocked as it dawned on me what I'd seen. I had been totally conscious in my dream, seeing through my own eyes yet observing myself like a movie, and thankfully the darkness had gone. I knew I'd influenced the outcome! Years later, I realised that I was lucid dreaming.

I kept wondering what had happened? Whatever it was, it had been linked to my dream.

On a practical level, there was so much to do. The whole apartment was completely covered in a black layer of soot; it was even inside every drawer, cupboard and wardrobe. Nothing had escaped. My insurance company were great and a massive clean-up operation took place. There was no evidence there had been a fire in the apartment, and I didn't have a regular coal or gas fire. My only heating was electric night storage heaters...

Listening to and acting on my intuition may have saved my life, who knows? But I still didn't believe in myself or in my inner knowledge and guidance system.

Some weeks later the apartment was clean, painted, fresh and shining. It was wonderful to feel the sunshine streaming into the lounge and onto my face and body; to enjoy the silence and gratitude of the moment. For once, my mind was still and I felt peaceful within the moment.

Fire!

'What?'

Fire! I heard it clearly as if someone was standing right next to me.

'What? OMG there's no one else here! What does that mean? OMG I'm hearing things!' Yet there's a feeling of knowing in my body and I'm not sure what to do with the information. It feels imminent and close by. It plays on my mind and I wonder what it means. So I check the rooms and recheck the rooms, even though I know they will be ok.

My partner arrives in from work as I'm getting ready to go out for the evening with him.

'Hey, had a good day?'

'Yes, you?'

'Er, well… something weird happened earlier…'

'What?'

'Well… I heard something, and I don't know what to do about it.'

'What do you mean?'

'I heard "Fire" really clearly, as though someone was standing here next to me and giving me a warning.'

'Fire?'

'Yes. I was just enjoying the moment and suddenly it was there. I heard it clearly and no one was around and now I feel like I need to let people know…'

He smiles. 'Who?'

'I don't know… People… in the farmhouse.'

'How's that going to work out? Do you think they'll believe you?'

'OMG, I see what you mean… So, what do I do?'

'No idea, they'll think you're nuts.'

'Probably… Maybe I was daydreaming?' I convince myself that was it, yet I have a nagging feeling I'm trying hard to ignore.

'Ready to go?'

'Yes,' I reply. I grab my bag and we head out of the door, get in the car and drive out along the driveway. I glance at the farmhouse as we pass; we turn onto the road and the thoughts slip from my mind as we enjoy the evening and each other's company.

After a wonderful meal, we head home. It's dark and there aren't many people or cars about, which isn't unusual as it's a pretty rural area. It's been a lovely evening. Driving through the village we turn the corner and head up the hill. We both see lights. As we get closer, I catch my breath: 'OMG, there's a fire engine… There's two!' I'm shocked; I want to vomit. So much emotion is rising in my body, I need air.

My partner explains where we live and the fireman lets us turn onto the drive. I remember driving over the hoses, feeling total disbelief. We park up, get out of the car and stare at the scene. I feel totally helpless, in shock and I start to shake. I have to go inside whilst the emotion I'm feeling comes up; tears and waves of emotion move through.

My partner suggests we go and see the neighbours, to see what we can do to help. I follow out of the door. They are huddled together covered in coats and blankets. We walk over, check if everyone is ok and ask if we can help in any way. Thankfully, everyone is fine, although shocked. We hear one of them fell asleep and their curtains caught fire from their candle.

Much later we get to bed. I'm confused by the situation: why was I warned? What should I have done? Would it have changed anything? My mind has only questions and scenarios and no solutions. Sleep comes in the early hours and I wake in the morning, feeling like I don't ever want to be clairaudient, clairvoyant, clairsentient or psychic, or have anything to do with conscious knowledge ever again. Because, what do you do with that kind of information?

And that's exactly how it's been for years. I've ignored it. I want to know but I don't want the responsibility.

Yet the Universe always has other ideas and keeps knocking till you take note and listen. It took me a while to realise I held the keys to my own happiness and that I could help others find theirs. I retrained and began to understand the mind and its patterns. To be in your awareness and follow your intuition, you have to break down old barriers, really look at your beliefs, and challenge who you really are and what you've been told. Then you can begin a search for your own fire, your own spark, your true passion, creativity and purpose, which is mostly, I have found, usually hiding in plain sight.

www.nikkifinch.com
nikki@nikkifinch.com
INSTAGRAM: @nikki_finch
VERO: @nikkifinch

Our loved ones never leave us, even when they pass. They still love us and want to help us. Alexa's grandmother made sure she was reunited with her favourite bag.

I ALWAYS KNEW SHE WOULD HAUNT ME

Alexa Whitten

I always knew my grandmother was special. She was a big part of my early years as she lived next door to us, and I would often find myself in her kitchen, helping her make chocolate eclairs or baking cookies. She also introduced me to the wonderful world of writing; she wrote a book about me and my donkey on a gorgeous Olivetti typewriter, which I loved to type on when she let me (supervised mind!).

Unfortunately, she died all too early (I was 12), but she always told me she would watch out for me. (*'I'll come and haunt you'*, were her actual words, and I knew deep down she would.) In the story I'm about to share it's very clear she kept her promise.

We were on our second leg of our sailing trip – sailing from the West coast of Canada, down the coast of North America, into Mexico, Costa Rica, and eventually to Panama en route to Europe. We had taken a side trip to visit Guatemala and the wonderful market of Chichicastenango and I bought a fair few clothes and embroidered bags – one of which I used so much it developed a hole, and I had to fix it with mismatched thread. Those were the woes of being on a boat with no shops at hand.

It was here, in Panama, that something quite extraordinary happened, and I can't deny the synchronicity of events, which opened my eyes to a higher power.

My friend and I were enjoying the markets and bars of Cartagena, and one evening we found ourselves in a taverna, which was full of dancing and merriment. The people were so friendly and we bumped into a couple of chaps who we'd already met at the marina where we were moored. We found ourselves sitting at a table drinking the local beer with them, and we were so grateful that most were able to speak English.

A favourite tune came on and we were soon on the dance floor, boogying the night away. It wasn't until closing time that I realised my bag (the one from Guatemala with mismatched thread) had gone missing, and panic set in. In my bag was a watch my dad had given me – a rather distinctive swatch-type, which I'd taken off earlier to have a shower – my passport (yep, how silly was that?), my Canadian bank debit card, and some money.

Within five minutes of me alerting the group that my bag was missing, the owner, a rather nice chap called Jose, turned off the music, turned on the lights, and we had the whole bar looking for it. I wasn't bothered by the money, but I was bothered about my passport, my watch and the actual bag itself as it was a reminder of the wonderful streets of the Guatemalan market.

After ten minutes of frantic searching, nothing was found. I left my details with Jose, who promised to contact me if anything turned up. Interestingly, a man who was drinking at the bar was fingered for the theft (blessing number one). He was questioned by Jose, to no avail, and eventually got kicked out. However, no bag was in his possession. He kept saying he was innocent and we spent the next few hours scouring the streets nearby, seeing if the bag had been dumped. Unfortunately, no luck. We went back to the boat, despondent and upset. I was also kicking myself for being so stupid as to take my passport. I mean, how the hell was I going to get that replaced?

The next day, after keeping what had happened the previous evening from my parents, my friend and I decided to go to the local market to see if we could find a replacement bag. We trundled off and, even though there were lots that were similar, nothing quite compared to the one I'd found at Chichicastenango. By this time, we were hot and sticky, and both our tummies were rumbling, so we decided to get some lunch. Liz (my friend) needed to get some money out of the bank so we went back to the main square, where all the banks and bars were located. The first bank we tried was shut (second blessing) so we nipped across the street to the second bank, for which you needed a bank card to access the cashpoints. Liz (who incidentally had the same type of debit card as I did) used hers to get in. We waited in line whilst a rather officious 'girl' who was holding a clipboard stood beside us. Liz went and used the machine.

This girl then approached us and, in halting English, asked if Liz could show her how to use the bank card (third blessing). Trying to explain to a girl who doesn't speak English that you don't share details like this was quite frustrating. I mean, she was asking Liz for her PIN number!

Huh?

She said she was from the bank and needed the information.

Something wasn't ringing true.

That's when I noticed the bag she was wearing.

It was mine.

I told Liz. She looked at me. 'Nah, can't be. There are lots of those types of bags...' I pointed to the sewn-up hole and mismatched thread.

'Where did you get this?' I asked the girl. She was somewhat confused by me looking at her bag and inspecting it.

I then noticed her watch – my watch. Yup, she was wearing the swatch-type watch my dad had given me.

I said to Liz, 'Look! She's wearing my watch!' Liz conceded, and I grabbed the girl by the wrist and marched her to the bar from the night before, which was just across the street.

On the way there, the girl, who'd now realised we'd cottoned on to her antics of theft, was resisting somewhat. I wasn't going to let her go but she was putting up a fight. As we approached the bar, the chap who'd been wrongly accused the night before was loitering in the entrance. He recognised me, and then saw the girl. His face fell, and he quickly helped us push her upstairs.

Jose appeared (blessing number four) – the bar should have been closed – as he had come in early to do a stock take. He saw the huddle of people: the girl, me, Liz and the chap who had been at the centre of attention last night.

I let go of the girl and explained the situation.

I showed him the bag, the watch and ultimately the bank card (with my name on it), at which he looked ashamed and totally forlorn.

This girl was his daughter.

He was asked if there was any punishment I wanted inflicted – the thought of the Panamanian police filled me with dread, so I declined. But not before explaining, with tears flowing, how she had ruined a wonderful evening, and that theft is not the answer to anything. I hoped my compassion would be the teacher – but I can't help but wonder at all the blessings that fell into place for me to be able to get my stuff back: the closed bank, the timing of our visit to the second one, the fact Liz had the same bank card as me, the chap who was at the entrance to the bar, and Jose being at work when he wasn't supposed to be. All of this? I got all of my stuff back, including my passport and all my money.

I think it was the hand of my grandmother... Her looking out for me manifesting itself, for sure.

www.bookrefinery.com
alexa@alexawhitten.com
FACEBOOK: @gettingyourbookpublished
INSTAGRAM: @lexafit_wip

Chris eventually learnt to accept her gift of mediumship after listening to her 'inner compass' and experiencing a true miracle.

LEARNING TO TRUST

Chris Gill

I remember quite vividly running up the stairs and reaching the landing. And as I turned to go past the bathroom door, I met my grandmother. There she stood, as plain and clear as could be, which wasn't unusual as she lived with us. Only difference was that she had died three days earlier.

As I stood still in my tracks, I reached out to touch her and she was gone! I was around 12 years old then, and I recall thinking to myself, did I really see her or was it just wishful thinking? Or my imagination? I wasn't frightened by this experience as I had a great relationship with her, and loved to sit at her feet while she recalled stories of when she used to take my mother and her 14 siblings hop-picking in Kent when they were children.

Only a day or two later, when I entered the lounge, I saw her sitting in her chair by the fireside, where she always sat. It was only for a few moments, but I just knew what I saw was 'real' and NOT my imagination. What was I going to do now? Who could I tell? Who could I turn to, to share my excitement that my nan wasn't really dead at all? That she was alive – I know, because I'd seen her!

There was no one. My mother was grief-stricken, and dealing with her brother who wanted to know what had happened to my grandmother's money. What money? There was just about enough to bury her with, and my mother made up the rest. An argument ensued and my dear mum was so distraught and enraged that she threw a plate at him! Well, she was attempting to serve our dinner up at the time. He left with his tail between his legs and at speed.

Calm returned only for a very short time as, in the afternoon, my aunt arrived, demanding my mother account for my nan's lack of savings. She upset my mum so much I asked her to leave, as she was sobbing. I recall her being so shocked that I'd dared to ask her to leave, that she refused. I, on the other hand, was determined she would leave, so I grabbed her and pushed her out the front door. There was a scuffle and I hit her before closing the door in her face. For days after, I was petrified she'd come back, and my vision and excitement of seeing my grandmother was never to be shared with anyone.

A year had soon passed. My sister had moved into the bedroom that had been my nan's, which meant my younger sister and I shared a bedroom now. We had more space. We had a telephone installed in the hallway, which was a luxury then, as the whole street would have to use the phone box at the end of the road if we wanted to make a call. In the next nine months, my mum would lose seven members of her family, and I became petrified of that telephone, as I knew that when it rang someone else had died. The feeling was so strong that I used to run upstairs and hide when it rang. This fear of telephones has stayed with me throughout my life. Silly really, because I use the phone a lot, but there are days when I need to make a call, and can't. I've learnt to either leave it for another day, or I have to write down what it is I want to say before I pick it up.

This 'knowing' that something was about to happen, or my intuition, is something that I've learnt to embrace and trust beyond doubt. I wish, looking back, that I'd 'listened' earlier, but then everything happens for a reason, and I accept that I'm in the right place at this time.

It was only a short time later that my mother was diagnosed with breast cancer, and it was inoperable at that time. She was treated at The Royal London hospital with radiotherapy, as chemotherapy hadn't yet been developed. She was an extraordinarily strong woman, and I know she wanted to live long enough so myself and my two sisters would be able to look after ourselves, so she fought for seven years to stay with us.

I met my husband when I was 14 and we were planning our wedding when I was 19. Mum was so very ill and she had great difficulty walking. We were planning a July wedding, and like most weddings, it had grown in numbers, from a small group into about 100 people; from a quick trip to the Registry Office, to a church wedding. It was March time when I took my mum out to buy some material to have something made for her to wear for my wedding. Her left arm was huge; she had lymphedema and wanted a dress or outfit that would fit her but hide her arm. She had to use a wheelchair then, as she couldn't walk very far.

We searched around the shops and came home with some material that she liked. During the next couple of months, her health deteriorated considerably and I feared she wouldn't make it to the wedding. She spent days in bed and, when not lying down, sitting in the armchair. She was on steroids and her face and body were bloated. She had no energy and was in pain. And it was then that I asked for help. I made a solemn vow to follow in the belief in God if he would grant my wish and give my mum a year of my life, so she could witness my marriage and have the strength to enjoy it.

The 28th July arrived, my wedding day. My mum walked down the aisle, unaided, and took her seat in the front row. No sign of her wheelchair, no stick, nothing. She looked amazing in comparison to two months earlier, and she even managed one short, slow dance with my father. I was enlightened to the power of prayer and thought.

On returning from honeymoon, I found my mother in bed. She had used all her energy to make it on that day, for me. She died the following June; one year after I'd set my intention and bargained with the Great Spirit and the Universe.

Lots of things happened so quickly after my mother passed to Spirit. Six months later, my father became engaged to my aunt – yes, the very same one I'd thrown out of the house, and he married her exactly a year after my mother's death.

We decided to quit the rat race here and bought a £10 ticket to emigrate to South Africa. It was my way of dealing with everything; just get away, as far as possible. I didn't belong here anymore. What I didn't know was that, a year later, we'd be returning, as a war had broken out in Angola and there was talk of ex-pats being called up to do National Service. My husband started making bomb casings at work and troops moved into our town one Sunday afternoon. Armoured vehicles and tanks rolled down the road past our apartment. The shopping precinct was filled with troops for days. To say it was unsettling was a huge understatement; I was petrified. Would we get out in time?

We hastily sold our possessions and booked a flight back to the UK. We stayed with my younger sister for a few weeks before setting off again in search of another home, somewhere we could put down roots. We ended up living half way between Coventry and Leicestershire, in a small village outside Hinckley. We both found work, bought a house and were happy and contented.

It was one Christmas time when my trust would be tested again, as I was taken ill late one evening. I was in excruciating pain, couldn't stand and felt nauseous, and my whole body was shaking. I was never ill, not even as a child, so this was certainly a new experience for me. I didn't like it; the pain wasn't going away and I didn't know what to do with myself. My husband called for a doctor, who, after examining me, diagnosed appendicitis. He asked if we needed an ambulance to be called or could I be taken to hospital by car. I said immediately, 'By car!' The doctor telephoned the hospital advising that we would be on our way…

This wasn't right. I had visions of people standing around a table with knives and forks, as if to carve the Sunday joint, but it was me lying on the table. I had no medical background, and yet I KNEW I didn't have an appendicitis! I wasn't going to be carved up! Was I being totally stupid? I was in pain. I could die, if the doctor was right and I was wrong. Anyway, I didn't go, and obviously have lived to tell the tale.

This isn't something I would advocate anyone else does, but it was my decision, with the help of my guides, not to have an operation, and I quickly recovered once I'd asked for help. The doctor returned later that morning, and to say he was angry would be an understatement. But this wasn't to be the only time I'd ask for help or question medical decisions.

I was approaching 25 and thoughts of starting a family were beginning to crop up. My husband was keen to start straightaway, but I was hesitant. I had to plan this; I had so many 'what ifs' that were unanswered. It was several weeks before I got my head around motherhood, so I thought and trusted that my child, who I hadn't even been conceived, wouldn't encounter any great dangers in their life. And almost ten months later, my first son was born.

When my son was roughly 20 months old, our thoughts once again turned to having another baby. It hadn't been an easy pregnancy or delivery the first time but I didn't want him to be an only child either, thinking four would be a good round number. However, the thought of having to go through all that four times seemed daunting, so I decided to again 'ask' my Great Spirit Guide and the Universe, this time for twins. How wonderful that would be: three children and only two pregnancies. My family would be complete.

It was when I was going for my first scan that I turned to my husband and said, 'Wouldn't it be funny if they found out I was having two babies instead of one today?' as I just KNEW that might well be the case. He wasn't amused as he was working a three-day week and people were being made redundant from their jobs at that time. It would be really hard.

The scan took place in silence and, as I watched on the monitor, I could see one complete baby – a body, head, arms and legs, a heartbeat – perfect! It then picked up another outline. I could see a head and torso, but no limbs. My God! What was that? The nurse then again went over to the first baby – yes all there – and then to this second outline. She quickly turned off the monitor and turned to me and said, 'Congratulations, you're expecting twins!' I didn't know whether to laugh or cry. What about the limbs? That's when she quickly explained that the baby had its back to us and the limbs were facing inwards. What a relief!

I went outside to the waiting room, in hysterical laughter, as I told my husband we were expecting twins. He fell off his chair. Another gift was given; my thoughts and desires had been answered again.

The pregnancy went fine. I reached my 40 weeks and they should have been born, as most twins come early, but not mine. Without going into too much detail, my intuition kicked in again. After being in labour all day, the midwife wanted to give me something to make me sleep so they could increase the contractions by drugs. I was adamant I didn't want or need any drugs – I was fine. So I told her that unless my babies were born NOW I was leaving. Hastily, the matron was called and then a consultant, and after an extensive examination, I was told my babies were stuck and would never be born naturally. One child had put his hand above his head and was entwined in the legs of his brother. I was then rushed to theatre and given a C-section, and my beautiful boys were delivered fit and healthy. In the coming months, I often looked back to that very scary time, and the 'what ifs' played in my mind. Thankfully, I trusted once again, refused medical intervention, and I feel that saved my children's lives and possibly their future health. I'm eternally grateful.

Bringing up three children under three years old wasn't easy, especially as we had no help whatsoever. My in-laws, or out-laws as I often referred to them, never came near nor by, and family thought we lived at the other end of the Earth instead of off the M1. But I had my children, my wonderful, funny, mischievous, happy boys. I had often 'looked' for my mother at times, longing to see her again, but she never showed herself to me as my nan had done those years ago. My thoughts would often take me to the how, where, why, and when could I discover all I yearned to know about Spirit, the 'other world', intuition and about the power of the Universe. I had no idea what the bigger plan was for me, what I would be doing or how I'd be able to communicate with the spirit world in the future. Little by little it would unfold, not in weeks or months, but in the years ahead.

Who Am I?

What do I see when I look within
What is there beneath this skin
Where is my Spirit
Where does it hide
What gives me a sense of pride?

What makes me 'get up and go'
What is it that drives me so
What gives me pleasure
What makes me sad
Is this the life I should have had?

Have I done enough
What's next
What drives me on to do my best
What gives me hope
That 'knowing' deep inside
I will be given enough to survive?

I put my trust in the spirit world
For there's my guardian and my guide.
They'll not forsake me, and always by my side
They give me strength when times are rough
They give me hope when nothing seems enough.

I will never walk alone
My trust in them has simply grown
From small seeds into fields of green
My strength, my hope, my everything.

chris.medium@icloud.com
FACEBOOK: @chrisgill
INSTAGRAM: @chrisgill5567

'Corporate girl turned cosmic girl', Dawn leaves the corporate life to share her gifts with the world. You may have to read her story more than once to believe the miracle of the healing of the broken ankle.

KEEPING IT REAL WHEN LIFE SEEMS SURREAL

Dawn Alexander

I incarnated this time around in 1968. I feel like I've lived many lives within this one. I was always a sensitive child and at times when I found the energy and circumstances challenging, I would look up to the sky and question this reality. I always felt that there had to be more to life than what I and others were experiencing. I often found other people's energies to be extremely harsh and although I know there are many wonderful people out there, I experienced situations in childhood that came from the shadows; the abusive underbelly of all that is hidden. Years later, I pondered over writing a book, and I began many times, yet always knew there would come a day when I could tell my story as the survivor and not the victim. At this point in my journey, it doesn't feel like I'm meant to go into all the finer details, yet some background helps in comprehending how I went from shy, sensitive child to working with thousands of people, helping them heal and move forward in life.

I was in my early twenties and I remember going for a reading. This was by an elderly woman, here in Aberdeen, but as much as I attempt to recall all the details, I seem to have retained only what would be important for me to look back and reflect on. I have vague memories of some of what was said, but what did stay in my mind all these years was her saying, 'One day, you will do what I do.' I had received messages from a loved one who had crossed over, and she seemed to know things about me that she couldn't possibly have known. When she uttered those words, 'You will do this too', I no doubt gave her the eye rolls and look of disbelief that I became so familiar with myself years later, as others sat in front of me. I heard her say that I was not to give it too much thought and 'when it comes on, it will just come on like a rocket'.

I left her house that day and the words played over in my mind. I'd always been curious about the concept of life after death, ETs and all things a bit 'out there' to some. I was intrigued by these men and women who claimed to be able to 'talk to the dead' and know things about our past and predict the future. I had, and still have, a logical, analytical side too. I was heavily into reading, researching, learning and wanting to know everything about everything. My inquisitive nature had me peering into every corner and continually asking questions. I was still like the young child who asks WHY? every few seconds. My soul never felt settled and I didn't know why.

After that day, I simply got on with living my life. I was in a corporate sales job, working long hours and climbing the career ladder, as well as going out partying most weekends. I was making the money and having fun yet I didn't feel fulfilled deep within myself. I was head-hunted by another company, as they'd heard I was really successful within my role, and I ended up being the only female sales representative within the company I moved to. There was no thought given to any of what was said at that reading, yet the lady's words were filed at the back of my mind; files that would one day be recovered, dusted off and fully paid attention to.

Fast-forward to when I was 30 and I discovered I was pregnant. This too was not part of the plan. I had always wanted children yet my 'career plan' was interrupted. The company car and corporate meetings were to come to an end. I can look back now and laugh as I see where I attempted to plan out the path, yet another path was being carefully carved out for me. I had to let the logical, over-thinking part of me be quietened at times. I could feel that there was something stirring deep within me; I couldn't put it into words and often I still can't. We are thinking and feeling Beings. Sometimes our thoughts can override our feelings; our mind becomes stronger than our heart and it's this which is one of the biggest lessons I had to learn along the way. That of trusting my heart, my intuition, those gut feelings; the knowing things without knowing how I know them. I just did. I just do.

I've always been a plain speaker; I can 'channel' or connect to an aspect of me that can use spiritual jargon, fancy words and flowery sayings, yet I've always been more 'corporate girl turned cosmic girl' than headscarves and halos. Some of what I would see over my years of immersing myself into the 'psychic' arena would make my toes curl; I cringe a lot but that's me. I may dot about a little whilst sharing my story yet I prefer to go with the flow, and that always works out for the best. This would be another key quality as I went through life; do not stay rigid but be open to all potentials. Stay curious and question everything.

When my son, Robbie was two years old, I was drawn to a Body and Soul Fair here in Aberdeen where we live. I received a Reiki session and thereafter felt the call to further my own training in Reiki, and subsequently I would go on to train in many healing modalities and complementary therapies. The word 'psychic' still conjured up images of fairground fortune tellers, crystal balls and those sorts of people, and I definitely 'wasn't one of them'. This reluctant psychic never wanted to have any label put on her or to be put in a box, yet as these 'kinda weird' things were happening to me, I needed to find a way to let others know. I felt as if I was meant to help them, I just wasn't sure exactly how. I would always have my street cred in mind. There were people around me who just didn't believe in 'talking to the dead' or tuning in to others to give them messages. There was a part of my psyche giving me that pep talk too; the reluctance to embrace what was happening and the speed at which things were unfolding.

'When it comes on, it will come on like a rocket...'

The words were reverberating around my mind once more.

I would often get a gut feeling and it would prove to be spot on. I know now we all have these innate abilities yet a busy life and a refusal to 'go there' can put the dampers on a glorious connection, with so much more than we are led to believe. I've always had an inquisitive mind so, once the metaphysical mirror was held up in front of me, I was drawn to explore further. I would listen to the voice in my head that, yes, sounded like me, but at times seemed so wise and profound, I wondered who on earth it was. We do have, around us, what many will refer to as Angels, spirit guides, Ascended Masters and Beings of Light. Ascended Masters are those who have incarnated in a physical body like you and me. They walked this Earth and lived that life of integrating and embodying a 'higher' awareness of consciousness and knowing that we are souls inhabiting a structure, a vessel, a form. They were able to remember who they were and the 'super-human' abilities they had.

These Ascended Masters walked the Earth for a specific timeframe to leave their footprints and energy on the tapestry of life. We can walk over these imprints and intuitively tap dance our way along the path of remembering. Angels, guides and many other Light Beings are expressions of this consciousness, light and energy; they are vibrational markers on the cosmic map of life; illuminations of the light that we all are. I like to keep it simple. For me, I see the branches on the Tree of Life and we are all exactly where we need to be in any moment in time and space. Some of us are nearer the ground; we are physical. We are rooted here on Earth in a body. We can walk and talk and be active participants in reshaping this physical expression of life. Our original spark of light is like a star twinkling in the sky, guiding us as we walk the Earth.

Twinkle, twinkle, little star, how I wonder what you are?

I kept exploring and will always do so. My human doesn't always have all the answers, yet my soul always does.

In 2003, I felt a strong pull to travel to Ireland to learn/remember more about connecting to Angels and working with my psychic abilities, and to open up to the possibility of mediumship. I could feel a layer of reluctance and avoidance being removed. Suddenly I had to know.

During this week, an experience happened that would prove to open me up even more than I could have ever imagined. The story of this was shared in a national magazine and, to this day, I often have to remind myself that this actually happened to me.

Throughout the week, we did yoga every morning, we were guided through meditations, we were put into pairs and into groups. This was intensive 'development' and yet my sometimes shy, sensitive inner-child would come to the fore, and a room full of around 180 people could feel a touch overwhelming at times. I was there for five days and I knew there was a reason I was so strongly guided to go. I had a young child; his dad and my mum made sure he was well looked after. And I had to borrow some money to enable me to attend this retreat, yet I knew I had to be there. I've always been extremely sensible with my finances and I would never have left my child on a whim, yet the feeling within me that I HAD to be on that retreat/course was so palpable I simply couldn't ignore it.

On the fourth day, we were all down by the river as we were about to take part in a ceremony; a releasing of all that no longer served us. As a surprise to us small number of Scottish contingents, one gentleman, who unknown to us had taken his bagpipes with him, appeared at the top of the hill. As he played, my friends and I began dancing around in excitement. The next thing I knew, I'd slipped and went crashing to the ground in excruciating pain. My left foot was twisted out at an angle; it literally looked as if my foot was hanging off. An ambulance was called, I was put on a stretcher and taken to the local hospital. I did not see that coming!

My friends who I had travelled from Aberdeen with me accompanied me in the ambulance and I was screaming in pain the whole way there. Some of the memories are still vague yet this stays strongly with me. We arrived at the hospital and I was taken for an X-ray, which confirmed that I'd broken my ankle. Bagpipes and a broken ankle; if I hadn't laughed, I'd have cried.

I had moments of haziness in amongst the pain yet others witnessed what happened next. I was placed in a waiting room; I was in a wheelchair, waiting to be seen by another professional. Sitting near me was Jim Allen (he has published this story on his website so is happy to be mentioned here), who was on the same course as I was. With so many participants, we hadn't had an opportunity to get to know everyone on an individual basis in the days prior to this.

Another woman at the same event had fainted during the ceremony and had also been taken to hospital as a precautionary measure. As she'd attended the course on her own, Jim had offered to travel in the ambulance with her. He sat there waiting, looked over at me and asked what had happened. He then said, 'Would you like me to heal your ankle for you?' Although I was already attuned to Reiki and had begun exploring many areas, I still held some healthy scepticism. Jim continued to tell me that he channelled Archangel Raphael, the Angel of Healing, and that he could channel that energy to help heal my ankle.

He saw the look on my face... Cue eye rolls and disbelief once more.

Jim then spoke gently yet firmly: 'It won't work if you don't believe it will.' I smiled in between wincing at the pain that shot through me. The nurse hadn't come back to get me yet and I had absolutely nothing to lose.

Jim advised me to say out loud several times, 'I believe, I believe, I believe.'

Either I was hallucinating, dreaming, in a surreal fairytale, or something really profound was happening here. As much as part of me felt a little embarrassed sitting there in a room full of people, I wanted the pain to go away. As I repeated those words, Jim carefully placed his hands on my ankle. I would find out later that I blacked out. I was gone. It felt like a long time yet it was merely minutes. I heard a voice, in what seemed like the distance, calling my name. A nurse was stroking me to bring me back round to consciousness. I glanced at Jim and he had the happiest, cheeriest look on his face. He already had that kind of look about him that seemed slightly 'other-worldly' and the glow on his face said it all.

I looked at my foot. Where it was once at an angle it was now back in place and the pain was subsiding.

My logical brain couldn't take all this in. My friends were amazed too; they had witnessed it first-hand as I was knocked out to allow this miracle to take place. I was then reassessed by the medical team, who said that all they could see was what looked like an old scar of a hairline fracture that had happened years ago. I had never broken any bones prior to this so this 'scar from years ago' seemed to be the break I'd just had hours ago. The 'miracle healing' had happened so phenomenally that the break had been 'healed' and moved on from in linear (past, present, future) time to a mere past event that was no longer here in my now moment. It's only now, with my present-day awareness and consciousness, that I can travel back in my mind and feel into those emotions with varying perspectives and aha moments. I've laughed so many times over the years at the surrealness of this and many other events that have happened in my life since.

The day after this miracle healing, I still felt tired and somewhat bewildered. We had been at the hospital until the early hours of the morning and had to be up early to attend the final day of the course. A vegan breakfast was served before yoga even before the day's teaching commenced, so it was an early start each day.

I hadn't had much sleep at this point. My foot was still bandaged up and was bruised, yet it was back in place and 'healed'. I realised later that our 'healing' takes place on many levels; we have an energy field (our aura) around us, which reflects our mental, emotional, spiritual and physical wellbeing.

This experience would be my precursor to fully knowing the link between our thoughts, emotions and energy and what we perceive to be 'reality'. My delicate human self couldn't quite wrap her head around it all.

I spent that final day of the course being pushed around by others in a wheelchair as I absorbed and integrated it all. Prior to that day, I'd spent most of the week blending in with the crowd. On this last day, I was wheeled to the front and the woman who was hosting the course handed me the microphone and asked me to share my experience with everyone. Suddenly, all eyes were on me. Everyone listened to my story and of course, those who knew my sense of humour didn't find it a surprise when I told everyone I'd 'been tripped up by a leprechaun' (when in Ireland, lightness is the order of the day).

I also see now how this was preparing me for what lay ahead: 'the journey of 1000 miles begins with a single step.' Never was this quote more apt.

Back home and still taking in all that had happened, I began to use Angel cards to give friends and family readings. I was particularly intrigued by the concept of Angels and Archangels (varying streams of energy, consciousness and light that can assist us).

Another thing I want to remind everyone here is now, even after all these years, I have moments when I think I made the whole thing up. You know when you have a really vivid dream and you wake up in the morning and can't remember if it actually happened? Well, it did. In another dimension. Another reality. There are many, but I don't want to go too deep here. Not that we can't go there but it would be a longer journey than 1000 steps. At the same time, as you read these words, the energy held in my story is also held in yours. You are a soul. You are a Light Being. We all are. We are amazing super-human Beings.

I often sit and think about creation. I look at my own body and feel my breath and I give thanks for it all. The diversity of us all. The beauty. The intricacy. The capacity to feel emotions. The intellect and the intuition.

As I 'practised' Angel card readings on those I knew, I would read the cards intuitively and, as I did so, I would often hear words in my head; I would feel sensations in my body. I would keep getting those 'I know but I have no idea how I know' moments. I would have words come flowing out of my mouth without any time to 'think'; I couldn't 'make it up'. Some of what I would say would seem so random to me and there's no way I could formulate such a rich dialogue, often filled with words I would never use in my daily life. This was how I began to distinguish between what I call my 'human' and my 'higher Self' (my soul, the part of me that is energetically connected to everything).

I generally speak with a local accent and don't use eloquent and elaborate words as the norm. I would feel an energy shift within me and I had to learn not to step in and shut it down. When you begin to open up more, you can also experience more resistance. I would often say to myself, 'What if I'm wrong?' As I said, street cred. I say this with a sense of lightness and humour yet there was always a feeling of stepping from a corporate career into a completely different arena; the two were literally worlds apart and I had no idea how my somewhat 'sudden to some' transition into communicating with Angels and giving messages, insights and guidance would be received. I knew that I couldn't go back to my corporate career.

The miracle healing in Ireland and the months that followed changed my outlook on life. I knew I had to follow this feeling deep within me. I was to keep taking that one step at a time. If I attempted to look too far down the road, I could get frustrated or talk myself out of it. My innate inquisitiveness was relentless and a million questions could go through my mind. I would replay the scenario over and over again in a quest to see why my life had taken a quantum leap into another reality. One I was only beginning to step on.

Over the coming months, I did readings for friends and their friends. There were those I was familiar with but I never knew everything about them, their lives or their loved ones prior to sitting opposite them for the session. I had learnt to say exactly everything I heard, saw and sensed. I would hear words in my head – sometimes a single word at a time, other times a flow of words. I would see pictures in my head too and sometimes it was as if my third eye (centre of my forehead) was a projector and it was shining that image to beside the person. I would feel sensations in my body and I began to be adept at interpreting what these were. I would sense an array of emotions, from anxiety to elation and depression to delight. I could feel what others were feeling.

I was having to trust that even if the recipient didn't make sense of it all at the time, if I didn't let the words flow through me, they would stay stuck in my throat like a giant fur ball until I coughed them out!

I soon saw and felt it was easier to simply say it and to put to one side any fears or thoughts about what others were going to think or say about me. This didn't always come easily yet on many levels it was effortless; when I stayed in my heart and knew I was to help others heal, it kept everything in perspective. This was not about me; this was about the message. I had to be brave enough to put myself in front of others and listen, trust, share, love and support. Over the years, I've felt the presence and encouragement from my Light Team; these beautiful benevolent Beings that are here to remind us all that we are Divinity. We can call in their assistance in every moment.

One evening also stays strongly in my heart and mind. I had joined some of the mums from my son's school at one of their houses; a social gathering and I took along my Angel cards, my only pack at that time many years ago. I asked if anyone would like a short reading and, one by one, they would come through to a conservatory area. As usual, I would go to shuffle the deck, select a few cards or ask them to; I always went with what my intuition told me in every moment. I remember one woman asking that evening, 'Do you get messages from people who have crossed over?' I responded to let her know that I was still getting used to reading cards and adding in anything else I saw or felt and, no, I didn't get messages from 'the other side'. No sooner had I said that than things were about to get even more interesting. As I went through my routine of connecting into my own higher self, calling in the Angels and asking for messages of love, support and guidance to flow through, I became aware of a man standing next to the woman sitting opposite me. I blinked and I looked again. He stood there looking at me and, in my head, I asked who he was. He then began to talk; a telepathic connection, yet I heard it as a dialogue as if I were conversing with you right now.

It all happened so quickly and I remember telling the woman that this was her grandfather, who had passed over several years ago. He told me his name, how he'd died and other details. The woman sat staring at me. I had a moment of sheer surprise and elation at this and yet I knew if I stopped for too long and began questioning it, it would shut down the communication and stop the flow. For every woman who sat in that seat that evening, I saw, heard and felt a loved one who was no longer here in the physical. They all confirmed the accuracy of the messages they had received; these were not generic but specific and unique to each individual.

Afterwards, as the reality of it hit me and all the women were excitedly discussing all that I had relayed, one woman remarked, 'I thought you said you didn't do that.'

I felt myself shaking a little as I replied, 'I didn't.'

This was yet another turning point and a verification that this new path I was now walking was the one I would stay on.

The following year, in 2004, a friend said to me, 'When do you think you will ever be good enough to do this professionally?' She knew the feedback I'd been receiving was brilliant yet I'd not yet committed to letting the wider world know that I was now coming out of the psychic closet, let alone 'talking to dead people'; that's how many would see it. Many would be intrigued and would want to come for a sitting; others would struggle to comprehend my doing this. My friend could see that this was a gift I was to fully unwrap. She could see that my moments of self-doubt or apprehension regarding fully being seen in that capacity would hold me back forever if I didn't simply take the plunge and dive right in.

In November 2004, I set up as self-employed and the rest is her-story. My story. There is so much I could share, yet I'm listening to that quiet inner voice that guides my words as I type.

Being psychic, intuitive, a medium, a conduit, a channel, a messenger, a bridge between heaven and Earth; being me; being brave yet being gentle. I still have that shy, sensitive side and I've also embraced the parts of me that can and have stood up in front of small groups and larger audiences, and spoken. I've never felt comfortable with giving readings in public as, for me, discussing people's personal lives and emotions is a sacred connection. It is never entertainment and I hold my integrity and what feels right for me always. We will all embrace and utilise our gifts and abilities in our own precious way; helping others feel better, supporting others, reminding others that there is life after life and that we are so much more than this earthly existence. Giving people hope, encouragement, a positive momentum. Sharing love and shining light.

I, and others, am here to help you see that when these seemingly unusual, weird, spooky (many words are used) things happen, that is, in fact, our true, natural way of being. We are being switched back on. We are being 'activated'; if you can, imagine lots of strings of fairy lights inside you. You are plugged into a SOURCE and electro-magnetic energy is running through you. Each light bulb holds part of your potential, your power and, of course, your light. Some of these bulbs are already on and the others will gradually be activated and switched on when you are ready.

The Source is infinite potential: a cosmic culmination of all that is, beyond our logical linear comprehension. You are plugged in and connected to a quantum field that contains everything. You are a field of electro-magnetic energy within that field, within a field. We are all expressions of this one Source. From Angels and Ascended Masters to Gods, Goddesses and Galactics; we are it all. Energy. Expression. Evolution.

As you begin to trust more, another light bulb illuminates within you. Another facet to your diamond is polished up. Your fairy lights shine bright. More light is reflected and seen not only by others but you begin to see it in yourself too.

I went on to do thousands of readings with people not only in my local area, but there were some who would travel hundreds of miles to attend an appointment with me too. I always aimed to stay humble, grounded and in integrity. I had to find that fine line between being confident enough to let others know who I am and what I can do, and trusting that those who were meant to find me would do so.

After 16 plus years and meeting so many amazing people, I continue to listen to my inner and higher guidance. I moved away from mainly psychic/mediumship readings and now focus primarily on the 'healing' aspect and empowering others in their own sovereignty. Remembering you are a Sovereign Being simply means that you don't give your power away to anyone else. Your thoughts and energy are yours; you don't look to anyone else to tell you what to think, believe or do. You intuitively and innately know how to be an honest, authentic, loving person. You know in your heart why you are here and the path you have to walk. Physical and non-physical Beings will walk alongside you, bringing you back home to you.

I can still see, hear, feel, sense and know Beings that are not in the physical world as many perceive it. I can also 'read' and sense deeply those that are here in the physical; all of us here in this earthly experience, doing the very best we can in every moment.

I've amalgamated all my 'abilities' with all that I've learnt over the years, as I went on to be attuned to various healing modalities and trained in several complementary therapies. With the 'healing', as much as I was attuned to Reiki and more, I now feel that these are innate abilities in all of us that don't necessarily require an attunement or a certificate. We all have an infinite pool of resources within our soul.

I feel the energetic pulse of humanity; love is the life-giver. Love is the Source. When we plug into our own source of love, we fully activate, illuminate and radiate.

Our love lights the way.

Lessons learnt:

- Trust yourself.
- Maintain a sense of humour.
- Take one day at a time.
- Breathe.

www.angeldawn.me
dawn@angeldawn.me
FACEBOOK: @dawn.alexander9231
INSTAGRAM: @angeldlight

Out of Body Experiences

Out of Body Experiences (OBEs) can be scary. Imagine being woken up at night to see yourself hovering over your body. This is not uncommon and actually nothing to be scared about. Read these two stories and rest assured, 'all is well.' You are simply evolving.

Sarah, or 'Rei' as she wishes to be called, shares her out of body experiences and how she didn't feel she fitted into this world.

REI'S OF ASCENSION

Rei

To all the enlightened Beings – Indigo, Crystal, Rainbow and Starseed.

Your soul's mission is to usher in a new wave of light, love and vibrational energy, to help raise Earth's frequencies and humanity's consciousness. To those of you who have accepted this mission... we welcome you.

Muses From a Mystic

These are the words that echo in my soul.

For as long as I can remember, I've always felt like a visitor watching the wonder of humans, their emotions, their funny ways and relationships; the way we live in funny boxes and transport ourselves around in funny machines with wheels – and the observations go on. As a young child, I would spend my time reading, choosing my own company. My mother talked about the frequent visitors during the night and people would say I could see into their souls. And they were not far from the truth.

I have come here to assist humanity and experience a human existence for myself. I also remember too much. Most people who experience having an

Awakening in their lifetime are often closed down as children by conditioning of some sort. You see, we came here awakened. It's just finding our way home. This was the case for me.

I have always been a lucid dreamer. For as long as I can remember, my dreams have come in all sorts of different experiences that usually leave ripples I can recall for years. Some come and visit me for a day; others can bring the full force of emotions and can consume me for days on end. However, I suppose the most interesting dreams are the visits and journeys that I experience often. I have loved ones, and other loved ones who visit me but who have not been with me in this lifetime, yet my soul recognises them. And then I have the Astral travelling. This has been a journey that has taught me so much, but most of all to let go of fear.

So, my Awakening Began...

Let's rewind the clock back to my late teens. For as long as I could remember, fear, anger and hurt had shrouded my day-to-day life. It was woven into the tapestry of my living. The daily service of disempowerment and victim consciousness I delivered myself, was a way of life. I had simply learnt how to survive. I was a single mum, trying to cope – and then one night, it happened.

I went to bed as normal, fell asleep and the lucid dreaming started. But this time, people began arriving. Or, more accurately, lost souls. They were upset and panicked as they were unsure where they were, and they kept coming, in my half-asleep state. I fully woke up. But every time I shut my eyes after that, they kept coming until, eventually, I started being pulled out of my body. I began experiencing what is known as 'Astral travelling'.

Every night, with fear consuming me, I would sit up, trying not to sleep. And every time I dozed off, the inevitable would happen, like a vacuum being sucked out of my body. Sometimes there would be people there; other times, a dark shadow at the end of my bed.

What I knew was that I needed someone to help me. I searched and sat in groups and met many healers. I knew one thing: I was tired of living in fear and starting to get angry (this was another form of victim consciousness, I later came to recognise). I turned to Angels for help; I practised working with them daily until my flow of communication came as naturally as breathing. They would show me signs, until eventually I could hear them. I never gave up hope.

I found Alison or, more to the point, the Universe placed her in my path for my growth, to assist me with my development and learning. I was coming to understand that everything was placed on my journey for a reason; for my inner healing.

I went on to do my own healing development, and studied Reiki and different forms of energy healing, and gained empowerment over myself and my life. I recognised that these gifts were a purpose for me to help others. What I've also recognised is who I am and where my soul truly has come from. Some souls wake up slowly from their slumber and others are woken up with a mission. Every day, I practise these tools as a healer and a teacher. I know I am here to help others and lead people along the way to love.

My gifts are that I see and receive information from people's lives and souls. Sometimes their souls will show me past lives they have experienced; sometimes they will show me only an aspect of their journey. This gift of awareness has come through trusting in my inner knowledge and purpose as to why I am here. The Universe talks to me in many different ways through different Beings; masters from our human race, different realms and Angels. I see, feel and connect with the life force of this planet, absorbing the humming of her vibration through me. I feel the connection to the stars and every life force within this Universe and beyond. I feel at one.

This is something that makes me feel very different to others and is not something I share lightly. But I believe it is time now to help other souls who may be struggling with new gifts and understanding a new way of seeing the world. So, through gifting this information from my life, I can go on to help others understand how beautifully wonderful they are. And when you fear something, it may just be the gift that shows you something so much more beautiful about yourself.

Reisofascension@gmail.com
INSTAGRAM: @reis_of_ascension

Linda's journey shares her opening up to her psychic gifts, OBEs and tingles of love and joy.

LINDA'S JOURNEY

Linda Yakaitis

Like so many of us, I remember many times in my childhood when I was connected to Spirit. I had a lot of premonition dreams, one being about a tornado, where I woke up screaming my brother's name and falling out of bed. Years later, I was in a tornado in my house with my brother. When the house started coming apart, I heard my Guardian Angel behind me say, 'Go into the foyer closet.' While in the closet, I opened the door and screamed out my brother's name, since I didn't know where he'd gone.

I also had an out of body experience in my teens. I was extremely sick and got up to get my mom, and I passed out in the doorway of my bedroom. Suddenly, I found my consciousness floating pain-free near the ceiling. Looking down, I watched my parents lift me and put me back into bed. They kept calling my name to wake me and suddenly, I opened my eyes up, back inside my pain-filled body, lying in my bed.

So many, many stories – but I had no one to share them with. I didn't dare tell anyone. And as I got older and busier with 'life', these experiences faded away.

Then I became pregnant at 27, and I started to feel an inner tingling. I was scared there was something physically wrong with me. Shortly afterwards, I started to notice the tingling happened when I experienced love and joy. Then I felt a longing: it was as if there was a part of me that wanted to be discovered. That longing set me on my path of discovery of who I truly am!

One book about psychics led to another book, which led to another. One day, I was guided to stop at a local new age store in town I had passed many, many times. It was as if I were in a trance. I walked around the tiny shop not knowing what I was looking for. I found a book that I thought was fiction and bought it. Turns out it was a channelled message, and I ended up going to a class held by the writer; which led to a journey to India and Darhmsala, and many more classes taught by her (she is now one of my closest friends).

Years later, I found myself signing up for a five-year class where I learnt about plant spirit medicines, chakra clearings, past life retrievals...

And throughout all of these 26 years, the thing I've learnt the most is to trust. Trust that each step you take to discover who you really are is an important step. Trust that you are not walking this path alone – your guides and Angels are always with you.

And pay attention! Really open your eyes and see the beautiful messages that are always around you. And know that all you ever need is inside of you – your feelings, your 'knowings', your visions are all real. And don't take it all so seriously. Remember to stay in love and joy and behold the childlike wonder throughout your journey to self-discovery.

Blessings of love and protection to you.

Facebook: @linda.yakaitis

Finding Your Soulmate

Many of us dream of meeting our soulmate but all too often it happens when we least expect it. Experiencing an abusive relationship often teaches us to let go and allow love in. That is when our soulmate experience is ready. Don't force it to happen. Forgive, let go and be open to receiving love.

After enduring an abusive marriage, Jan left, found her soulmate and was awakened to spirituality when she received a 'spot on' reading from a stranger.

AN ANGEL SAVED MY SOUL

Jan Taylor

It was 2006 and I was 41 years old. My life as I knew it had completely changed, beyond all recognition. I'd lost all my close friends and some family and felt completely lost and alone. Why was I feeling like this? Should I not be feeling better after ditching the man who'd made my life hell for 18 years? Should I not now be feeling free and ready to face my new life with vitality and enthusiasm? Why, oh, why did I feel so desperately alone and full of fear and anxiety?

I felt so bewildered and lost that I started ringing psychic lines, desperate to find some answers; to know that I wasn't alone in this world. None of them felt like they gave me anything; none of them felt like a spiritual connection. None of them gave me the hope and trust I yearned for that there was something else out there other than this mundane life.

The more I felt they didn't satisfy my curiosity for Spirit and my hunger to know that my future was going to get better, the more of them I rang till I drummed up huge debts; not good when you've now suddenly become a single parent with no support from your alcoholic, abusive ex.

Then, one day, I turned to a lovely friend of mine, who lived a couple of hours away from me. One thing I remember that she said to me has stuck in mind for years: 'Whatever doesn't kill you makes you stronger.' I've never forgotten it because it has got me through so many difficult times over the years. She was lovely and, despite being friends with both me and my ex, she seemed to 'take my side' and be more sympathetic to what I'd been through with him because she'd been through it herself.

To my surprise, she believed in Spirit and psychics and mediums, and she put me on to a psychic she knew. She told me the psychic lived a few hours away from me so she could do a reading for me over the phone. Well, I had that reading and it totally blew me away! This woman, who I'd never met and who knew absolutely nothing about me, actually knew loads of things about me and about how my ex had treated me. Things that I hadn't told anyone. I remember I cried that day on the phone, but I now had hope and I now knew that my loved ones in spirit were watching over me and looking after me. I no longer felt alone and I could start to heal. In fact, I knew I wasn't alone and I felt the presence of my loved ones in spirit cocooning me with their love.

I had many more readings after that but rang no more psychic lines. I had the readings every six months to a year from the same psychic, and also from a lovely medium that my friend recommended. Every time, I was blown away by what they picked up and I became more and more interested in psychic and Spirit work. The medium told me I should pursue it myself as I could easily do it. To be honest, at the time I just laughed as I thought I'd never be able to do that.

My psychic friend – yes, she had become a really good friend and still is to this day – told me that I'd meet the man of my dreams just before Christmas 2007 and, low and behold, I did. I met him on 15th December, 2007 and we got married in 2010 in an idyllic castle in the beautiful Shropshire countryside. He told me he had actually seen Spirit as a young child and the night we met, I knew he was my soulmate. In fact, I was told he was a match made in heaven, which I totally believed.

A few months after we met, as we were both interested in spiritual stuff, we decided to embark on a spiritual development course together. It was a six to eight-week course if I remember rightly and we did learn a lot, but many of the people there were experienced. I felt so frustrated that I didn't think I was doing as well as they were that I cried in the car on my lunch break with my husband. He too was picking up loads but I felt I had some kind of block or something, or just wasn't cut out to do it. So, once the course had finished, I didn't do anything for a while and my husband just lost interest. I did pass though and I was amazed how much I picked up when reading objects in sealed envelopes. It just came to me totally out of the blue and I was spot on. We also did some spiritual healing on each other, and we were both told by the course leader that we were healers as the recipients could feel heat coming from our hands.

Fast-forward to 2012 and I was advised in a reading to get some Reiki, as I was off work with stress and depression, mainly due to a very stressful and lengthy court case with my ex. I saw a post on a local yoga Facebook page and booked a session. Yet again, I was blown away by the close spiritual connection I felt whilst receiving Reiki and, after a few sessions, I asked the practitioner for information to train in Reiki myself.

In 2013, I did my Reiki first level course and, my, oh my, this was the most amazing experience of my life! Whilst receiving one of my attunements to be able to do Reiki on myself and friends and family, I had vivid visions of Jesus and Angels and I felt like I was soaring through the clouds like a bird. I'd never experienced anything like it!

Still ever curious, I came across a lady who did Akashic readings, which tell you about some of your past lives and what your soul contract is for this life. A soul contract is something that many believe you agree on before you are born on the Earth plane. I was told that mine was a destiny soul contract and also that, when I'd gone through the trauma of physical and emotional abuse from my ex, my soul partly went off to heal and a higher energy like a lower Archangel had stepped in. This can be called a 'walk in' and I was absolutely blown away. It did make a lot of sense though, and explained why I'd suddenly become interested in the spiritual path. The lady who did my reading also said that I needed help to retrieve my soul as now was the right time. She performed a soul retrieval healing on me the very next day. I literally felt the healing taking place in my body and the energy coursing through me. It was amazing!

I've since gone on through the levels of Reiki to become a Reiki Master Teacher and a Crystal Therapy teacher. After also completing a Develop Your Intuition course with my Reiki teacher, I started my own business in 2014. I began drawing cards for my page and channelling information from my guides for each one. I now do psychic oracle card readings and teach spiritual development, and have an oracle card reading course. I still have to pinch myself that I've come so far and grown so much. Despite my reluctance at times to believe I could actually do readings, let alone teach others how to do them, I've pushed time after time through the doubt and the fear and just got on with it. It's taken me a long time to heal from the trauma of the past, including healing from past lives with associations with my ex, but I've come out the other side with a renewed sense of life and confidence. I've been able to build up my self-esteem again and, although I still waver at times, I'm getting there, and it's my mission to help other ladies do the same.

I absolutely love what I do and I believe everyone is psychic and can gain a close spiritual connection. All it takes is practice and belief in yourself. I love helping people to believe in themselves so that they too can embark on their own spiritual-awakening journey. I'm still developing myself, we all are. As many famous spiritual leaders have said, it's a journey not a destination and, believe you me, it becomes more and more magnificent the further along the path you go.

www.indigosoul.co.uk
jan@indigosoul.co.uk
FACEBOOK: @indigosouljantaylor
INSTAGRAM: @indigosoul_jan_taylor

After a clairvoyant told Katie she would, 'soon be swept off her feet by a Knight,' she literally found Mr Knight and became a Knight herself.

BECOMING A KNIGHT

Katie Baxter

In 2011, I had my tarot cards read. The lady told me that soon, I'd be swept off my feet by a knight. I remember feeling, wow, I wish that was true! I was currently in a five-year relationship that I was unhappy with. Later that day, I thought about the knight card and it made me giggle... When I was a young girl of around eight, I used to sign my name as Mrs Knight, as I was in love with John Knight from New Kids on the Block.

Three months had passed since the reading and I'd left my fiancé. A few weeks later, I found myself sitting in a field having a picnic on a first date with the most handsome man I'd ever met. I was instantly head over heels. As we sat there, we discussed what song we'd have for our first dance when we married.

Fast-forward three years and I was still with the guy from the picnic, and still mad about him. We'd decided we'd like to start a family. Everything was going great. We both shed tears of joy when I fell pregnant, and we moved to a new home in readiness for our new family life.

After a hard five-day labour, I had a beautiful baby girl who was eventually born by C-section. When I finally arrived home, I felt exhausted and low. Whilst my husband was at work, I'd often spend time sobbing when my daughter was asleep. I really wanted to feel well and enjoy motherhood. Every time I looked at my little girl my heart swelled with love... But was I enjoying being a mum? No! And that was the hardest thing for me to admit to myself. I felt so alone; my family lived miles away and I had no friends in the area.

My mood didn't change after a few weeks so I went to see the doctor. I kept repeating to her, 'I love my little girl with all my heart but I just feel so depressed. Please help me!' I thought she'd judge me as a bad mum and think I didn't love my daughter. She prescribed me some tablets and I went home, feeling like I'd failed my family.

One day I was feeling the lowest I had ever felt. I managed to get myself and my daughter ready and headed out for a walk. My daughter fell fast asleep, as it was a hot summer's day. I chose to walk down a country path that I'd never walked down before as it looked quiet and I needed to cry. I came to a bridge overlooking a busy main road and spent a while looking over the wall. I thought, 'How low do people need to be to throw themselves off a bridge?' Was I that low? I looked back at my daughter and knew I couldn't leave her.

Out of nowhere, without warning, there was an enormous clap of thunder. It shook me and I suddenly felt like I'd woken up. I started to see the view in front of me clearly. It felt as though, before the thunder clap, I was wearing sunglasses, but they'd been lifted from me. I covered my daughter and began to cry. As I did, it started to rain harder and harder. The rain washed away my tears and made me feel comforted. I began walking home, faster and faster with this new energy.

When I got back, my daughter was still asleep. I was soaked through but felt cleansed and happy. I can honestly say that, from that moment on, I began to enjoy motherhood. My daughter is now a happy, kind and beautiful six-year-old.

And... seven months after she was born, I got married. Yes, to the man who I had a date with in the field. I became Mrs Knight, and we danced to the song we'd chosen on that first date.

kvbaxter@hotmail.co.uk
FACEBOOK: @katie.baxter.1297
INSTAGRAM: @baxter_halloween_queen

Believing in Archangel Michael, surviving a car crash, finding and marrying her soulmate, Natasha doesn't do anything by halves.

MY STORY

Natasha Lea Mills

I think in some aspect, I've always had a knowing that there is something more out there, something more within me and something we can all tap into. I grew up in a home where 'religion was the root of all evil'. My mum wore a metaphorical 'absolute atheist' on her sleeve like a badge of honour. I, however, was obsessed with churches and would even find myself bumbling into town as a kid to sit in the glorious Coventry Cathedral, just admiring the Angels. Looking back now, I feel I was drawn to them. I mean, I do have to admit that, as kids, we found the famous Archangel Michael lording it over the devil on the front of the new Coventry Cathedral absolutely hilarious, because the devil's manhood was there, giant and fully out for us all to see and point and giggle at. We were kids, after all.

I paid particular attention to a mosaic Angel hidden away in the cathedral, Angel of Agony, by Stephen Sykes. In writing this, I researched this Angel, and it comes to us in the hour of agony to offer inspiration, so that even in suffering we can find bliss. Which is maybe a message I was meant to deliver to you all right now.

I remember the moment I realised I could call upon the Angels to support me and, once I did, they really showed up for me and opened my eyes to even more magic. I first learnt of Archangel Michael and his powers to protect us, to help us have courage and integrity, things I value highly. I called upon him, as many people should, to help guide me when I was friends with someone, who, let's say, was less than ideal. We hung out a lot when I returned to my home city from where I was living in Leeds. He was obsessed with religion and his nickname, amongst many, was 'Abel'. And a shepherd he was. He led many a poor lamb astray and he constantly let his rage get the better of him. He'd hit self-destruct more often than I could keep up with. I'd heard about his reputation since I used to know him before I'd left Coventry for Leeds over nine years previously, and I couldn't quite piece it together. That wasn't the lad I'd known all those years ago. He always wanted to be a 'bad boy', a bit of a misfit, a criminal and was always fighting. He'd been made an example of by a court of law as a young person and it was as if he'd then decided to create a persona out of this bad boy image. At heart though, you could see right through it all. I would just see a lost soul; a bit of a gent. I still believe I was put there for him at that time. We can all relate to an element of martyrdom, can't we?

We hung out a lot, and I could feel myself being sucked into his energy, like a spell had been put on me. Surely I didn't actually have feelings for this guy? He was an out-and-out wrong'un for me, and I could lose my profession if I was around anyone with criminal behaviour. So I asked for Michael to protect me. And I kid you not, every time I was around this guy, I would see Archangel Michael show up. That was the first time I remember seeing the feathers.

I told him about Archangel Michael and it's no surprise that he thought I was 'bat-shit crazy'. But that's all part of it – I was actually starting to act crazy around him. He would bombard me with companionship, fun and attention I wasn't even looking for from him, and then there'd be massive rejection, ignored calls, texts, lies. It was a complex and bizarre time. It took a while of intermittent hanging out and crazy adventures, and then I had to take notice of the signs. I decided to cut him off. The signs were all there and I was being shown I had to listen.

I've only seen him once really since, when he called in desperation after a huge accident (I still don't know the full story there). I raced hundreds of miles with my medical kit to help him out, with DVDs and food supplies, and to ensure he had someone in the house as he had massive concussion, had lost his teeth, and had scrapes and scars all over his hand as if he'd been dragged for a mile by a car. And he'd self-discharged from hospital.

I cleaned him up and bandaged his hand, which I knew would get infected otherwise and he'd risk losing it and therefore his profession as an artist. Then, after all that, he said I couldn't stay as his ex-girlfriend was coming over and she hated me. Now, there was no reason to hate me as I was a friend, but this summed up the level of rejection from this person. Archangel Michael protected me so well, I was emotionally able to be there for him but also not let him get under my skin. I drove off, knowing sometimes you are the Angel in other people's worlds and you just have to accept that; they may not always show gratitude and you might not always need it.

I started to make a life for myself in Leeds again. 'Right, maybe I'll stay here,' I'd say to myself. It wasn't time to go home to Coventry. So I began dating again, kissing frogs to find my prince, always guided by my intuition. I then met this guy – nice, respectable job, which aligns with my values…TICK; car that was functioning and capable of making trips… TICK; he was even on the speaker and personal development circuit… TICK TICK TICK. Then, in stepped the signs…

One day I was with him, randomly walking past my old house, which was near an old youth club where I used to teach dance, and he told me he knew me back then. At that point, I saw a graffiti tag on the wall that said, 'Pause 4 Thought'. I couldn't believe it. It just so happened to be the name of my first dance company. This was a sign. Now, the thing about signs is they're open to interpretation! Watch this space.

A month or two later, we'd had some lovely dates. Finally my luck was changing, I thought, and I accepted his invitation to take a trip to Devon. It was really fun hanging out but on arrival in Devon, we pulled into a car park and to this day I've never seen anything like it. The car park was littered with black feathers.

I remember turning to him and saying, 'This is weird. When I see black feathers, it's usually a massive warning to me.' I brushed it off (as us reluctant psychics do). From that moment on, he was different. He was on edge; he was disconnected. And my instincts were going haywire in my whole body, telling me something was wrong, but I couldn't quite put my finger on it. Meanwhile, he kept saying the words, 'Nothing is wrong'.

I'm unsure how long we dated after that, but I'd been getting visions for years that I'd move back to Coventry to be there for my grandad and that I'd settle down. This guy was supportive and agreed to come and visit and have a long-distance relationship. He'd pop down to see me and then, a few weeks after I moved, I was invited to meet his family for the first time and stay at his parents, to attend a christening. I went up to Leeds and he again was disconnected; he kept walking off and leaving me alone.

We later went back to his parents' house because he wanted a nap. I was sitting there on my phone and he lay sleeping. Then I looked at him from the end of the bed, and I noticed his nose was full of white powder. I confronted him, as this guy had told me he 'didn't do drugs and didn't smoke'. Those were my conditions on dating someone in the very beginning: the very first date, in fact, I put it out there. And anyway, we were at a christening. What an earth does someone need to be doing lines of 'coke' for?

He lied to my face right there and then; tried to convince me it wasn't what I thought it was and that I was mistaken. I got up, walked out and left; stayed at a friend's and ended it right there and then. He tried to send me gifts to get me back and, months later, he had a child with someone. I never found out the full story other than that he took drugs most days and smoked 20 plus a day, and the dates of the child suggested he'd been sleeping with someone else during our relationship.

But my instincts had been kicking off throughout our time together. However, again I had to take note. I'd been shown a car park full of black feathers and, for me, it hadn't been enough to make me walk away… It was time to fully trust the signs and the instincts.

During my move to Coventry, I'd taken a job. It was supposed to be my dream job, something I'd worked towards for years. When I rocked up for my first day, guess what was waiting… That's right – a car park full of feathers. This time they were white. This is a sign, I thought. This is the job for me.

Having taken the job, my heart was filled with joy. It was like all my dreams had come true. I was working with Professional Premiership Rugby Club. I'd made it. This was what I'd been visualising for years.

I then used to see feathers little and often. But the mood began to change and I quickly realised I was in the wrong culture for me. The players were lovely and so were some of the staff, but I was a starshaped peg in a very square hole and it was noticeable. I didn't drink enough, I didn't bitch enough, I didn't agree enough; I dared to challenge the point of view of people and that marked the end of what I could achieve. I experienced bullying that I never would have allowed to happen to me at school. I was watching people in charge of a career I'd worked so hard for, start to chip away at my future working in that sport, and my confidence. I would walk into a room and people would stop talking; the atmosphere was so frosty. They thought they weren't being obvious with their behaviour, but the thing about instincts and guidance is, you know even before the actions are clear. In that job, I would have the absolute trust of some of the best players in the country, yet the staff were getting angry and questioning my intentions. I remember one day being shouted at in front of players, to the point where I couldn't stop shaking. I had to drive around in my car for 45 minutes after the incident to try to stop myself crying and trembling enough to walk back into the building to do my job. I would shake and have to control my anxiety. It took all I had to walk into a room, and I was making more and more mistakes to be blamed for because I was so anxious.

You see, I can link this all, now I have clarity, back to the trauma I experienced as a teenager, when I was locked in a bathroom by a man who was a real predator. I'd protected my friends from him like a guard dog as he kept trying to isolate them in a room. Then, he decided to solve the problem, which was me, by locking me in the bathroom with him.

He and his brothers had a fierce reputation for a variety of crimes, including robbery, assault and carrying fire arms. The brothers have since been convicted of kidnapping a local taxi driver and one is on the sex offenders' register for brutal assaults against women.

The 6 foot plus tall ex-rugby-player-turned-coach shouting at me, had invoked a fear I didn't know was possible, because just like a teenage girl all those years ago with a grown man locking me in a toilet, I was a grown woman who had made something of herself and this man was taking it all away in an instant. Ah, the feathers… They were there to show me I needed protection and it was all around me.

During this, one of the worst times in my life, with a boyfriend who turned out to be a massive drug addict and pathological liar, and a job I'd worked my whole life for hanging in the balance, I found something that made me sparkle with joy. With the help of my mum and a friend, we reignited the 'Inspiration Club', a monthly event that allowed me to connect with some of the most enlightening souls, and we shared stories of triumph over adversity. This became my light at the end of the tunnel and I'm sure was the key to helping me start to manifest my dream job.

At the end of the season, it was clear I needed out. I came back from Tony Robbins's 'Unleash the Power Within' like a lion, with energy, clarity and passion, and I remember walking in with my head held high that day, high-fiving my colleagues. They all responded with enthusiasm, except my line manager. He had a face like thunder at even the suggestion I could walk in so happy after the week before, when the coach had shouted at me.

I stood with sheer confidence next to the coaches, and then watched them start to turn on me even more, just like a lion around a pack of hyenas. I was threatening their very territory with just my presence.

My boss called me in for a meeting. I remember saying to myself, 'Don't quit, don't quit, don't quit!' I'd come too far. I was working 70 hours per week and financially I couldn't afford to jump ship. As I walked into that room, which was a conference box overlooking the amazingly green pitch, I can't remember what my boss said. But the words flew out of my mouth like someone else was in charge: I QUIT!

Within days, the dream job with the most amazing manager and sport popped up like magic. It was exactly what I was manifesting. I just needed to let go of what was no longer serving me to open up the gateway to amazing opportunities. This job was part-time and would allow me space to heal, as I was burnt out. With my cortisol levels extremely high, I was on the pathway for Chronic Fatigue diagnosis.

As soon as I landed the job, my boss put me on garden leave; no goodbyes to anyone, no end of season ball; just made to disappear. But for me, it was a key chance to rest, reflect, repair and reinvigorate.

Now, it would be easy if I could say life had been plain-sailing ever since. However, it just doesn't always work like that. I started my new job part-time and also began a physiotherapy business, renting a room off an old friend I'd bumped into in a coffee shop. I was full of hope and optimism. By the summer a year after I'd begun to live my new life at a slower pace, I was seeing friends and genuinely building myself back up, healing emotionally, physically and spiritually.

I said yes to attending a charity event where the aunty of a school friend, who became my friend too, was shaving her head for charity. I went along to support her and, for the first time, her nephew (we'd known of each other for years) spoke to me. He sat down beside me and chatted. I got a few goose bumps but denied to myself that he was interested. I told him how I went to salsa with his aunty, and his sister, who I knew well, said this was his attempt to flirt with me. And he invited himself dancing with his aunt and his friends.

We hung out a few times. He was practically everything I'd always wanted: amazing values, kind, sporty but not competitive, handsome, piercing blue eyes – the quiet one at the back in a group of people, fun and family-orientated. Then I noticed a tattoo on his arm. Guess what it was… Archangel Michael. Oh no, not a warning about this guy. He then showed me his other arm, and I couldn't believe it. It was a symbol of the phoenix. Now, growing up, I was a gymnast and my club was Phoenix gymnastics club. My gymnastics coach was like a second mum and the symbol meant so much to me. And here was a guy with a warning, yet with a symbol that was so precious too. It was a sign, but I had no idea this time whether it was good or bad. All I knew was this guy gave me the butterflies I was looking for.

Six months later, we moved in together. The signs were all positive and I started to see fewer feathers and more animal totems and Angel numbers. He has learnt to believe in them all too.

Everything was going well: the new work environment was all I'd ever wanted. I had an amazing boss, was part of a great team who supported each other and with a set of coaches who respected our opinions and were kind and fun. I was travelling the world with the job, from Japan, Korea to all over Europe. It was amazing.

I was also enrolled on a Personal Performance Coaching Course. This was it. I was living my best life; everything was aligned. Although one key thought kept going through my mind: 'I don't want to be a physio anymore.'

One weekend, I was away on my coaching course and, as money was tight, I decided to drive the two-hour trip back home and sleep in my own bed, then drive back the next morning for 9.30. I'd arrived for the course on the Saturday morning. It was a cloudy, blustery day for July and there was a black feather next to my car. I acknowledged it and accepted I would have to keep my eyes peeled for something that may crop up. Nothing really did.

I left at 5pm, walked to my car and the black feather was still sitting there. 'Oh, ok,' I thought, 'I'd better take extra care driving home.' I got in the car and, sure enough, there was so many near misses: cars flying by at 100 miles per hour, undertaking and overtaking, everyone was rushing somewhere on a Saturday evening in July. I also kept having moments where I didn't feel in my own body and I had to keep pulling myself back in. It makes sense to me now. I haven't had that feeling much since.

I called my other half on speaker phone, something I never normally do whilst driving, and I told him my estimated time of arrival of 7.30. I also sweet-talked him into getting me my favourite takeaway, and told him I loved him and couldn't wait to get home to see him. I then stopped at a petrol station for some painkillers, as I remember having the most uncomfortable stomach cramps.

A few junctions from my home, on a rather busy M40, I was overtaking in the fast lane when, ahead of me, a car smashed into the central reservation. I swerved and I remember clear as day thinking, 'I've got this.' All those years of listening to positive mindset books! I remembered Tony Robbins talking about racing drivers learning to look in the direction they want to go, not at the up-and-coming wall at high speed, and the car will always travel to the open space... I looked to the centre lane and got control.

Months later, I pieced together what had happened with flashbacks, and I think that following that, I made a second decision to brake at high speed due to debris in the road. I spun to face on-coming traffic to then hit a grass verge. I told myself, thanks to advice from my mum's car accident years before, 'I must relax now.' I then remember saying, 'Cover your head', as the car flipped onto its roof, with the sound of metal crushing around me. Everything went into slow motion. This covering my head is possibly how I chipped the bone in my arm, but protected my face and eyes from all the broken glass. I then, as if by a miracle, woke up, with the car smoking but the right way up.

I'd travelled well over 100m from the central reservation, spinning into on-coming traffic, flying off a grass verge missing all other cars, in between trees, through a fence and into a lush, newly ploughed field, and had landed the right way up! Now if that wasn't someone looking after me, then I don't know what is.

I woke up to thinking my car was on fire (it happened to be the smoke from the airbag) and, before I knew it, was out of the car window. And I truly believe I was pushed through it by a force behind me. I grabbed what I could and I walked towards the road. Having worked in professional rugby, I knew what I needed to do and check: pelvis, spine, abdomen. I'll never forget a rugby player once saying to me he doesn't mind getting knocked out as it's a nice feeling, being concussed. That thought often crosses my mind and now I totally understand. For those split seconds, it's like your brain is rebooting, trying to make sense of the world; make sense of what's happening, and everything is quiet, with a ringing and blissfulness. As your eyes refocus, everything looks vibrant and like the first time you've ever seen the colours – right before incredible pain and then shock set in. I hope never to experience anything like this again. I wouldn't wish it on my worst enemy. But that moment changed me forever. This was my Awakening (Angel Alison Ward).

That day by the roadside, a man with a beard was there. From what I can remember in my haze-like memories, he was so Jesus-like. He provided me with a duvet and a camping chair; he helped me check my neck, with my guidance, and, eight weeks later as my memory came back, I remembered he'd put something in my bag. It was a religious book. He'd just happened to be there for me at that moment and he and his family must have been the ones to call the ambulance. A nice little reminder that there is magic out there. At that moment, I remember I was joking (pumped full of morphine by the paramedics), and shaking like I'd been dunked in ice-cold water, unable to control my body as I was fully in shock. Needless to say, I couldn't remember anything in that moment. My head had taken such a blow as it rattled around while the car flipped like a gymnast into the air a few times.

Months later, I recall the police officer reminding me I'd asked him every few minutes how the other guy was in the car that had crashed into the barrier. I remember trying so hard to recall the names of the paramedics and the guy who'd looked like Jesus. I think I must have asked their names every few minutes too, by the looks I remember on their faces. I remember clear as day saying, 'Crazy shit happens to me all the time. I want to remember you as one day you'll feature in my book!'

Alas, I can't remember their names, but another nod to knowing one day I would have the opportunity to thank them! So, thank you, random strangers and paramedics and Archangel Michael!

What were my key learnings from this moment? Be careful what you wish for: I'd been saying more often than I care to remember, 'I don't want to be a physiotherapist anymore', rather than asking for what I did want, which was to be a coach. The Universe delivered by breaking my arm in a massive accident.

It reminded me to trust my intuition. It's the best gift we have and it allows us, even in dark times, to know that ultimately there really are amazing things out there looking after us. We just have to trust.

My favourite lesson is that, even in my darkest hour, I have a cracking sense of humour. We humans can survive anything life throws at us, and believing and trusting allows us to live a more abundant, happier, fulfilled life than we can even dream possible.

Finally… I married that blue-eyed boy. It turns out it was a sign and it's more than I ever could have hoped for!

Call to action: work on your mindset every day. It's a skill that will be there when you need it most. And why not invite Ascended Masters and spirit guides into your life and see what shows up for you?

FACEBOOK: @natashamillsmm
INSTAGRAM: @natashamillsmm

Healing Journeys

These following stories share illnesses, Near Death Experiences and Awakenings, allowing the authors to start seeing the world differently. People who have overcome illness, experienced NDAs and Awakenings are much more positive and focused when they 'wake up' to their psychic gifts and abilities.

A lonely child, Sue developed an illness. This led to her healing journey where she discovered Reiki, reflexology and homeopathy, which opened her up to her gifts and her business.

MY LIFE PATH OF TRUTH AND LOVE

Sue Crowe

As a middle child with an elder sister and younger brother, I found that I wasn't really part of their world. I was different – thought different, did different activities, enjoyed dancing with my parents. People my own age weren't really interesting. I didn't read much, so their discussions on books left me cold. They discussed boys – wasn't really interested. Went to a few discos, but was bored with the childish games they thought were fun. I loved ballroom and Latin dancing, both with my parents or with a girl partner who joined me in competitions. I went to church on my own, Brownies on my own; never with my brother or sister. We even went to different high schools.

I loved sharing my dad's love for football, watching him at matches and practice sessions. I'd help him deliver to farms, holding the eggs on the way back after delivering the meat. Then I'd help in the shop when he had his own shop. I'd work on the veg side at weekends.

But at 60, my dad had a heart attack and died less than two months later. My life underwent a massive change from that point forward. I developed an illness that took a while to diagnose. My GP had no idea what was wrong. I lost my short-term memory and started with a muscle spasm in my neck. With little help from my GP, I went to a physio, who tried to help me. After some time, she asked me to see my GP again and gave me a letter for him, explaining how we'd proceeded over months without success and she felt I needed to see a neurologist. He disagreed and sent me away without any further assistance.

So, I booked a private appointment with a neurologist, who diagnosed Dystonia. Again my GP was unhelpful so after one session of botulism toxin injections with Professor Williams at a huge cost, I went to see a homeopath who was helping my husband with side effects from a drug given following a heart attack. I was also recommended to see a healer by my physio. She gave me medium messages from my dad, which was something she'd never done before.

I went to the spiritualist church to get treatments from Sylvia, as well as other healers working there. I was also recommended to a hypnotherapist who was in Penkridge, a journey worth taking as each healer gave me such positive insights into my illness, as well as connecting to my dad.

With the holistic world truly opened to me, I took up Reiki with a lady who used rooms at the homeopathic practice, before moving on to a lady I studied with from 2005 until recently. She taught me Reiki I, II, III, and how to be a Reiki Master Teacher. I also went to college to learn reflexology, which allowed me to help my sister when she had a stroke in her late forties. My siblings taught me the truth of 'you can only heal others when they're ready'. My sister preferred her illness and the attention and benefits of income support and a car, to being well and self-supporting. My brother has taught me how lucky I am to know love and light, rather than darkness and anger with how the world is.

Having read very little as a child, as the holistic world took off, I read books on healing, non-stop – different modalities of healing: Louise Hay, Eckhart Tolle, Doreen Virtue, Vianna Stibal, whose 'Healing with God' course I did, my first course of many. I learnt from Louise Hay that we are 100 per cent responsible for everything that happens in our lives. That took me years to fully understand.

Trance medium, Jan Higgins, came into my life through a crystal talk she gave at a seminar run by the hypnotherapist I'd found, who also channelled

White Feather in trance. Shortly after I started going to spirit church, I then ran a development group with Jan and began going to her retreats in Wales over a week, immersed in like minds, sharing love and new learnings. Standing up to speak, writing, channelling words, messages. Playing spiritual games to enhance our buried gifts and abilities. It was a whole new experience that I loved. It made me feel so good that I found adjustment to coming home again was challenging. Doug, my husband, has no interest in sharing my world, although he does have intuitive abilities he uses without any realisation. He seems to know how best to deal with situations without much thought. His heart attack at 34 was an opportunity to change his habits around smoking and drinking, and change his friends who didn't want to be a part of his new life. He used homeopathy instead of drugs, which again left him 'out on a limb', the title of a book by Shirley MacLaine. He gave up his medical support, trusting that what he was doing served him much better. We supported each other through these challenges and grew more spiritual along the way.

Now I look back on 30 years of life's ordeals, I'm pleased to have been assisted by my dad, as well as the rest of his family in spirit, who have helped me grow. I've discovered that my family are healers through generations, not something that had ever been discussed. Through working in trance, I've been working with Spirit on a regular basis. The development group has brought out my confidence to use my spirit poet – my Goddess Durga, who is a powerful energy, stepping in during trance to allow me to appreciate her size. I feel she is teaching me to stand up and appreciate my power, to give up being small. I love writing my poetry, channelling words and writing without my mind engaged. I've used my poems to give messages from Spirit during our 'stand and deliver' sessions on retreat.

The benefits of the current time have been that I've been able to meditate more often: sending love out to the world and the fear pandemic to negate the situation. Sending lots of distance healing to help those dealing with the situation of losing jobs, being unable to visit elderly relatives in care, those in chaos over being isolated. Talking to people in need of support in understanding their situation. I'm grateful for the understanding I hold with the creation of our world situations linked with control. I also understand my Atlantean connection, and both my brother and I now know the underlying reasons for our experiences with fear. My confidence grows with understanding, plus there's a sense of deeper connection with my guides and guardians.

In a recent course on Aura Cleansing, I've learnt to find attachments, and about psychic attacks. This has uncovered a darkness I wasn't aware of within a teacher I'd worked with, which has helped me with my work on current energies. I keep my mind positive as much as possible, as I don't wish to add to the energies that are encouraging the fear around illness and death. I understand our vibrational change to 5D and above releasing the heavy 3D energy we have lived in. I've experienced many of my healings in the 5D energies, loving my life and the whole life-change situation.

Lessons learnt: today, I feel a different person. The biggest lesson has been that I'm not insignificant and everyone doesn't know more than I do. Education comes from life experiences, not just from school, college and university. As a child, I was never good enough, always striving to please others, be a good girl, avoid confrontation and keep the peace. I now appreciate how important it is to be honest with myself, even if I disagree with another's point of view. We all hold beliefs and aspects of our knowing and social conditioning. Not all people are what they put out to the world. We have our own lives to lead, in our own way. Our choices are always there for us to make in how we respond. Every day is our gift to live as we choose; if we choose not to set our intentions, then others will set them for us. Life and death are intrinsically woven throughout life: we can exist day to day, or thrive and live fully. We can set our day as being full of wonder and joy, making every moment count. When we experience events, it's our choice how we react. If something is causing us frustration or anger, there will be a teaching within, so I will sit and ask, 'What am I learning from this?'

My spirit teacher says, 'If you're not having fun, you're not doing it right.' I choose to be response-able and aim to be at ease, not in dis-ease.

Life and Death

Every end brings in a new beginning. What is death?
To those upon Mother Earth it is the final breath
But to those in spirit it is a return back home
Certainly not the end, but back to family, not alone

We are born with Free Will to live out our life
Gifted every day, our present to embrace and live
Freely and joyously, fulfilling our Earth experience
Dancing, running, feeling the vibration and hence

We emotionally flow, or block our way ahead
With empty pathways or boulders to block us dead
Stuck in the fear, emotional dread, no free will vibration
Giving our life away. Stuck in another's migration

Heaven or hell, living or dying, our free will
To live fully engaged, embracing the walk or stuck still
Learning to be powerful self or diseased and sick
We can give away our power, or live fully and slick

Hell upon Earth, is this a human creation? A power control
Life as a slave to the race of masculine energy toll
Harshness of fear, mindless being, kept stuck and ill
Instead of feminine freedom, opening up to free will

Joyously skipping forward, enjoying our life of fun
Helping each other to bring together each and everyone
Out of the prison, releasing the slave's chains
Nothing to lose, everything to gain

How To Let Go

No word or thought my head is empty
Let the flow of spirit bring plenty

See nothing, feel nothing, in limbo I sit
Why is the energy balance difficult to hit?

Plant vibrations and human vibrations align
Feel and acknowledge the elemental sign

Go deep, let go of fear, take that leap of faith
Into unknown territory, make it a date

No illness excuses or dead feeling within
Close by open, no such belief in sin

God holds us in light, never anything to fear
Angels surround us always ready to appear

This world is not always visible, not heavy or dark
Meditate, connect in silence, jump aboard this ark

Fly freely, be joyous to align the two frequencies
Divine energy, perfect aspect of Divinity

suecrowe59@gmail.com
FACEBOOK: @reflexsue

I was 'knocked down by a feather' when my husband offered to write a piece for
Reluctantly Psychic. *Wayne became gravely ill a few years back; I could see his
life force energy leave his body but eventually we got the help he needed. Wayne
describes how he used 'mind over pain' to not feel pain when fellow patients were
crying out in agony.*

MIND OVER PAIN

Wayne Ward

The first signs I had of stomach bloating was on a flight to Arizona, USA. My
stomach blew up and went hard as a drum. It deflated within a couple of hours
of landing.

I put it down to the long flight and drinking loads of water.

Over the next six months this bloating was to reappear several times but
without any actual pain.

The following further six months saw the bloating disappear and no new
symptoms took their place. In October 2016, Alison, my wife and orchestrator
of this book, went on *The Jeremy Kyle Show* on TV with our son, Sam to share
their inspirational story of their Awakening. They weren't the typical Jeremy
Kyle type of guest, but they hoped that hearing their story might make a
difference to at least one person.

That night, I awoke in the early hours and just knew I didn't feel right. My
stomach was bloated again; this time it was much bigger. Calling a cab, I quietly
slipped out the door. I didn't wake up Alison as I didn't want any fuss, and I
didn't want to worry her or the boys; Sam in London or James who still lived
at home with us.

I arrived at Solihull hospital and quickly saw a doctor, who advised me that
there was nothing wrong with me and that it could be irritable bowel (I'd not
been to the toilet for a week). He supplied me with co-codomol and sent me
home.

A new symptom arrived; pain in the base of my stomach. Pushing it to the back of my mind, Alison and I drove down to Herefordshire to stay at our static caravan, a place we loved and called 'our heaven on Earth'.

Over the next few days, the symptoms not only persisted, they got more intense. I still was unable to go to the toilet. Alison called the paramedics, who arrived swiftly.

Alison was clearly fearful as she knew something was wrong with me; she later told me she saw my life force energy leave my body.

The paramedic arrived, took my vitals and told me nothing was wrong, but he advised me to go to Hereford hospital to be checked out. Alison told the paramedic she knew something was very wrong and that I had an odd odour, but he was unable to sense that.

After arriving in Hereford hospital, we went straight in to see the doctor as, fortunately, there were no other patients waiting to be seen. He checked me over and said I was constipated and needed to take a suppository.

He then sent me home.

By this time, Alison was getting considerably more worried, and called in the help of her spiritual friends, who urged her to seek more medical help.

The next day we drove back to Birmingham and went directly to Heartlands hospital A&E department.

They obviously could see I wasn't well and took me straight in for a scan. They told me my appendix had burst and had become attached to the bowel; it was actually growing over it, enveloping the bowel from clear view.

Unknown to me, they told Alison that I was seriously ill; my organs were shutting down.

The next morning, I was taken into surgery where they removed what was left of my disintegrated appendix. My stomach was full of bile that had to be drained off.

They were amazed I was still alive as I'd clearly been ill for a while. The peritonitis had occurred a good while ago. The poison in my system had made itself at home for months. How could I still be alive? And how come none of the previous medics were able to see how ill I was?

My time on the post-op ward was an eye-opener to me. All night long I heard moaning from the other patients who had undergone similar surgery, yet I didn't feel the pain. I made a decision: to block the pain out. My mind was made up; I was no longer going to feel pain and therefore not have to take a load of tablets.

The Asian guy opposite was amazed that I didn't let the pain get to me, enquiring how I didn't feel it. I shrugged my shoulders.

The ward was my home for five days. I still didn't feel fully well on discharge, but I just wanted to get home and have no fuss.

That evening, I developed a deep pain in my back. No matter how I sat or lay I couldn't get comfortable. We used every single pillow and cushion we had to keep me propped up but still I had pain.

I spent the night sitting upright in the lounge, concentrated on breathing deeply and again tried to tell my body I did not feel any pain.

The next morning, Alison and my younger son, James took me straight back to A&E.

Upon arriving, it was evident there had been a big car accident on the nearby M5. They put me into a side room on my own whilst they dealt with the emergency patients from the car crash.

I was to remain there all day. Alison and James joined me but I insisted they leave at 3.30pm, as they were tired and hungry.

Sitting upright on the couch, the pain deepened. I once again decided to try a new tactic to ease it; I was determined to get a grip of the pain and overcome it, rather than it overcome me.

I sat on the edge of the couch, used breathing methods that just 'came to me' and told my mind to stop the pain. It worked; I felt it slowly leave my body, replaced by a powerful energy that told me I had conquered this. I knew in the back of my mind that my body was in pain but I also knew I was now in control of the pain and me feeling it.

At 5pm I was taken to see a doctor, who diagnosed double pneumonia. I spent the next week on the cystic fibrosis ward where my health and strength returned.

I eventually went back home to my relieved family and got fully well once more. Returning to our holiday home, I was able to rest and breathe in the fresh country air.

This experience taught me that I wasn't afraid of dying and that if I had to go through any future painful procedures, I had the capacity to reduce pain, as I now knew that telling my mind to do this could be done.

Does this make me different from others? I'm not sure. All I know is I wasn't fearful, and I wasn't prepared to be in pain. I suggest that this mixture of strong mental attitude kept me pain free. It makes you wonder what else the brain can do.

A former trauma and orthopaedic team leader, Jayne was used to being in the operating theatre. Little did she know that she would nearly lose her life during a life-saving operation and see 'Davy Crockett' at the bottom of her bed.

FROM THE HEART

Jayne Passey

A Few Years Ago, I Had My Awakening...

I was seriously ill in hospital after having my gallbladder removed. Little did we know at the time that the surgeon had damaged my bile duct beyond repair whilst doing the surgery. As the days went by after my operation, I was getting sicker and sicker... The surgeon kept saying it was normal but I knew, after working in theatre as a trauma and orthopaedic team leader, this was not the case!

This eventually led to me collapsing at home just 12 hours after being discharged and being rushed back in by ambulance. Fortunately for me, I was then under the care of a different surgeon, who took one look at me and sent me to the Queen Elizabeth hospital liver unit. Nothing could be done in my local hospital as I was too sick.

When I arrived, I had many tests. They were trying to find out what was causing me to be so sick. For the three nights I was there, at first, all I knew was that I was poorly and I felt I was gradually slipping away. On the second night, this is when my Awakening started. I was asleep (so I thought I was dreaming). I saw a man, who didn't speak but was standing at the bottom of my bed, smiling at me. This man looked like he'd walked out of an old film, as he appeared and was dressed like Davy Crockett. At this point, I must add that, due to me being so poorly, I was in a room on my own with my own bathroom. Standing at the door, there were also three nurses from the past. They looked like what I can only describe as 'Amish' in the way they were dressed with their uniforms. They stood in a line at the open bathroom door, beckoning to me to follow them. At this point, I woke with a jump and presumed I'd been dreaming.

The following night, the same thing happened again, with the same man at the bottom of my bed and the three nurses. This was when I got out of bed and started to follow them towards the bathroom door. I again woke with a jump and found that I had actually got out of my bed and was half way to the bathroom door! So I got back into bed and went back to sleep, presuming that I'd been dreaming – again.

I'd like to say that I was totally lucid at this time and hadn't received any sedatives or medication any different to what I'd been on for the past two weeks. As a very experienced health professional, I was quick to assume these were just dreams. But then I'd never had a dream like this that was exactly the same as soon as I closed my eyes.

The next night, my husband visited me and I said to him, 'If you hear me talking to someone if I drop off to sleep, don't panic!' He left for home and, once again, I went to sleep, and quickly, the same people appeared in my room. It was so real; like they were there. I was speaking to them, asking them what they wanted me to do, but they didn't answer. They just kept smiling and beckoning me towards the nurses, who stood at the doorway of the bathroom in my room. I remember seeing there was a very beautiful white light beyond them. I must have got out of bed again and was nearly at the door when I awoke with a jump, and it was just as if my family had been calling me from behind me (where my bed was). So I realised I'd again got out of bed but this time, I'd nearly got to the bathroom door.

That day, I had a special P.E.T. scan and the surgeon came up at midday and said I was so sick they were taking me straight to theatre. I didn't have time to call my family and was rushed down to surgery to have a huge operation on my liver. My non-existent bile duct had to be replaced with my bowel. This had given me billary peritonitis and I had sepsis and was dying.

After eight hours in surgery, I was moved to the critical care unit. When I came round, all I wanted was to see my family. I don't remember this, but I do remember seeing my husband and daughter's faces briefly late that night. I think I wanted to make sure I was still on Earth and hadn't followed the people who I'd seen for the past couple of nights!

That same night, I had a visit from 'Davy Crockett'. This time he was on his own; no nurses with him, just him. I must point out that I was now in a side room in critical care and not on the main unit. He again stood at the bottom of my bed, smiling at me, on his own as if he was saying goodbye. He waved and I didn't see him again after that. From which point onwards, as the operation to repair my liver had fortunately been successful, I was slowly but surely improving day by day and getting better. From that night, I didn't have another visit from Davy Crockett or anyone else. I just continued to gradually recover and eventually, after five days on critical care, I was allowed back to the ward for another week before being well enough to go home.

When I returned home, I couldn't do anything and this is when my mind started to realise what I'd actually been through and, as everyone says, a little inside knowledge is dangerous! I knew as soon as they transferred me to the liver unit I was critical, but it all happened so quickly at the time.

This feeling, and thoughts about what had happened on those nights before my operation, started to make me feel very scared and uneasy. My mind began to play tricks on me and every time I closed my eyes I could see it and was reliving this over and over again. As you can imagine, this had a drastic effect on my mental health.

One day a while later, purely by chance, my mum took me to meet Alison Ward. I'd never met her before but as soon as I did, it was just like I'd known her all my life. I just started telling her what had happened and how scared I was and I couldn't stop! I've never experienced this before with anyone. I started working with Alison as, before I met her, I'd been diagnosed after my surgery with Post-Traumatic Stress Disorder (PTSD).

She asked me what was bothering me and why I was so frightened every time I closed my eyes and saw this man.

As a health care professional, I had, during my 24 years in the NHS, unfortunately seen a few people pass away. Three of these were children on one day. That was the worst day in my professional life. You don't realise how you hold these feelings with you and just what trauma it causes you.

I explained that I knew I'd been dying. I also knew why these people were there as, during my time at work, there were many people who, just before they'd passed, had spoken to others and smiled, and also spoke about seeing lights etc. So, as I had seen this, I knew WHY they were there but just couldn't understand WHO they were! I was expecting to see my gran or grandad or some other family member, certainly not Davy Crockett!

During my life, even as a child, I'd always 'seen' things and people, and had déjà vu all the time. I also, never seemed to get lost, even when I'd not been to a place before. It was almost like I had been there at some point. I just thought this was how everyone felt and I never spoke about it.

After working with Alison, it was quickly revealed that this 'Davy Crockett' man was my father in a previous life, and the nurses who were there in the room were also there when he passed over. This was my 'lightbulb moment'. All those souls who were lost in my work, Alison explained to me that they chose me to take them there. So I was doing the ultimate in care by holding their hands as they passed over.

Well, this was like a bang on the head. Everything just dropped into place! I totally got why I went into the NHS to help people and why I was chosen to help souls cross over too.

This face still gives me comfort now it's been explained to me, and all my childhood 'visitations' etc. fell into place too.

My daughter is very 'aware' and I think this is something that's been in the family for a long time. We speak to each other about things we see and how we know who's going to be on the other end of the phone when it rings without answering, and many more!

My husband, who is my soulmate, and my family, who love me so much, were the anchor to this life for me when I was gravely ill. I know that Davy Crockett was there to guide me as I also know that no souls go over on their own. If it wasn't for the love of my family, I wouldn't be here today.

Life After The Awakening...

Well, it's taught me to be grateful for what I have and who is in my life. It's also allowed my inner artist come out!

I'm now in my happy place with myself and enjoy the blessings I have in my life with amazing family and friends. I'm a lot more 'aware and open' and have much more understanding of the 'psychic' things that happen in my life as I feel every day is a blessing and, instead of being fearful of them, I now understand what they are.

Since the Awakening and the peace that I've found from understanding my role here to help people and guide them to the other side, I've been given the gift of time now, as I'm retired from the NHS on ill health grounds. This has allowed me to reawaken my inner gifts and I've been drawing and painting. I mainly paint animals and do pet portraits. Now I've started to do this, everyone has said how the eyes in my paintings have so much 'soul'. This, I feel, is a superb compliment. I love animals and, as a child, was able to be brought up with many different ones. I always had ponies as a child, and horses then going forwards. I would always talk to my animals and I had such love for them all.

I've been very fortunate to be contacted by many people to recreate their loved pets, who have passed over rainbow bridge. Rainbow bridge, for all who don't know, is where all animals go when they die to wait for their loved owners to reunite with them when they pass over too. I really feel that this is my connection now, and so many people cry when they see their loved ones brought back to life. I feel this is now my new role in helping people heal and bringing happiness and love to them, by putting the 'souls' of their animals into my drawings. Many people say that their eyes follow them around the room! Now I'm not sure if that's a comfort, but I'm blessed and it fills my heart with so much joy to give them happiness and to be able to reunite them with their loved animals again.

Lessons learnt:

- I know I'm here to help people – you are too.
- After having to give up the career I loved, life made way for other things.
- Never take anything for granted.
- Always be grateful for what you have.
- Love, love, love, everyone.
- There are always two sides to a story – it depends how you choose to interpret it.
- Always be open to anything you're given.

www.andromedart.co.uk
andromeda.art24@gmail.com
FACEBOOK: @andromeda art
INSTAGRAM: @andromeda art 24

A born sensitive, Mike had visions from an early age, but an abusive childhood led to depression until he was introduced to energy and energy healers. Mike is now a renowned healer.

MIKE'S JOURNEY

Mike Neville

As a child, I was always hypersensitive to other people's energies, which was and is the only real memory or sense I have of my early childhood years. But there was a good reason for that and it became clear many years later.

When I was 14, two very distinct and separate things began to happen.

The first was that I started to have visions of the Virgin Mary and of Jesus, and I thought for a while that I may be having a vocation to the priesthood, as I was brought up within the confines of Catholicism. At about the same time, I found myself increasingly drawn to aspects of the occult, and indeed began to read books on it. These two opposites in some ways dictated the level of conflict that I lived with for many years afterwards, as I pursued my career in the corporate world, and pulled away from anything that seemed 'dangerous'.

The corporate world is a complex place, full of values that have little or no meaning, and with an over-focus on profit, money, cash and power. Within this paradigm I existed and worked, but was never fulfilled, always feeling separate and alone, not 'inside' or aligned, and with little or no joy.

When I was 42, I experienced an epiphany, which started one dark Christmas day afternoon, by the side of a canal. I was going through a divorce and felt very alone, and at that time was considering my physical state – that is to say I was considering suicide. Quite by chance, I came upon a beautiful white swan floating dead in the canal, and this image, which has stayed with me since, actually turned me around.

Very soon after that I was introduced to someone who trained people in reading and interpreting energy, and although I flourished in some ways during that time, I found myself let down quite badly at moments of vulnerability and uncertainty.

Notwithstanding this, my journey continued, with dreams, which were electrifying in their detail and colour, and consistent themes of psychic happenings on multiple levels.

It was when I was circa 45 that I began to have the return of some childhood memories, and this created a major hurdle for me in my journey. It became clear that the reason I had no memories was that I had suffered systemic sexual abuse, at the hands of people who were in positions of influence. This was excruciatingly painful, but also began to build part of the new foundation for me going forward. Thus, I had to do the hard and difficult internal work.

As I worked through the deeper internal issues of my psyche, I began to experience profound development of my own innate skills in reading and interpreting energy, beginning to understand where my alignment was wrong; where I wasn't living in accordance with my own values and my own soul contract.

During this time, the number of people I was seeing quadrupled, and most of them were experiencing multiple complex issues, which I felt drawn to helping them with. I didn't advertise, and still never have. Everything I've ever done has been word of mouth, and at one stage I was working seven days a week, which of course couldn't continue because of the potential for burnout.

My development continued. I became qualified in many holistic therapies, but they were only tiny fragments of what was needed to get me on the right road. What was more important was my own ability to channel and formulate spiritual matters that were in true alignment and ethically correct in their composition.

Now I spiritually mentor people all over the world and I provide guidance on their path. I still provide healings but that's a smaller part of what I do. I work very much on the empowerment of the divine feminine and the rise of the spiritual matriarch, two aspects that are of significant importance going forward, as humanity can only evolve its consciousness through embracing the true essence of that divine feminine. In addition to mentoring, I teach others how to read and interpret energy, how to channel safely, and how to align their values in accordance with their own soul contract.

I am dedicated to providing a genuinely safe container for people when they are opening and developing, as my own experiences of that were somewhat lacking in that area, and it's really important when you are first opening and becoming conscious.

The path of spirituality is not an easy one at times. It's littered with aspects of our own traumas, embedded non-serving patterns, paradigms that do us no justice, but with help and favour, one can reach a state of certainty with regards to one's path, and with that comes alignment and ultimately fulfilment.

mike@mike-neville.com
INSTAGRAM: @mikeneville1

Kerry's had a tough life, but she has overcome abusive behaviour, loss of her dear mum and has found her purpose in healing by accepting her gifts. So many healers have overcome such things. It gives them more empathy, compassion and connection thus making them great therapists.

MY SOUL JOURNEY

Kerry Bavin

I wasn't like most children my age growing up. Instead of going to the local club discos or get togethers, I was either at church or an event involving church. My nanna was a Christian and I guess I was too, or at least brought up as one as I was then confirmed at the age of 11.

When I was around 12 years old, I remember having an extraordinary dream of going up stairs that were familiar to me as they were the stairs in my senior school that led to my form classroom. When I got to the top, there were two people either side of the entrance doors, which still looked like school. There was nothing angelic about them. I was told by one of the people to go back and that it wasn't my time. When I woke up, I was very confused and confided in my nanna about the dream. She explained that she thought I may have had an out of body experience (OBE). She also told me about reincarnation and spirits, and how they can come back to look after you. She then proceeded to tell me that, at four years old, I'd seen my grandad and she'd seen me talking to him (unfortunately, I don't remember that far back in my life). As there was no internet (or I didn't have access), I went to my local library and started researching OBEs and more. The more I read, the more I was hungry for knowledge, and the more I went down different avenues and subjects.

For the next few years of my life, I dabbled in and out of spirituality. I taught myself to read tarot (although I could never grasp them, I did try), and I did candle gazing and mirror gazing (that made me jump – going from having long blond hair as a female to brown hair and a beard as an old male). I was known by all my friends as the spooky or weird one and, to be honest, I felt proud to be different.

However, I did some things I wasn't proud of in college. One was dabbling in drugs and getting involved with a drug dealer. I started to take cocaine and, wow, what an addiction that became very quickly. Within weeks, I was doing it every day. But one evening, after being out with friends, I went to a party and was on the cocaine. I got talking to a friend and realised he was very spiritual. He was telling me how we are living in a matrix and that nothing around us is real.

Suddenly, I noticed two blue lines in my friend's face and I just thought, wow, this cocaine is crazy. But my friend had obviously realised I'd seen something and asked me if I was ok. I told him that I was imagining blue lines in his face and that it must be the drugs. He started to laugh and showed me a newspaper clipping. I wasn't aware, but when my friend was in his twenties, he'd been involved in an industrial accident, which meant his face had to be rebuilt with plastic surgery, and underneath it were two metal plates! I had absolutely no idea at all. Then, as I turned around, I saw a child-like figure in the corner of the room, sitting on a chair – a ghost!

By now I was terrified, and then, all the walls around me started peeling off as if the wallpaper was coming down. That was enough to get me off the drugs and to cut all contact with my old acquaintances. Years later, I actually had a clairvoyant read for me and she confirmed that, if I'd carried on along that path, I wouldn't have lived. I took the right path and survived.

Around 2003, I met my daughter's father. I'd stopped using my tarot and other divination practices around 2000 and settled into life as a full-time working mum. Things were great for a couple of years, until I realised I was living with a man who was mentally draining me. But three affairs (that I know of) wasn't enough to make me leave him. Until one night when my life changed forever.

I'd been out with a friend for the evening and I walked back into my kitchen to find two bowls in the sink. I knew intuitively he'd had another woman over to my home. I walked upstairs to find two black hair bobbles on the bed. That confirmed it – yes, there had been another woman around. It may sound innocent, but I was blonde and these were black, and all women know we wear bobbles the same colour as our hair.

I approached him about it and an argument erupted. I followed him into the kitchen asking him who she was and why he'd done this to me again; the usual questions I'd asked in the past. Then suddenly, he turned to me and he looked dead behind his eyes, almost evil. I felt threatened and grabbed the first thing I could, which was a knife from the knife rack. I held the blade towards him and told him not to come any closer. He looked at me with a smirk (I still remember that today) and said, 'If I push myself on that knife now, you'll never see Janine again.'

I quickly realised then that he'd been manipulating and controlling for all our relationship and I'd played into his hands. I spent that night in a police cell and I've never felt so low and embarrassed in all my life. I knew I had to change my life around and get out of the relationship. I left him, finally, and moved into a lovely little apartment with my daughter. I felt great having my independence back, and gradually started to date again.

Turning Point

I was now happily settled in a job I loved, Janine was thriving and I'd met a wonderful man. My daughter still got to see her grandparents and dad whenever he was in the area, as he'd moved away with a new partner. Things were going great until my lovely mum was diagnosed with terminal cancer. Then my daughter's dad split up with his girlfriend and started to contact me again. He wanted to start afresh 'for Janine's sake'. I knew that, although I wanted Janine to have a family, and I also knew I was very lonely and cried most days over my poorly mum, I wasn't prepared to go back into that life again.

That's when the abuse started. I was followed, I received hurtful messages, I was threatened. I was even burgled and all my personal items were stolen. To this day, I know he had something to do with it.

Awakening

It was a November evening and freezing cold. I'd met up with friends to see a band, but the more text messages I got, the lower my mood went. After receiving more abuse and threats, I decided I couldn't cope any longer and didn't want to be there anymore. I ran out of the venue and down towards the beach. I ran onto the sand and remember how cold it felt underneath my bare feet. There was ice, and it cut through my soles. I was crying and screaming at God, blaming him for Mum being ill and for all the pain and hurt I'd gone through. I remember saying he was evil and that he wouldn't put people through so much if he wasn't.

I dropped my shoes, neatly placed my phone in my bag on top of them and ran into the sea. My heart was racing as I could feel the cold sea air getting closer and closer. When my feet touched the icy water, it sent adrenaline running through me. I continued to run until all I could do was swim. I was determined to end my time on Earth there and then. I lay back and remember looking ahead at the seafront and the lights. I'd been dragged out to sea. There was no way I was getting back now.

And I waited to drown... Silence...

When I woke up, I felt like I'd been having a nightmare, but quickly realised that wasn't it. I was still in the sea but I was at the sea wall. I'd somehow swum back but I couldn't remember any of it. I quickly clambered up the wall and, after falling back twice, I finally managed to climb to the top. I was overlooking the seafront and alive! I ran into the closest night club and collapsed to the floor.

The last thing I remember was being covered like a turkey in the back of an ambulance and rushed to hospital. Then I must have fallen asleep. I awoke to find two police officers around my bed, asking me how I was feeling. Apparently, they'd seen me run into the sea and had run after me but, once I was swimming, they'd had to give up and had radioed the office that I was gone and would be found further down the shore. They said they were very shocked to find me in hospital and that someone had definitely been watching over me.

I realised then how lucky I was and that I'd been given another chance. To this day, I can't explain how I got back. It was as if I was just picked up and moved back to shore. I do know one thing, though – that night I had a Guardian Angel save my life. I'm sure I'll find out when the time is right who it was, but for now, I just appreciate that I was saved.

In 2010, I met my now husband, Karl, and was so pleased to learn that he too believed there was more to life and the Universe. We had a son together (my second child) and we got married in 2014. My beautiful mum lost her battle to myeloma not long after.

It had been a week since I'd let her go. I say let her go and I did. She was still alive while the paramedics tried to bring her back. I told her to leave and find peace.

A few days later, I was sitting at the computer talking to a practising medium friend. He asked me how I was coping and although I said in the message, 'I'm fine', in reality my heart was breaking and tears were streaming down my face. He said to me he had someone with him who wanted to give a message to me. I've always believed there are gifted people in the world but for some reason I didn't believe him. But I gave him the benefit of the doubt. He explained that there was a lady and she was wearing a floral yellow wedding dress, and immediately I knew he had my mum with him. He went on to say that she knew she'd asked for pink to be worn at the funeral, but she only wanted me to wear a bit of pink as she knew I usually wore black. He then said she was sorry and that she loved me; that she would always be proud of me, even if she didn't agree with a lot of things I did, like my hobby. She said it didn't matter as long as I was happy.

I was absolutely elated to realise that our loved ones really are around us, so I asked my friend if I could go to the next mediumship circle with him. He agreed. The day came round, and I was so excited to meet people, even maybe just to get a reading from them. I was surrounded by all these gifted people, and then there was me, who couldn't even feel the vibrations of crystals! But I persevered and completed the course.

I went back to normal life but started practising divination again. I was shocked one day to find my tarot had completely disappeared out of the box it was in, so I decided to try oracle cards. I still couldn't seem to understand them, but then I was given some, and these are cards I still use today to read for friends. I was given a pendulum too and I started using this. I couldn't believe how accurate it was and how strongly it connected with me. I started to meditate daily. From seeing nothing, this gradually developed into beautiful swirls of pinks and purples and then into images. Sometimes the vibrations I felt were so intense it was like I'd moved into another world. I was then told about Reiki and how amazing it was to help a person to heal. I decided that, after I received my inheritance, I was going to put it to good use and help myself to heal. I did some research and found the most beautiful Reiki Master, and my amazing soul journey began. I practised Reiki on myself daily for about six months, but then life once again got in the way.

I was happily working full-time, and then my health took a turn for the worse. I was in constant pain and I learnt that, because of the trauma I'd suffered giving birth, I needed an operation. A year later, the pain was unbearable and, although I still meditated and practised, I didn't do it as much as I'd like to have done.

I started to use my Reiki on myself again and was surprised to find that, wow, I was hardly ever in pain. I was given notice in my job and then my operation was booked for a few months later. Once my job finished, I knew I'd have spare time so I decided to enrol at college and study Complementary Therapies. I was a living example of how holistic therapies can change your life. While at college I decided that, as a therapist, I also wanted to incorporate Reiki into my practice with my future clients, so I decided to train and be attuned to Reiki practitioner. Wow, once I was Reiki II-attuned, so many things changed for me.

I had always been sensitive to people and, years later, I realised there was a name for this. I was an Empath, but since being Reiki-attuned, I was so much more sensitive. I could walk into a room and sense the energy in there, whether it was negative or positive. I started to read people. I knew when someone was trying to pull me down – they were literally draining me of my energy. I learnt about protection and how to pull your aura in if you feel uncomfortable around people.

Then friends started to fall away from me. I'd begun to take back my power and no one liked it. But I didn't care because I knew deep down they weren't going to be in my life anymore. It wasn't easy and I'm ashamed to say that a few words were said, but when I received a sign from the Angels soon after, I knew I'd made the right decision. One example was that, for years I'd been pulled down by a group of people and if I was ever around them, I always felt drained. Anyway, one day I just snapped. Everyone was shocked to see it of me but I knew it had to be said. The following day, I walked into my son's bedroom and found a yellow feather on the floor. I looked up the meaning of a yellow feather and it basically gave me the confirmation that what I'd done had to be done.

After this, the synchronicities I experienced went into overdrive! It was 11.11 all the time. Equally as common was 13.3.3 (my birthday date and time). It even got to a point where I knew what time of the day it was without looking at the clock. I kept waking up at 3am, too, feeling like I was being watched while I slept. And I had some pretty amazing experiences. I still don't know if they were dreams or not.

09.03.19

I woke up at 3.20am to go to the bathroom. It took me ages to go back to sleep, all sorts of things going through my head about my interview today. Then I felt like I was falling asleep again. I could sense the energy all around me like when I meditate or practise Reiki. I could feel my crown chakra tingling constantly (but I feel that a lot before sleep). I was then in a lucid dream where I was in a laboratory. There were all these scientists around and there was one standing at a board, telling everyone the benefits of meditation and how it improves our health. I remember floating upwards and saying, 'It allows you to do this', and messing about, tapping the scientists on the head from above. Then I felt myself go higher. I quickly woke myself up. I was in my bed with my eyes shut and could see all these other eyes looking at me as clear as day.

Next thing, I was lying in bed quite still, and again I felt all the energy swirling around me and like I was floating. I was aware of Karl snoring, and the pigeons on the roof, so I wasn't asleep. Then I heard a dog come into the room and round to my side of the bed. I could hear a sniffing. I remember thinking for some reason that we had a dog. I leaned over to stroke it and fell out of bed. But I fell out in such a way that I didn't feel like it was me. I looked up at the dog but it wasn't a dog anymore – I was looking at myself! I quickly used the window sill to pull myself up. I could see my reflection in the window and I saw big blue sockets where my eyes should be but I didn't see eyes, just the glow of the blue. I felt a pressure in my head and suddenly I was flung to the floor and there were all these images going into my head. I could literally feel the pressure. I was curled in a ball on the floor because I couldn't physically get up. And I remember asking for protection. The next thing I knew, I'd woken up, but in bed, with a pounding headache and feeling sick.

12.03.19

I was awoken at 2am feeling like someone was sitting on the bed. I was communicating telepathically with Karl; I didn't feel asleep. But I was seeing images in front of me. One image was of Albert Einstein. When it stopped, Karl went to the bathroom and I was properly awake.

I was woken again at 3am by some sort of 'woom woom' noise and when I turned my head, although I didn't feel like I had, I could see myself in what looked like an energy field. I could feel it all around my body. When it stopped, I felt like I was swaying, as if my body was trying to stabilise although my physical body wasn't moving.

At 5am, I was awoken once more, this time by a feeling of being watched. I turned to see a floating being beside me. It just looked like static energy and I felt what I can only describe as warm liquid been poured into my neck, before falling asleep again.

By now I was using Reiki all the time and I started to meditate on and off, and my dreams were becoming even stranger…

18.04.19

I went to sleep around 11pm. I was aware of most noises through the night as I was sleeping. My husband was suffering with his chest so I kept turning to give him Reiki while he slept. I asked to be cloaked so nobody was aware I was healing and proceeded with Reiki on his back. As soon as his breathing changed, I turned back round to go to sleep. I remember dreaming that I was in some sort of shopping mall and was talking to a lady who said there was a special load of shops that I'd like but I'd have to go down a scary walkway. I agreed that I would. As I walked through the door, I saw that it certainly did look scary and it smelt musty.

I came to a guy with a big stall selling Levi jeans and various other clothes and accessories that I love. All around me, it was like I was in some sort of horror movie. It was like a yard with wood everywhere, not the sort of thing you'd see in a shopping mall. As I got closer, I could smell the guy's body odour and suddenly he grabbed me. He had me in a headlock. I remember then waking up from my dream and seeing in front of me thick black tentacles trying to wrap around my face while I was in bed. I quickly asked for protection from Archangel Michael and for him to sever the attachment to me, and I sent it into the violet flame with love.

While I lay in bed awake, I realised that I wasn't afraid and that the entity wanted me to be. So I closed my eyes and went straight back into the dream. I don't know if I was asleep and dreaming or just had my eyes closed to imagine, but once I was back there, I went straight up to the man and told him I wasn't afraid of him and that light will always win over darkness. I put my hand up to him and lots of blue energy just radiated out of my palm chakra, and he disappeared in a puff of blue smoke. I heard telepathically, 'We will not be beaten'. When I came back to my awake stage, or out of the imagination, I looked at my clock and it said 04.44. I took a mental note of this to remind myself to research the spiritual meaning of that number when I got up. As I was falling back asleep, suddenly I was seeing lots of blue energy around me, surrounding me. I could feel my hands, feet and head all pulsating to match the energy frequency. Then my husband started coughing again so I turned to give him Reiki. I woke again at 05.55.

I've always felt drawn to Egyptians. Maybe I was one in a past life. But the more I do research, the more downloads and wisdom I feel, they present themselves to me. I was browsing social media one day and saw a class for Seichem training. I'd never heard of it but I decided to research into it. I contacted Elaine of Inner Peace Healing and asked her about the training and costs etc. I was very shocked to learn that the initial attunement and training were less than £100, and that it was about working with all the elements and can possibly help you connect with Spirit more. So I decided to book myself on the course. It was very informative and amazing to learn about the Egyptian deities, and I immediately started practising Seichem on myself. After about three months, enjoying every minute of healing with Egyptian energies, I decided to go to the next level and be a Seichem practitioner, which meant I could offer the treatments to my clients, along with Reiki. In November 2019, I became a Seichem practitioner, and suddenly I was seeing beauty in everything around me. I feel that the training I received was basically making my soul remember an energy I had in a past life.

Once I was qualified in Level 2, I started to see Spirit in human form. I even started to see animals in my house and have since done research and learnt that my home is built on farmland. I also began to sense if I'd picked up anything while in a dream state and had to constantly cleanse my aura, and I was seeing portals physically open in my home and therapy room, with white energies stepping out. I loved the idea of having portals in my home and a direct connection to Spirit, until the not-so-nice spirit started coming through and the energy in my home changed. My husband started to notice dark shadows and was being woken at 3am hearing a knocking on the bedroom door, which he said made him feel uncomfortable. This made me realise that I wasn't meant to have the portals open. I meditated and went within, questioning my higher self about what I was meant to do. I was guided to close the portal and to send the spirit into the light with love and light. I did this and realised that this is what I was meant to do: my role was to help spirits cross over should they so wish.

26.12.19

It was Boxing Day at my in-laws and, having had a fun-filled second Christmas, I retired to bed at around 9pm. I was lying there awake when I recognised that there was someone in the room with me. I sensed she had white hair, was small and quite plump. She told me that she hadn't crossed over because she was worried about her family that were left behind. Telepathically, I told her they would come to find her when the time was right. I then asked someone from the other side to come and take her so she'd realise she wouldn't be alone. When I saw a flash of light on the mirror, I felt as though she'd gone. And I asked for the portal to be shut.

I woke up at 5.30am when Karl went to the bathroom. We had a chat before going back to sleep, then I started to dream. I dreamt that I was in a house and we had a dog. The dog was medium-sized but I was unsure on the breed. Into the house walked a fox. I love foxes and it came up to me, rubbing up against me, so I stroked it. Then the fox went up to the dog and started nuzzling into him. I thought it looked cute until the dog seemed to go very quiet and wasn't moving. I went up to the dog and realised he was bleeding badly on his legs. The fox had been attacking them without me realising. I pulled the fox off him and instantly it ran straight back to the dog and started attacking him again.

Suddenly, the fox ran upstairs into another room – and I was in bed again and thought I'd woken up. But then I felt something drag at my legs, trying to get me out of bed. Something was trying to pull me into a badly damaged wardrobe. I screamed to be protected in a white ball but it wasn't having any effect and I could still feel I was being pulled. I then cried out for protection from Michael, Metatron, Raphael and Jovial, all the Angels I could think of. As I did so, I saw flashes of what looked like small orbs in blue, gold, pink and green. I felt the loosening of the grip as whatever had me, had let go. Then, when I looked towards the end of the bed, I realised it was a young blonde child or very young woman. And she disappeared.

I went back to sleep but woke up again to the feeling of my legs being pulled once more. This time I thought I was out of my dream because I could hear Karl snoring. But I wasn't; I was still dreaming. I felt like whatever she was wanted me in the wardrobe and would stop at nothing to get me in there. Again, I asked for my guides to protect me from the girl. She was pulled off me and ran into the corner of the room. She tried to talk to me and I felt she wanted me to feel sorry for her. As I got closer to her to help her, I felt a feeling of much dread and I knew instantly she wasn't of good intentions. I grabbed her and threw her into the wardrobe, and then realised it was a portal at the back. Part of the wardrobe was falling apart but behind it was a big white light and surrounding this near the entrance it looked like red brick. After I'd thrown her in, I screamed at the portal to close and never open again.

Recently, I started questioning my role here on Earth. Yep, I know it sounds crazy but this is really the kind of thing that goes through your head once you awaken. I knew I was a healer and I researched and discovered that I was a Sirian starchild or Starseed, and had lived on the planets Sirias A, B and C. Once I started expanding my awareness, I began seeing visions, either before I went to sleep or just as I woke up. I've walked into my bedroom to see blue orbs around my room and recently a blue beam. I just class this as normal now. My therapy room is my haven to get away for my time to meditate or read. Sometimes while in there, I feel a very cool energy and when I acknowledge it, I see gold and blue flashes of light. Once, I was massaging a client and the walls in front of me changed into what I can only describe as gold grids. I believe I was seeing the matrix. Other times I see something I call 'Reiki fog'.

It's literally just like a fog above a client. I acknowledge it and then continue with the treatment.

So here I am now, 39, an Energy Healer specialising in Reiki and Seichem, a Holistic Therapist and, on the odd occasion, a Rescue Medium. I feel I would never have got to where I have today if it hadn't been for the pain and suffering I'd been through in that earlier relationship. I'm a massive believer in the fact that you have to go through hell to be in heaven. I still have friends who think I'm crazy to a certain extent, but they love to hear about my experiences. I know I've a long way to go and that I'll not be using all my abilities in this life, but this life is a journey and I'm loving every ounce of it. Don't get me wrong, sometimes I feel negative and alone, but then I only have to call upon my spiritual team, and immediately I feel so much love that I know everything is happening for me in the way it's meant to.

www.soultriage.co.uk
FACEBOOK: @soultriage
INSTAGRAM: @soul_triage

Chris, one of our five male authors, overcomes self-sabotage to form self-acceptance and his love of connection to the Earth and healing energies. He offers his energy therapies to the world.

KNEE-JERK REACTION

Chris Batchelor

There were gifts I noticed and recognised but chose to ignore in place of the old patterns that I'd programmed for myself throughout my childhood and adulthood (adolescence 12 – 42 LOL).

I came to realise that the hurt I had and continued to create for myself, the permanent target I painted on the wall for my head, and the hand positions to stabilise me whilst I actively went about the sabotaging of my life, had become my pattern. The ostrich head-in-the-sand viewpoint (classically known as checking out!) became the huge hurdle I had to overcome. That was my gate to get over. I had to wake myself up to all the twists and turns in the road that I'd distracted myself with in taking the path most easily travelled. Why did I never take the most direct route through the power of seeing value in myself and wanting to achieve a level of love beyond all others I had received? I had to make a decision to no longer receive from others the love I wanted, or distract myself with seeking acknowledgement or affections from others, but rather to give that love to myself – right back to the child I see in my eyes every time I look into the mirror.

But how would I do that? How could I give that which I had no clue how to receive in the first place? Well, all I can say is that when I turned 42, I began to question even my existence.

With all the procrastination and debating with myself as to what I wanted and how I wanted it to be, through all the years I'd lived so far, and the mental chatter of self-sabotage patterns, I'd reached a point of surrender. I knew I could no longer live the life I had. I knew I was more than just this physical being. I had a knowing, an unbelievable drive that found me stepping into my current self.

I received energetic flashbacks to past lives, guides, protectors, even those that had hurt me or that I had hurt. Sensitivities to the invisible world from my magical years of connection with Spirit/Faeries/Angels (whatever you wish to call them) had all presented themselves again. A knowing... a chance to trust and believe in myself; to welcome myself into my heart and to receive the joy from the divine... from the Source... from God... from myself!

Every day, I am so full of gratitude that I'm alive, that I'm abundant in so many ways. And it only happened because I chose me. I chose to love who I am – my lineage, my beliefs – and to empower myself.

I was the only way. IT IS THE ONLY WAY. I am the divine within. I am within the divine.

Much love and blessings.

balancethespirit@hotmail.com
FACEBOOK: @lightrays01

An 'old soul' in a young man's body, Mike never fitted in with other kids. He was, however, able to connect with adults. Overcoming bullying from being different at school, Mike has used his challenges to become a mental wellness advocate and therapist.

MIKE MEETS LIFE

Mike Fairbrother

As with most people, my memories of being younger are very sparse, ranging from very early memories of family holidays, to washing my parents' car outside of the family home. I often wonder if the memories I hold are from genuine memory retention or whether in fact they are events, over the years, that I've been told about or have seen on the old VHS (remember those) when reminiscing with my family as I grew up. One thing I do remember and still feel from my time growing up though, is the pain of being bullied; the feeling of being alone and upset at never being good enough for anyone and never fitting in, or never being surrounded by friends like the other children in my class. I was always the odd one out; the one sitting on his own; the one who walked home alone and never had anyone call for him.

Growing up on a quiet, beautiful road in the North East of England had its advantages. I was able to enjoy playing with my cars in the front garden or the back garden. I had friendly, older neighbours, who always spoke to me if they saw me, and I was safe enough to cycle my bike around the block if I felt brave enough.

The disadvantages for me were that the street also had a lot of other children; some older than me but mostly my age or a little younger. They all generally had a good relationship with each other – good old British summers were spent by them playing bulldog in the street or hide-and-seek for hours on end. I used to watch them through the window from dawn till dusk, enjoying the outdoors, only briefly disappearing when the calls from their parents echoed down the street. 'TEAAAAA!' parents would shout – and without question, one of them would respond to their mother's call and flee home to throw the food down their neck, before returning to the outdoors to be with their friends.

I remember going outside a few times, when I'd pluck up the courage, to see if I could play too. I was usually ignored, which was hard and I always wondered why. So instead, I'd just stand in my driveway or by my wall to keep out of their way, but try to have some enjoyment myself at watching them have fun. Sometimes, I did get to play and it was amazing. The feeling of being involved was elating and euphoric.

I remember one day I went and sat on my front wall. After a few hours, someone asked if I wanted to play. I was dubious – this had happened before and it was usually to try to draw me in to then pick on me. I'd been tripped up, pushed off my bike, pushed over a wall, punched, kicked and shoved. They used to have a game within a game. There were even times when they'd invite me to play hide-and-seek – they'd all go hide, or so I thought – but in fact they'd go to someone's garden and leave me looking for them whilst they played elsewhere without me. I remember looking for them once and finding them all playing football in someone's garden. I just ran home crying because I'd been so foolish again.

However, this time, I didn't need to be dubious – they must have had an epiphany because they were treating me like anyone else. We played for hours, in and out of each other's gardens playing hide-and-seek, capture the flag, British bulldog. I remember coming in that evening smelling of the outdoors, needing a good shower – but being absolutely high on life. It was the one and only time I remember this happening.

The good times were rare; most of the time I was an outsider, for no known reason to me. I spent years trying to understand what it was about me that people didn't like. From school to the street I lived on, other children just generally tried to hurt me, through their words or their actions. Bizarre really, because I'd never have hurt any of them. I remember once having a conversation with a primary school teacher about other children and especially those who hurt me. I don't recall why but I told her, 'I don't know why they hurt me. If they were on the side of a cliff and needed help up – I'd hold on and never let go and pull them up to safety.' I told the same thing to a peer of mine within the class, who responded, 'Even though they're always horrible to you?' And I said, 'Yes, I'd have to help them.'

Despite my lack of relationships with my peers and being very isolated and lonely, I always had an indescribable connection with others, children and adults, which I never understood growing up. I could tell if they were upset, hurt, happy, withdrawn. I noticed subtle changes in their behaviours and their moods. I remember often asking people if they were ok for them to reply with, 'Yes, thank you', only for them to be off sick the next day.

I could talk to adults on a deeper level than to my peers and found that sometimes, adults even confided in me as a young teen. Not to an unprofessional or unacceptable level, you understand, but on a personal level. They knew I was mature enough to chat openly. Whilst, through years of bullying, I was very shy and reserved and would happily sit quietly reading a book, I was also very polite and pleasant and would talk to people.

My grandma used to work in an office block as a cleaner. On a Saturday, she was given permission by her boss to take me with her to work. I used to sit in the kitchen whilst she cleaned and then we'd go and do her shopping in the afternoon before heading home. I felt very grown up and mature being able to go to a big office block and sit in the kitchen. I sometimes got funny looks and I knew what they were thinking: 'Why is he sitting there? He can only be ten. Who's he with?' But they soon got to know who I was and would start to say hello.

I remember one lady, called Lorna. She would always say hello to me and was always telling me how lovely my gran was. We once sat in the kitchen whilst she had lunch and she began talking to me, just about general stuff. I remember asking her if she was ok and the nervous feeling I had with saying to her, 'Excuse me for seeming rude, but you really don't seem yourself today.' She was always a bubbly character, laughing a lot and smiling loads. This day was different.

After she'd looked at me with a mixture of shock and confusion, she replied, 'Well, actually, Mike, my dog died yesterday and it's upset me a little. But thank you for asking. You're very kind. I can't believe you noticed that.'

We didn't dwell much on it – but I expressed how sorry I was and I think, if I remember correctly, I drew her a picture of a dog and gave it to her before my gran and I left for the afternoon's shopping.

Moving on to secondary school and later in my teens, I always had a knack for understanding people. I started to realise I was an amazing judge of character and could tell you a lot about a person from seeing them physically, in a photo or even from reading their 'bio' on social media. I always felt you can tell a lot about a person by the way they look or the way they write. It became scarily accurate on too many occasions. By secondary, I had two friends in the school: Sean and Jonathan. I still speak to Sean to this day and he's one of my closest life-long friends. As we've grown, Sean has asked me on several occasions what I think about various people. Whether he's curious or has a genuine belief that I'm accurate, I don't know – but he saw the gift in me, I like to believe.

When I was midway through secondary school, I had an awful time. My mum was having difficulties in her marriage, which was obviously affecting me at home. I had upcoming examinations and the stress that came with them. I was being bullied quite intensively around Year 9. Previous years it was the same stuff, different year group – but from Year 9, for a good year and a half it was very intense. I felt like I had no friends. I did have friends, two of them, but to me it felt like I was so lonely, so excluded from everything. I was nervous in corridors; I was particularly nervous in P.E. as I got bullied in changing-rooms, pushed around, my bag stolen from me, and no one could do anything. I had people attempt to fight me on my way to my grandma's after school. I tried to avoid it on several occasions, and often went the long way home, sometimes an extra 15 minutes out of my way to avoid people. I even waited back after school for a full hour one night to avoid a particular individual, who was fucking horrible to me at every opportunity. He made my life absolute hell. I knew deep down his insecurities about his own severe obesity, ginger hair, terrible attitude, lack of compassion and lack of academic ability were the reason for his jealous behaviour resulting in him targeting me, but why me? I had no issue with him. I didn't see him for everything he was physically. His hair was ginger and he was overweight, but so what? Those things mattered to others, but not to me. I knew what it was like to be treated differently. He was just another boy in my year – yet to him, I was a threat. He absolutely hated me and I knew it.

I never really understood why people felt I was a threat. I used to believe I was just an easy target but, over time, I've learnt that bullies are vile individuals who are just jealous and threatened by you in some way. They'd laugh if you said that to them – because of course, they don't believe it's true. But it is. They're jealous of something, whether they like to admit it or not.

I never understood it because, well, I was just less than average. I wasn't sporty or cool. I didn't have loads of friends, or posh clothes, or expensive trainers. I didn't care about those things. I had bog standard blond hair with, at one point, circle glasses and an overbite. I wasn't overweight, I wasn't skinny. I wasn't athletic but I wasn't a couch potato. I didn't struggle in everything academically, apart from mathematics – I was literally the Milkybar kid. I was nothing special. I never had girlfriends and I didn't really exist in the classroom. What was there to be jealous of?

The rough time I had led to some, at the time, odd events occurring. I remember one day sitting in my grandma's house after school and I just started uncontrollably crying. She immediately comforted me and asked me to explain what was wrong. I just kept telling her I didn't know – and I genuinely didn't know. I knew I felt really shit. I used to walk to school feeling sad, leave school feeling sad. I remember a time when I just didn't smile anymore, at anything.

A few days later and my grandma checked in on me.

'How're you feeling at the moment?' I remember her asking.

'I don't really know, I just feel sad all the time,' I replied.

It was then that I very first heard the term, depression: 'I think you've got a touch of depression, son,' she told me, with sadness in her eyes.

Time passed and, to be fair, I probably went up and down when I look back. Exams take over, people grow up – we move on from school and the people in it, thank God. The term depression never hit me again until I was in my twenties, when a vile individual targeted me in a professional setting. My offer of help and being taken up on that offer made him seethe with jealousy. I saw the jealousy in his eyes, I could 'feel' it pumping around his veins. The way he spoke to me, the way he looked at me and the way he spoke about me to others just oozed hatred and jealousy. It was a really tough time for me. I had to second-guess everything I did to protect myself, and I had to live every day not knowing what was coming next. This led to a severe bout of depression and anxiety; I even planned ways to end my life, my misery and my sadness.

This was the peak of every bit of abuse I'd suffered at the hands of others. I'd had enough.

Through this and various other difficulties, I visited the doctor, who confirmed that I was indeed suffering with anxiety and depression. I was placed on medication and the dosage was increased to maximum levels very quickly. I started therapy, which was very difficult to engage with, but eventually I began to see some light at the end of a very dark tunnel. This wasn't easy, I might add. It took a lot of hard work, a lot of changes, a lot of soul-searching and a very unhealthy weight loss. At 6 foot 2 inches tall and around 25 years old, I was down to around 9 stone in weight. I passed out several times in secret and ate very little.

How on earth it happened, I'll never know, but it was then I met my, now, wife. Her energy was positive, calm, reassuring and understanding. I saw genuineness in her that I'd rarely seen, but pain at the same time. I saw independence and strength, but vulnerability and insecurity. Through discussions and friendship, we grew into a couple. She is beautiful, kind, caring, considerate and independent. Her strength and her own wisdom helped me grow and develop. We laugh together like I've never done with anyone before and I love her more every day. With her, I flourished into a different person. Through her energy, I became a stronger, more confident and independent person. I still had lots of work to do – but I had enough to rise above what I was going through and heal. She was my saviour.

Over time, my personal strength developed. My knowledge, experience and understanding of mental illness also developed, to the point where I felt I had to give back. The way people work, the things that make them tick; my ability to listen and connect with people on different levels, and to understand, were all factors that led to me starting my brand, 'Mike Meets Life'. It began as a way of talking about the way I met life. The way I flourished and developed. The way mental illness and the factors that had affected my life had changed me and had helped me to understand that, in the words of Rocky Balboa, 'Life isn't all sunshine and rainbows'.

I knew I had to give back to people; I had to help others, to help them find light like I had. To help them overcome issues so they never had to feel alone, like I'd done in the past at times, so low that the option of death by suicide was a serious contender. I want everyone to know that it's ok to not be ok, but that no one is ever alone.

By 2020, I'd developed some amazing knowledge through learning. I'd become a trained crisis counsellor, a therapeutic counsellor and CBT therapist and I was thirsty for more. Mental illness doesn't switch on and off. You have it and you will battle forever. You don't stop experiencing negative situations but you do learn how to respond to them better. I wanted to share my knowledge and help others.

One sunny day, a beautiful soul and friend, Alison, reached out to me. I'd made a comment on her Facebook post and, without realising, had been negative about myself. We spoke on the phone for some time and Alison explained that she had been guided to reach out to me, to help me and take me to the next step in my journey. Even after that 30-minute phone call, I was so motivated. I knew what my vision was but had never acknowledged it. Alison knew she'd been guided to me and knew how I was ready; how this was my time.

Through a number of conversations with my now mentor and friend, Angel Alison, I came to realise that my ability to understand and connect with people on a deeper level was down to energy and it made sense. Alison helped me come to terms with the fact that I was reading energy. That I was right to question the niggle in the back of my mind all this time about, 'How do I do that? How do I just know stuff about people?'. It isn't just a weird coincidence I know things about people so very quickly: I read energy and I'm guided. I'm guided to people, to answer questions they may have; guided to information about them so that I'm tooled up to support them in a way they deserve, in a way that the Universe wants them to be helped so they're on the path that was made for them. It was a revelation. An answer, if you like, for all the questions I'd had over my time. This isn't a special gift from God – in fact, I'm an atheist, but I am connected to the world around us. The energy is readable if you know how and there's an answer for everything if you ask in the right way.

This is just the start of my journey, but I'm excited, motivated, inspired and energised at what is still to come. I have a passion to help people. My journey is to help people. Alison and Julie, two dear friends, have been guided to support me to achieve these goals. We all need mentors to bring us into the world of the unknown. I'm here now and what a beautiful family it is. What a beautiful side of the world I've found. A place I'm accepted and welcomed with open arms and where I am, for the first time in forever, valued for all that I am.

www.mikemeetslife.co.uk
mike@fairbrother.me
FACEBOOK: @mikemeetslife
INSTAGRAM: @mikemeetslife
TWITTER: @mikemeetslife
PINTEREST: @mikemeetslife

One of the lessons Empaths learn is being 'open to receive'; they constantly give to the world. Once Serendipity did just that, she realised what a gift it was to be on the receiving end after a period of great personal challenges.

HOW I LEARNT TO ACCEPT HELP AND LET GO OF CONTROL

Serendipity Ruth

We all need help sometimes. Yet it's one of the hardest things to do, to ask for it or to accept it. We are bombarded in modern Western society with messages about 'earning' and 'deserving', as well as moral tales about greed and laziness, those 'on the take'.

When we're struggling, we do our best to get by and make things work; to succeed. Asking for or taking help can feel like failure, when it really shouldn't be seen that way.

Those of us on a spiritual path, which really is all of us in truth, experience life lessons. It can be a gruelling way of life, from one lesson to the next. That's why I want to share this lesson of mine with you now.

I wear many hats in life. Amongst them, I'm a tarot consultant, psychic, and spiritual healer. I am also a lecturer in Psychology.

In the beginning of January last year, life was going pretty darn well. New year had been lovely, spent with my fiancé in my cosy home, with my pets. We were planning a spring wedding to coincide with our fourth anniversary together. I was enjoying my work and caring for my partner's mother and her menagerie of animals, including llamas and sheep. My fiancé was a man I'd known since my teens in high school. I knew him very well and we got on brilliantly. No rows or drama, we were best friends.

On 4th January a bombshell landed that shattered everything. A bolt of lightning. I saw The Tower card in tarot. A bolt from the blue, out of my control that destroyed life as I knew it. I cannot explain the events here, because I have to protect the vulnerable. What I can say is that, if you can imagine the worst thing that you could find out about your partner, the most unexpected and unforgivable thing, then you would not be far from my reality that day. I wasn't the victim in this story but I was collateral damage.

Everything changed in that revelation. My relationship with my children, my lifestyle and, well, my life. I lost my partner. I had no choice but to immediately and totally separate myself. I've never spoken to him since. Again, no details, but he was arrested and went to prison. He has to be dead to me. This was a bereavement although at the time I didn't recognise it as such. It was extraordinarily traumatic and the emotional and psychological effects have continued to show themselves as time has gone on.

Over the next three months, I was to lose my job, my income, my car, my home, my pets, some friends and family, and almost my sanity.

I refused to become bitter and hardened and I was determined to cope. Coping had got me into trouble in the past. I had always been the one that copes; the fixer of other people's problems. I'd learnt the art of sticking plasters over things and moving on. I'd never asked for or taken help from others.

After this horrendous outcome to a love relationship, you'd think that I would have given them a wide berth, but I'm a romantic and I had hope. I'd begun talking to a man online. Just talking. It helped me believe in a light at the end of the tunnel. I rarely do readings for myself but in the midst of so much chaos, it had seemed a good idea. This man was The Magician to me in my reading. It made me a little wary of him. In romantic terms, I worried that he couldn't be trusted. Actually, this certainly turned out to be true, but that is a whole other story!

I'd decided on a new life and fresh start. Early March, I got myself a job as a part-time teacher in a girls' boarding school. It wasn't great pay and didn't begin until September but it was a start. I'd been asking my guides for signs to guide me. Standing in Malvern in February I'd thought, 'I'd like to live here.' When I saw the job in my subject in Malvern advertised the following week, I knew it was mine.

Next thing was to move there. As these plans were forming, I was without income. I was driving a car I'd bought from my ex's mother and paying for the insurance monthly, but it was in her name. We'd become very close and

I regarded her as a close friend. Then I received a casual text message to say that she'd cancelled my car insurance. I didn't know what to do. I had to find somewhere to live and to move out of my place. I needed work. I needed transport.

By this time, I'd been having occasional phone calls with the Magician man but we hadn't yet met. When he called that evening, I couldn't contain my tears. I'd tried so hard to cope but I was defeated now. He asked if he could help me. I said no. Of course I said no. I didn't take help and from a stranger? No. 'What else will you do?' he asked me. I didn't know. He insured my car to keep me on the road. No strings, and I knew I had to trust.

From that moment came more help. I found that I could rent a room in a lovely house in Malvern for £500 a month including bills. I had no money. My first two months' rent came as long-term, interest-free loans from two amazing friends. Not the friends you might expect to help and both offered. I had no choice but to accept. I was taking help and it didn't feel like failure. Actually, it felt really good to know that people I never expected to care, really did. I felt loved and I needed that.

I had no income of any kind from January until October 2019. I was helped a lot. I went to a food bank once and that was one of the most wonderful experiences. A gentleman volunteer with such kind eyes went to such trouble to find food to meet my dietary requirements. At the end, he put in some bags of Mini Eggs, as it was around Easter. He explained, as tears rolled down my cheeks, that we all need a treat.

My car was eventually taken off me by my ex's mother, to give to him when he came out of prison. I tried to fight that and perhaps I should have stood my ground, but sometimes you have to let go. Maybe I didn't need the trappings of the old me. The Magician gave me £500 to buy a car to tide me over. Here was a man who was a typical magician actually. He could weave magic to make everything ok. He was charming and charismatic in an unusual way. Not to be trusted romantically and I certainly should have paid more heed to my cards on that. No regrets, though. He taught me a lot and his generosity, along with that of my other friends and that food bank, saved my life. I have no regrets about anything that happened in 2019. Events and experiences have changed me as a person. Somehow, they've changed my very DNA. I've had experiences and met people, been to places that I wouldn't have done. It's all good in the end.

I knew by autumn that I was being taught a lesson: you don't have to cope alone. It's not failure to ask for help. You're deserving. We all are.

There were a few more curve balls from 2019 yet, and, after dodging some of them, in October I had a true meltdown; the breakdown I maybe should have had in January. Unable to keep my home because of my low wage, I was to become homeless again. My ex had come out of prison, earlier than expected, and I was scared. I was only able to eat because of help I'd received. Life was tough. I had to go off work sick. I was a mess.

I packed up and went to stay in the home of the Magician in Wales. He was out of the country. I had at this point lost all control of my life. I could barely function. Slowly, I got myself together, meditating, taking country walks and talking to my guides.

One day driving along, daydream meditating, a voice said to me, 'You need to meet Mark.' I joked, 'Well, come on then, where is he?'

About two weeks later, I met Mark. He was a native of the English border town that I'd decided I wanted to make my home. I don't remember what card my tarot deck gave him actually. I could make it up but I won't. I remember seeing his vulnerability and past hurt but also the love that he could give and needed. The first week we met, I told him I had to move out of where I was staying as soon as possible. He told me that as long as he knew me, I'd never have nowhere to go. He didn't believe in tarot etc., until I told him what I'd seen about him. He was converted, of course. I didn't completely move in with him straightaway but I know now, six months on, that I've found home. I'm happy with a man very like me in many ways. Will it last forever? I'd like it to but I'm not afraid anymore. What will be will be, and it'll be right.

Once I changed spiritually and psychologically to accept help, and stopped trying so hard to control everything myself, help and opportunities have just kept coming.

Take last night, for example. I was selling some costume jewellery to a buyer in Germany. I messaged him to ask if he was definitely going to send the payment, in order that I could budget. He was very apologetic; hadn't realised I actually needed the money. I explained that I wanted to treat myself to something and, as I'm on a low income, this sale would allow that. So it wasn't exactly 'need'. He kindly went straight to the bank to transfer it.

'Is it enough?' he asked.

'Of course, it's what we agreed,' I replied.

'But if you need more, just ask,' he said. *'If you ever need any more help or support, just ask me, don't be shy.'* The words of one very kind individual and in them, I hear the Universe.

serendipityrutheast@gmail.com
INSTAGRAM: @ruthburt

Awakenings to Soul Purpose

Many of our authors have experienced loss, abuse, and pain, yet 'we all rise'.
When you choose to look at these tumultuous times as 'lessons learnt',
chances are your gifts will surface, bringing you joy and fulfilment.

An apt title for a beautiful soul who chose a nursing career to help those in need,
particularly end of life. Di Evans is a natural healer and has developed her psychic
and healing gifts with courses and practice.

THIS IS ME

Diane Evans

When entering a world of spiritual Awakening, awareness and psychic knowing, many questions regularly and normally get asked:

What is a spiritual Awakening? What makes people psychic? How do I know if I'm a reluctant psychic or not? And there are many more questions like this.

Do any of these resonate with you? If so, read my short resumé of my own spiritual journey; its highs and lows, the people I've met along the way who have inspired and encouraged me and, yes, even my reluctance, self-doubt and disbelief.

Where do I start? Probably at the very beginning, you might say, but defining that is somewhat difficult. I like to think and believe that we are all souls in a human body, as opposed to humans with a soul. I believe our souls are born awake with an innate psychic ability and awareness, as well as a spiritual purpose; each of us having our own soul contracts, if you like. This all sounds fairly uncomplicated and straightforward but – and for me it's a huge but – the human existence throws a vortex of differing energies, belief systems, cultures and religion into the mix. All of these combined with what I have come to know as the ego and, dare I say, our past lives, can throw us into psychic turmoil.

Human existence itself is constantly looking for ways to challenge us and derail us from our spiritual paths and purpose. I believe that the ego and 'life' can leave us in a push–pull cycle, creating situations where, at times, we are very in tune with our souls, while at other times, we are thrown into depths of uncertainty, disbelief and even despair about our existence. This is all NORMAL. Try to think of your journey like that of the butterfly's. We are born as the caterpillar – all different types, some smooth and long, others fluffy and short. (Haha, I wonder which you will liken yourself to? I like to think of myself as one of the fluffy ones.) Imagine then being eager to explore Mother Earth and all she has to offer: the beautiful colours, sounds, textures, love and positivity.

Then, suddenly, you are faced with cruelty, negativity and loss. This is the point when you retract, becoming more reluctant. Your faith and belief systems falter, causing you to cocoon (what I call our comfort zone). And this is where some of us may stay for long periods, under the illusion that our cocoon is a safe haven and the place to be. Yet this in itself denies us the opportunity to awaken fully to become beautiful butterflies, spreading our wings to take flight and grow, encouraging and inspiring others along the way. Some of us will prepare to take flight, falter and recede back into our cocoons, an occurrence that can happen many times at different points in our lives.

All of this I have discussed so far has relevance to my story. This is where my own spiritual journey comes in and why I chose to call it 'This Is Me'. Some of you will be aware of the film *The Greatest Showman*; it's one of my absolute favourites. The song entitled 'This Is Me' defines how beautifully unique we all are, despite our race, beliefs, abilities and disabilities. It enables us the space to see our own inhibitions and afflictions alongside our qualities and areas of expertise. It demonstrates that, by supporting and connecting with each other, how amazing our journeys truly can be. In order to protect ourselves from becoming lost or broken souls, we need to learn and be brave enough to rise above the negativity, cruelty, fear, loss and feelings of being let down. I firmly believe that we really have got this, even in this time of fear with the

COVID-19 virus, and I know that if ever there was a time to truly go within and awaken our souls to their purpose and contracts, this is it.

Right from being a young child, I suppose I always felt a little different, struggling at times with friendships and not quite fitting in. I was very skinny and shy, with pigtails, and was often teased for this 'affliction' (which is why I am now a fluffy caterpillar but, oh, to be that skinny now LOL!). I was often left out at playtimes, a fact that used to hurt and upset me. I would wander around on my own, talking to my 'imaginary friend' and watching the rock lizards and bugs (I lived in Australia as a child). I have always had an affinity with nature and animals and, on my journey, have discovered that I am in fact an Earth elemental, which explains a lot.

At night, while tucked up in bed, I always had a cry to God and asked for 'friends' to be kinder tomorrow. Then, when settling to sleep, I would regularly see many faces appear before me. Not knowing what this was at the time, I used to hide under my bedsheets, feeling scared. I was always told it was in my mind, just my imagination and to stop being silly. Little did I know that all of these early experiences were damaging my self-esteem and confidence, leading me to lose faith; to feel that God wasn't there for me; he didn't seem to be answering my prayers. I'd go as far as to say that they were in fact shaping my spiritual journey, guiding me to my own cocoon; the beginnings of peeling layers from my soul. Of course, now as an adult, I know that my soul, before being reborn, had made the decision to enter this human body and live these experiences. They were all leading me to my path of enlightenment.

When I was a teenager, we moved to England; a chance for new beginnings and friendships. By now I was very firmly tucked up in my cocoon. I would say that at this point I didn't really have any religious or spiritual beliefs, nor did I feel the need for any during these years. I was only focused on making and maintaining friendships, no matter what the cost. I would be the one who would act the fool for attention in lessons, actively seeking out detentions and reprimand, a small price to pay for the friends that I gained. This behaviour saw a drop in my academic achievements, to the despair of my parents, who felt at the time I wouldn't make anything of myself.

Somehow I pulled it back, gained my O levels (showing my age now!) and secured a place at my local college, where I met my wonderful husband; my soulmate.

Life continued, seeing me achieve the start of my nursing career, and engagement to my soulmate followed by our amazing wedding day. Twelve months later I became pregnant and had my firstborn son (Tom). This, I have to say, was one of the most incredible feelings of absolute, unconditional love I have experienced; that moment when I first saw him and held him, so overwhelmingly beautiful. Dare I say that I felt truly blessed even though I was still tucked up in that cocoon? After all, why would I want to leave this safe haven? Everything was perfect as it was… for now.

This is where I want to add one of those 'strange' spiritual moments that at that time I never realised or noticed. At three months pregnant with Tom, I had a sudden longing to visit Stonehenge, somewhere I hadn't even previously thought about. On arrival, I was awestruck and had a sense of belonging; of calmness even. That's where it became psychically strange: Tom was born on the winter solstice, which is linked to Stonehenge, and I now call him my solstice baby. He was born four days early so his soul was determined to arrive on the solstice! Tom himself is on his own spiritual journey and embracing his psychic awareness. He is one of the people who has supported and encouraged me on my own psychic journey.

In my 26th year, everything was just perfect. Little did I know that one of the most painful and soul-destroying experiences was about to be etched into my life. A dreaded phone call late at night, the long journey to the hospital but all too late, with no time for goodbyes: the news of the loss of my beloved dad aged 55.

Daddy's girl, his girl, his one. How could this be? Why, why, *why*? Everything crashed around me leaving me enveloped in loss. If anything, this is when I went deeper into my cocoon. There was no room for anything psychic or spiritual, the hurt running too deep. I remember the funeral day filling me with dread; the thought of my dad being placed in the ground, lying there cold and alone. I was so far away from believing in anything spiritual and couldn't see that this was only his body being laid to rest, not the essence or soul of who he was.

In the midst of all this, I was so unaware that this significant life event was actually going to be my first spiritual Awakening. My psychic consciousness was soon to be reignited; I was about to be launched from my cocoon whether I was prepared for it or not.

A couple of weeks after Dad's passing, I stood by Tom's cot in the middle of the night, awoken by him crying. I was comforting him and trying to settle him back to sleep when suddenly the strongest sweet cigar smell filled the room. It was so distinct and powerful that I couldn't mistake it or think that I was imagining it. (Being able to smell the spiritual world is known as the psychic ability of clairalience.) And I just knew that this was my dad coming to see if Tom was ok. I could feel it in my gut. (There are some words or terms that describe our psychic abilities and they are known as the clairs. This sense of feeling is termed clairsentience.)

The smell remained until I spoke out to my dad and said, 'I know you're here, Dad. It's ok. Tom is fine, he's just woken up.' As soon as I'd said those words, the smell dissipated.

This was the first of many visits from my dad, most often around Tom. I began to call him Tom's Guardian Angel, especially after the night when I was fast asleep and Dad came to me in my dreams. He grabbed my arm and was shaking, saying, 'Wake up! Tom, Tom. You need to wake up.' I woke with a start and sure enough, Tom was struggling to breathe. He was having the first of many what we found out later were asthma attacks.

This went on for a long time until one night in my dreams I dreamt that I was heading out of the front door but had to return to the house for something. Dad was sitting on my settee and smiled at me saying, 'I'm fine, I'm ok now.' I hugged him and woke up crying. This was the last time I was aware of Dad visiting for a while.

I might have thought that was it psychically for me – the visits from Dad because he was just that: my dad. My soul had other ideas. Those visits were the keystone or pivotal point of my psychic awareness. I started to have prophetic dreams about places and people I didn't know, only to find that either the next day or over the coming days, in the news, the events I had dreamt about had taken place; a thing that, back then, filled me with fear and dread. I could never understand why I would be shown these things if I couldn't influence or stop them from happening.

I also began to have what I now call my 'dream thing', where I would be aware of 'someone' coming in through my front door and up my stairs, until I could feel they were standing right next to my bed. During this experience, I would have a vibration sensation coursing through my body and ears. I was soon to become aware that each time this happened, I would receive news within a week of someone I knew passing to spirit world. I was never made aware of who it would be and when I reflect on it now, I feel it was a way of preparing me because we are not allowed to influence or change fate. In all of this, there were a few times where I began to think I was weird or that I was going crazy. This was when I started to tell my husband when I had the prophetic dreams and my dream thing. I so needed someone else to know and verify with me that this was real and there was a pattern to it. He always joked with me, asking why I got the Angel of Death instead of the lottery numbers.

Bit by bit, my psychic clairs were being awoken, but I had no understanding of this fact. This certainly was beginning to feel like a crazy journey. I had no control over it and little understanding of why it was happening or where it was taking me. Then along came son number two, Andrew; again, the most beautiful feeling of unconditional love the moment I met him. There were no Stonehenge moments with him, no solstice baby, but right from a very young age I knew he was psychically aware. He began to tell me about a little boy who visited him at night and how he liked the boy but the big ones scared him. He struggled to sleep in his own room and would wake up crying, saying the big ones had come for the little boy. We even set up a video camera to try to capture anything, but interestingly, at the point he called for us the camera stopped recording!

A funny little anecdote linked to this was one night when my husband was out. Andrew again woke tearful, so I carried him downstairs. Now, our pet rabbit lived in his hutch down the garden and I told Andrew I was just going to take him his food and he should stand by the door for me. As I headed across the lawn, Andrew shouted out very loudly, 'Mommy!'

I froze, heart in my throat, turned around not wanting to look in case I saw something. To my relief and current amusement, he pointed out that I had dropped some of the cabbage leaves on the lawn! Nothing spiritual-related with this one.

Another moment I recall was a time when I 'dreamt' that a neighbour's brother came to me in my dreams, telling me he was dying: it was his time. I woke up and looked at the clock and it was 2am. Sure enough, the next day my neighbour informed me that her brother had passed away in the night – at 2am! This was just another psychic experience that has completely blown me away.

The next wow moment happened when I was with Andrew in the November. He very sadly had lost a friend to spirit world and we sat up late one evening on his bed, talking about happy memories. Andrew told me that he asked every night if his friend was ok and happy where he was. I heard a voice in my left ear (I now call this my psychic ear) say, 'Yes, I am happy. I watch you on your scooter at the skate park.' I passed this on to Andrew but was thinking at the time, I can't prove to him that I heard that voice. At which point we both heard a rustling, fluttering sound.

What we saw took my breath away. Perched on top of a tiger's eye egg crystal by Andrew's bed was a butterfly flapping its wings! This was winter; the windows hadn't been open and the fact it appeared at that precise moment on top of his crystal was all the confirmation we needed. I will never forget that moment.

Another experience was one day when Tom and I were sitting in the conservatory talking about all things spiritual, saying how strange it all was and wasn't it amazing when signs appeared. Literally as we were talking, six white doves flew across the garden and landed on our roof. We went outside and stood looking at them, unable to believe what we were seeing. They stayed for a while and then disappeared. No one in our area kept doves and we have never seen them again.

I would also like to share with you a time when I dreamt about one of my spirit animal guides, my wolf. He sat at my kitchen door inside the conservatory and I asked him whether, if he had really visited me, he could leave me a sign in the morning. To my amazement, when I opened the door, there on the floor was a pure white feather, exactly where I'd seen him sitting! I thanked him for this.

There are so many moments to tell but I have selected just a few for this story.

I want to mention too that most but not all of my experiences tended to happen in the night and in my dreams. I have learnt since that, in our dream state, our energy vibration increases and spirit world lower their vibration plane, allowing us to connect. We let go of inhibitions in our dream state and are therefore less likely to block visitations and messages. As I was in the early Awakening stage, I do believe this is why these experiences happened in this manner.

As I'm writing and recapturing all these moments, I pause for a moment and wonder if any of you can relate to all or some of my story? Have you had any strange experiences like these or are yours slightly different or even very different? Where are you on your Awakening?

The next chapter of my journey was when I decided I had to find an understanding of why this awareness was happening. I knew by now that I was definitely psychically aware and was sitting on the edge of my cocoon, but was not sure how to use or understand it. I now wanted to begin to take flight; to be the butterfly. This was where my psychic development really started.

Until this point in my life, I had never had a spiritual reading, but with both Tom (now a young adult) and myself having an itch to try this out and see what it was all about, we literally stumbled across a wonderful, compassionate lady called Jacqui Brown, who ended up being my first Psychic teacher and has remained a close friend ever since. We found her on her Facebook page called, 'Hello from Heaven'. We contacted her, booked, and waited nervously for our first reading. While waiting for this reading, my beautiful niece, Laura had started telling me I needed to develop my psychic ability. She has always felt this is where I was meant to be and supported and pushed me to go with it.

The reading was amazing. My dad came through and gave me lots of evidence and advice. At the end of the reading, we chatted with Jacqui, and I told her some of my experiences. I do believe in right place right time. Jacqui was actually starting a beginners' psychic development group in the next two weeks! Tom and I were in and have never looked back. We had so much fun and learnt about everything from mediumship to psychometry, auras and meditation, to name a few topics. Meditation has to be one of the most important things in spiritual development, along with practice. It didn't come easy to me at first. My mind was all over the place. But now I can completely zone and connect with spirit guides and loved ones, or use it just to relax.

I was soon to find out that synchronicities and intuition were about to play a big part in my life. Luckily for me, I was now at a stage where I trusted and believed in these things. I started to see posts about Reiki appearing on my social media, and around this time met a lovely like-minded soul while on Indian Head Massage training. They told me all about the healing power of Reiki and how incredible it was. I had started to see double numbers like 11:11 (the numbers of the Angels) all the time, everywhere I went. Then, in one of my meditations, I received a message that I was a healer and I needed to step into my purpose. I knew then that Reiki was going to be part of my life.

When I met my Master Reiki Teacher, Alison Ward, I knew it was meant to be. It has been the catalyst setting me on the path to enlightenment, my soul purpose and my higher consciousness; not forgetting the absolute pure love and energy of the Angels. Alison is known as Angel Alison and this is so true: Angel by name, Angel by nature. Such a beautiful soul with a pure energy. Alison told me as I was being attuned to Reiki that 'Reiki is the glue that brings everything together'. How true this is.

I have been blessed with so many wonderful Reiki clients where I have been able to channel the universal healing energy. Reiki has enabled me to provide both physical and emotional healing, as well as to bring comfort into their lives with messages from loved ones to be conveyed to them.

I have listened to my inner voice and guidance in setting up my own development groups, so that I could share all the things I've learnt and help others on their path. The first group was meant to start in the January but had to be postponed and the actual first session just happened to fall on a start date of my dad's birthday. This was the affirmation I needed to say, 'Go with this, you are in the flow.' Being able to see others finding their own enlightenment and spiritual connections has been one of the most amazing things for me. I have so much gratitude for all those who joined me, for trusting in me and continuing to develop themselves.

I do want to share a funny moment from the classes and, while it is a bit naughty, I'm sharing because laughter is one of the best ways to raise our energy vibration. Spirit world live in a higher vibration to us and, when sitting in circles or development groups, this is important. It was on the week we were looking at chakras (which I love – colour is so important and again has an energy vibration of its own). As we progressed through each one, we arrived at the sacral chakra, of which one of its functions is around our sexual organs and creativity. One of the group members shouted out, 'Oh, does that mean you'll know who's having sex or not?' The whole group collapsed and roared with laughter, as I'm sure you can imagine.

We also had a funny moment when one of the group found it almost impossible to sit still and concentrate in normal circumstances. So, to ask her to sit for ten minutes in meditation was probably asking for trouble. We had the incense and candles lit, closed our eyes and took a few deep breaths. The music began gently and all was well – until some gentle pan pipes played out, at which point she suddenly began sniggering under her breath; her whole body was shaking with laughter. We paused the meditation and she said all she could see was the advert on TV where the dog danced to the pan pipes. Again, it's so important to embrace these moments of bringing in higher energy.

I feel I have come a long way on my psychic, spiritual journey. I have most certainly evolved from being an almost broken, lost soul, full of self-doubt, fear and disbelief, unable to leave my cocoon. My soul purpose and passion have been ignited.

I am now just at the start of another Awakening, after collapsing 12 months ago in the middle of nowhere with my amazing husband, who managed to get the paramedics to me. I am eternally grateful to both my husband and those paramedics. I'm not sure what happened on that day. I just remember hearing the most beautiful music and feeling like I was floating into a brilliant-white tunnel with four people at the end. The sense of calm was like nothing I had ever felt, so intense and warm. But that's a whole other story!

That day jolted me into realigning and going within again, and I am waiting in anticipation and hope for what this Awakening is bringing me; opportunities like this one to write and share my story, spreading love and light, sharing messages of comfort and healing. Maybe an ascension? I have already started having dreams with messages about our elders, the angelic realms, rites of passage and soul success. Boy, am I feeling ready for this – I'm not stopping here! I might have started out as a reluctant psychic but I have now embraced and stepped into who I truly am.

If I can leave you with anything from the lessons I have learnt, it would be to say, still your minds; look for positives in everything, even on the stormy days. Carry out random acts of kindness, remembering that you may be that one person to be the light in someone else's life. Lift each other up in difficult times and give each other hope.

We are all on our own soul journeys, at different points, and I have experienced being well and truly embedded in my own cocoon. I have now left that place of 'safety', stepped out of my comfort zone, spread my wings and have never looked back. Take that leap of faith, listen to your intuition and don't be trapped listening to the human ego, which will always try to hold you back. I can promise you it won't be something you regret.

You too can confidently sing, 'THIS IS ME!'

Dianeevans4@aol.com
FACEBOOK: @dianeevans
FACEBOOK BUSINESS: @destiny-divine-healing
INSTAGRAM: @_diane_evans_

Conversing and connecting with spirits from a young age took Zoë Owl into formal psychic studies. She has spent her life developing her gift and embracing her free spirit. This wise owl gives you, dear reader, some valuable advice.

SPEAK TO SPIRIT

Zoë Owl

My rainbow warrior spirit and soul bravely made her entry into this current lifetime incarnation and into the womb of Mother Earth, deep in the southern hemisphere, over Mosi-oa-Tunya, which translates from local indigenous tribal language as '*the Smoke that always thunders*'. It was later renamed under colonialism and world-widely known as Victoria Falls, in Zimbabwe/Zambia. What a truly magnificent sight and magical portal of energy this breathtaking place of natural beauty is, and that's where I decided to land. I almost drowned in the rapid waterfalls, but that's a side-track story, of which there are many in the wild adventure that is my life. My first name, Zoë, actually means 'Life', by the way, in the Greek language. (I've also had past life incarnations in Atlantis around various Greek islands). As you can probably tell, I'm someone that many people call a 'worldish old soul', and a very indigenously tribal one at that!

When I was a small child, I would naturally and often converse with Spirit on a daily basis, on all matters and subjects of importance. One of my favourite places indoors where I could actually manage to get some peace in a busy, and often hectic, household of family members, was the downstairs toilet. I could safely lock the door and chat away freely in my toilet sanctuary that was my safe haven, and where I received my most welcomed confession blessings. You see, at Sunday school, our local vicar had literally thought of me as quite mad (probably due to too much meat just like Oliver Twist!). I'm sure that when I used to say things like, 'Whenever I want to chat to my mate, God, I just go talk to him on the loo', it got me into trouble. Eventually, our downstairs lavatory did in fact become my very own little self-designated church, where I was accepted when I was otherwise deemed too inappropriate for traditional Sunday service. My preferred Sunday school service was, however, singing and discussing astrology with my beloved maternal grandmother, herself a natural psychic, along with my mother and sister as well, on my feminine family side, so there is a direct family inherited lineage.

Growing up, I vividly remember my first animal spirit guide, who was a pure white Indian elephant, somewhat smaller than the African elephants I was more accustomed to, but still enormous to me as a tiny, mesmerised five-year-old. Noma was beautifully decorated and an enchanting soul. Her name was planted with African and Hawaiian origins, having root meaning in farming. She came in as my first fully conscious guide to gift me roots in the path I was walking in; to give me courage and comfort in equal measure that, despite what the other children in the school playground were saying and that they were laughing at me, she was my trusted first real friend. She showed me that with time, I could come to trust the animal shape-shifting I saw and can now regularly see in people and things; that I've seen in fact for my whole 45 years of sacred life so far. This helped me with subsequent bullying in attempts to try to shut me down and play my gifts down, as I quickly realised that not everyone can see, hear, sense, perceive or imagine the energies that I could, and still can to this very day. So I just adapted and quickly learnt to go within when conversing with them. I later learnt, however, as a young adult working in mental health as a qualified psychologist, that this was not acceptable in this arena either. 'Inner voices' were deemed to be an unwanted curse and an affliction to be medicated, rather than God or Great Spirit simply speaking back. So naturally, I gravitated towards working professionally with an African shaman, himself caught up in the psychiatric web system and labelled as 'schizophrenic' for hearing voices from Spirit. Together we worked on de-stigmatising those inner visions, bringing them out safely into the mainstream for them to be both creatively expressed and seen for what they truly are.

My most vivid and conscious Awakening as an adult happened to me at the life juncture point when I was 22 years old and living in Scotland. I'd gone on a pilgrimage upon graduating with my first degree, soul-searching and seeking to connect deeper with my paternal Celtic roots and to reclaim my pagan past life ancestry and history. I had also diligently learnt about the Buddhist philosophy and way of life, and how to meditate and chant, going on various retreats with the Brahma Kumaris and the Hare Krishna groups worldwide, reconnecting with my Buddhist and Hindu past life incarnations. This was a result of my clairaudiently hearing softly guided repeated words in my left ear: 'Meditate, meditate, meditate!' So I bravely took action and learnt to go within, and it has honestly been my most treasured game-changer life experience to date.

My Great Awakening took place in nature, around a stunning Scottish loch in the mountain range of the Glen Ochils, where I was living and working at Stirling University as a psychologist, whilst undertaking my psychology Master's degree. A life-changing experience happened to me there, which took me literally years to put into words, and this is the very first time I've actually written about it! I was walking and conversing with Spirit as I had so often done many times before, but this time was different. My consciousness flowed into other higher dimensions outside of the third dimension, where my feet were physically grounded in walking amongst the rocks and earth. My head and my heart brain literally went way beyond the clouds and I spoke with the weather and all manner of elemental spirits, as well as the Elohim angelic realm. They showed me exactly how interconnected everything was and how I'm a part of a greater whole, and that was my most mind-blowingly powerful introduction to oneness: a soul purpose I have actively lived and carried with me ever since that major Awakening download.

It wasn't until a few years later, when I went on a solo, walkabout, around-the-world travelling expedition for a few years, to discover who I really was and am, that I made more sense of it and took more meaning out of what I had so profoundly experienced that fateful day around the Scottish loch and mountains. In Aotearoa, Maori for 'land of the long white cloud', otherwise known as New Zealand, I encountered a Wahine Warrior Woman or Medicine Woman, and went deep into the Maldi caves and spoke to the glow worms. I went walkabout all over Australia with Aboriginal and Torres Strait Islanders, and it was then that it all became more clear: my journey; my purpose.

I was in Broome, in north western Australia, watching the outside opening of *The Rabbit Proof Fence*, the book made into a film about three Aboriginal girls of the stolen generation following their song-lines back home to their anxiously awaiting native mother. I watched, with Mother Nature's great atmospheric delights of geckos running up the outdoor screen, and the lead actress's Aboriginal grandfather singing out for his ancestors. I camped out under the stars at sacred sites like Uluru, Kata Tjuta (The Olgas), and these rites of passage then prepared me for my Lakota Navajo Hopi Native Indian naming ceremony in a sweat-lodge, where I received my full spirit name: Chantè (Heart) Hin Han (Owl) Win (Woman) – 'Heart Owl Woman', or 'Inner Owl' for shortened ease. In my recollecting of the many missing parts of my soul, I was able to rebirth myself into wholeness, and my soul purpose became as crystal clear as pure water: I was to help people remember who they truly are – to shamanically and psychotherapeutically recollect their missing, fragmented self-parts and put them all back together again in wholeness, so they can be on their soul purpose and mission too, with integrated wisdom and ease of flow.

Fast forward to several years later – after formal study at the School of Psychic Studies and the College of Psychic Studies with renowned psychics from the world stage platform, as well as having become a Reiki healer at the Reiki Academy in London, further specialising in crystal healing, tarot card reading and Ayurvedic Astrology, hypnotherapy and past life regression therapy (which all came so fluidly naturally to me from mastery study in my past lives), in addition to having scribed four books on ancient wisdoms for a modern audience in modern language – and my path evolved. It became clearer to me that my purpose was to unite the tribespeople; to help them come together in their common unity and to celebrate their perceived differences, which really were not all that different after all.

The next life-chapter stage ahead of me would be very challenging. I would experience my darkest dark-night-of-the-soul experience. I fatefully crossed paths with a travelling gipsy soul, who gifted me soul liberation into my warrior spirit. I shall call her Tiger-Lilly. A young woman, she was in the physical and didn't know her date of birth. She never gave her name, preferring to remain under the surveillance radar. She brought me back to my most primal instinct, back to my roots, which allowed me to break free from the restriction and limitations that I was simply allowing others to hold over me. Not only did she help emancipate my soul, which was feeling trapped within the trappings of convention, via a mighty shape-shifting experience of my seeing through the eyes of the tiger trapped in a cage, she also inspired me to write about that encounter with her, which unleashed my writer within. She helped open my floodgates to express and tell my story of the woman I'm emerging into – a butterfly flying free, in full wing-span glory, and radiating my inner luminescence.

My first few books were born: *SOULutions: Soul Healing Poetry To Set Your Soul Free* was my first creative baby, followed by *Creative Locksmith: Helping You To Unlock Your Magic Within*, which is actually an ode to psychically, spiritually and creatively coming out. The opening chapter and poem entitled, 'Mozart Walks Me To School', is about Wolfgang Amadeus Mozart, whom also features in modern neon colours on the front cover, and channelling spirits. I then went on to write *The Kid's Book of Wisdoms… On All Kinds of Stuff!* and *Mama On A Mission: Giving Yourself Permission To Shine as a Woman, Mother and a Creative Spirit* as a collective book of several female authors. Creative writing is a preferred mode of mine and it's through my books, and teaching in my workshops and on creative spiritual retreats, that I know I'm here to reach, teach, empower, inspire and help many people across the globe.

So, what advice do I have for you, dear reader, about how to move out of any resistance or reluctance that you may have, or may be experiencing right now, towards attuning your psychic abilities?

Firstly, please rest assured that we're all naturally psychic in a multitude of ways and we only need to realign ourselves with our innate abilities, as our God-given, sovereign birthright. You may be any combination of clairvoyant, clairaudient, clairsentient, or claircogniant in your natural form. However, the third dimensional system that we've been living in, in the physical sense, is the most dense to the psychic sense, and can therefore compound our natural innate abilities and higher intelligences. So we have to go within, to ensure that we do not go without. Everything we need, all our gifts, is embedded inside us, and for many of us, that's the last place we may look if we're constantly seeking externally, outwards, according to the great native Indian fable. When we connect inwardly with ourselves and we journey to the seat of our soul, which you can get to via any combination of meditation, contemplation and prayer, we become who we really are born to be: our blueprint! We become awakened to our soul path, purpose and mission in its fully illumined entirety. It really is an inside job. There is nothing out there that you seek. It's all that's within that enables you to see, to really see, with your third eye and extra-sensory abilities, the truth of all that was, is and will ever be, that is Source.

Secondly, stay wild! In a third-dimensional system that is forever wanting to move us towards transhumanism and amalgamate our souls and nature with artificial intelligence, do the opposite. Remain raw, pure and raise your energetical frequency to the highest vibration you can. That will help keep your humanness about you, your natural instincts. We are not robotic machines; we are the people and human beings we are – not human-robotic doings. You are much more powerful than the third-dimensional matrix system has ever allowed you to believe, has told or taught you. If you can awaken to your true essence, your blueprint, then no one and **no-thing** can mess with you, delude or derail you off-track anymore. Furthermore, when you work with the light beings, rest assured that no harm can come to you when in their vibration of the highest order; you'll be safe and protected at all times.

Thirdly, ASK–BELIEVE–RECEIVE: you must set an intention to connect with the world of Spirit, through your Divine Free Will. You must give your permission as a sentient Being; that is just cosmic lore and how it works in the Universe. Then, once you've done this, you need to trust and have faith in the Universe to answer your request or prayer. A close friend, upon her passing over the rainbow bridge into Spirit, said, 'Believe' as her parting words for what she saw, experienced and knew in her profound passing. Then you are open to receiving what it is that you seek, but you must listen and be vigilant to the presenting signs around you. Don't think too hard, or too consciously about it; allow yourself to flow in your divine feminine aspects, as psychic abilities reside in the intuitive, imaginative right brain, rather than in the logical, linear left brain. So allow yourself space to drift in between the spaces and keep an open mind. It's in the void that the creation of all things happens and where Great Spirit resides, and that's where you'll meet and find your guides. Bravely allow your psychic journey and spiritual adventure to begin! Let the magic unfold…

MitàKuye Oyas'in.

We are all related as ONE LOVE.

Zoë is the author of SOULutions: Soul Healing Poetry to Set Your Soul Free *and* Creative Locksmith: Helping You to Unlock Your Magic Within.

www.zoeowl.com
info@zoeowl.com
FACEBOOK: @zoeowl.soulfree
INSTAGRAM: @zoe.owl
TWITTER: @zoe_owl

From a child, Nicki knew places she had never visited; her gift was awakening. It warned her with a sense of doom about something that actually happened. Sometimes we are woken up with a bang; awakened. In this case, the loss of her dad awoke Nicki to her natural born gifts.

SHE BELIEVED SHE COULD, SO SHE DID

Nicki Jayne Jones

From the age of four or five, I realised had a gift. At the time, I didn't know what having the 'gift' meant but knew I saw spirits and was able to communicate with them. The most memorable one was my uncle, who had recently passed away in his early thirties from a brain tumour. I remember seeing him clearly by my mum and dad's bedroom window; I still picture that moment some 50 years on. I remember speaking to him too and him answering, although, due to the passage of time, I can't recall what we said to each other, but I know I wasn't afraid.

I have memories of visiting places and knowing all the details of them – having this knowledge – but I haven't actually visited them in person.

My parents owned a static caravan in Stourport. We visited there every weekend to give our parents some respite from living onsite at their self-employed business. I clearly remember a little road on the way to Stourport that was to the left-hand side as we approached the town. I described everything in detail to my parents yet, years later, I learnt that I'd never been down that road. I told them about everything there down to the smallest detail, yet they swore I'd never been there. We decided to go there and see for ourselves: it was exactly as I'd described it.

I also recall a beautiful place with stunning scenery; little streams that my friends and I paddled in. We walked through the streams and splashed and paddled as kids do. This image is still fresh in my mind now, even though I don't know where the streams were and where we were walking led to. I can't remember who those friends were, but I realise now they were probably people

I hadn't actually met at that time; maybe they grew up to be friends I've met since my Awakening. I'm yet to find out.

Jump forward 35 years and possibly many similar experiences, to my fortieth birthday party. My parents had divorced when I was nine and had a very turbulent relationship thereafter. All the family gatherings that followed had been 'challenging'.

Here I was now, planning my fortieth party. I was unsure whether to hold it as I knew it was likely to kick off again between them. However, they both promised they wouldn't speak to each other and would stay separate throughout the evening.

The party was fantastic!

Towards the end of the evening, I was talking to my dad and his wife, Pam (she was the reason Mum and Dad had divorced). Whilst talking, Mum came over. I was filled with the usual dread. However, Mum stood behind Dad and Pam and placed her arms around both of them. She told them both she forgave them. I almost choked on my sausage roll!

Afterwards, I asked Mum why she'd said those words of forgiveness. She simply didn't know! She said she hadn't had any intention of doing that, yet her body had other ideas. It felt like she'd been taken over, so she went along with it, not feeling she could resist. She stated she felt a sense of peace that the forgiveness had given her.

My dad and I had the last dance of the evening to The Commodores' 'Three Times a Lady', a song I can no longer hear without the tears flowing.

The following week was spent preparing for our holiday to Malta, a place I loved, but the preparations were far from good. I didn't want to go. I couldn't explain why, I just didn't feel we should be going. I left the packing to the last minute (anyone who knows me will know this isn't me – I'm Mrs ORGANISED).

Crying all the way to the airport in the taxi, the feelings got stronger. In the departure lounge, I was an emotional wreck and when we were called to board the plane, I became very anxious and scared.

As I was about to step onto the plane, I felt an intense cold pass right through my body. I froze in that moment and knew I was being told not to go. However, my panic was causing others ready to board the flight to panic too so, against my better judgment, I boarded.

I remember being told over the tannoy to turn all phones off. I looked at the digital panel above: it was 2.01am.

Shutting off my phone, despite being scared witless, I tried to calm myself down. I was extremely grateful to be on terra firma again when the wheels touched the ground in Malta.

Going through passport control, I turned my phone back on to find 17 missed calls and loads of messages to call home immediately.

I discovered that my dad, whom I'd been talking to a few hours earlier, had had a sudden brain haemorrhage. Dad had died; his time of death was recorded as 2.01am.

The holiday and insurance company were unable to fly me back until the following Monday, seven days later. That feeling of knowing I wasn't meant to go will never leave me. I knew something was going to happen and, coupled with my mum's unintentional forgiveness, it still resonates with me today. She obviously had to do it.

My dad did return to me several times after his passing. He's always close when I need guidance. I believe it was him who brought Tony, my soulmate and now husband, to me when I needed him most.

These are just a few of my many experiences of spiritual Awakening. The years after Dad passed away turned out to be the darkest, most emotionally charged years of my life, for reasons I don't want to go into here. I was in a very dark place, yet I was able to focus on a few positives I could find in life at that point, in helping others. Throughout my working life, I'd always had supporting and empathetic roles in adoption, fostering work, and as a bereavement manager in the Children's Hospital, to name just a few. During my difficult years, I became a funeral director, helping and supporting families suffering the loss of their loved ones, and caring for the deceased to give them the dignity and respect they deserved.

Although I worked in an office on my own, I never felt alone. I was constantly surrounded by Angels who had grown their wings, and I spoke to each one of them every day. I felt so supported by them too whilst in the safety of my work, and I believe that all these Angels and my dad helped me to find my way out of the darkness and into the new world I was to find myself in.

Fast-forward again to happy years when I met my soulmate. I wasn't even looking yet we found each other when we needed each other most. Since then, we have both supported and helped each other through many difficult situations, each one cementing our relationship and subsequent marriage, and making a stronger and unbreakable bond. I now laugh where I used to cry, and see light where I once could only see darkness.

This brings us to a few years ago when we decided, on a day trip out, to look at buying a static caravan; an on-the-spot decision but nevertheless one of the best we were to make. We loved every moment we spent at our beautiful retreat enough to make my becoming ill and needing several life-changing operations bearable. We spent most of our time there so I could recover in beautiful and peaceful surroundings.

One evening last September, when I was feeling quite low, wheelchair-bound, fat and ugly, Tony persuaded me to go to the onsite bar's first karaoke evening. I didn't want to go if I'm honest and only did so as I thought Tony needed to let his hair down (not literally as he's bald, LOL) after caring for me continuously 24/7 for many months.

It was while sitting in my wheelchair that I met another Angel – Angel Alison as I refer to her now. She asked me if I was going to sing and I said, 'No, I'm crap at singing!' Then she told me never to say I'm crap at anything. She said, 'You are YOU and you are beautiful – be proud!'

That moment was another of those 'meant to be' moments. Over the following months, I met Alison regularly and on 25th October last year, I had my rebirth; and from my rebirth came more Awakenings; my realisations and finding my soul since that time. Many wonderful things have come since. I think it's because I now feel alive. We've recently purchased an upgrade on our retreat, which is beautiful and absolutely perfect for us, and we've moved house to a much smaller property to meet my physical needs. All of which happened with perfect timings.

Now I only think positively, not allowing any negativity in whatsoever. I have good quality sleep and wake each morning with complete contentment. The move from our old retreat to our new one, and the house move, have allowed me to declutter; physically, but also in my mind. I laugh until my ribs ache, I stay out of drama at any cost and I dream big with a cherry on top!

I've learnt the power of thank you. Gratitude has been a big part of my new life. I'm extremely grateful for this lockdown the world has suddenly found itself in. I see it as Mother Nature pressing the reset button, which was so desperately needed. Don't get me wrong, I still have moments of anxiety during the lockdown, but they've literally been moments. And I'm kind to myself if I stumble. I appreciate nature so much more. I've had the opportunity to experience nature at its best in local parks, which I've never noticed before. I've become so creative and realise how much patience I have. My life has been completely turned around thanks both to Alison and, of course, to me! I've learnt how bloody amazing I am. I bloody love ME! Wow, the old me would never have said that! I'm looking forward to all life has to offer as I continue to grow; hopefully emotionally and not physically, LOL. Each story is beautiful, but ours is my favourite.

The corporate world taught Julie that suffering with burnout was not how she wanted to live her life. Born sensitive to energies, Julie was shown she had to live and work in an environment that was 'sensitive' to her needs.

HOW AN ANGEL TAUGHT A TEACHER HER BEST LESSON

Julie Phillips

I was told as a pre-teen that I was highly sensitive… and not in a good way. In fact, it was fair to say my mother disliked this aspect in me. We were opposites. The louder she shouted, the quieter I became. I learnt to hide my feelings, to disconnect my emotions and not to utter a word about what I was feeling in case it made me look stupid or like I was drawing attention to myself.

As a young girl living in a small seaside town in the late 70s and 80s, I became silently aware that I was picking up on people's energy fields. I didn't understand it – it wasn't rational – and yet I sensed the ebb and flow of energy, so much so it was overwhelming at times. At school, I tended to hide in the library during breaks and lunchtimes just reading anything I could get my hands on – the lunch hall and the busy school yard felt too chaotic for me. I was beginning to recognise that I had a dislike of crowded places and that large shifts in energy made me feel quite ill.

During these teenage years, my respite came from singing in a local church choir – this felt like lovely energy to me and such a positive, enjoyable experience, to sing with others. I came to love my Sunday mornings in church; I felt replenished. No one else in my family had any time for church, which I was secretly grateful for, as it became such a comfort to me. I think other teenagers in the town thought of me as a little 'odd' at this point and there was some bullying. However, as I hid away in school and on a weekend in my room or in church, I kept myself safe and away from people.

I've always had a deep sensory load to my memories, so it's rather frustrating to me, a woman now in my late forties, that I'm quite absent-minded. I frequently forget where I've left my car keys, can't recall if I've fed the dogs or whether I actually replied to that important email. I think my forties will take longer to get through as I tend to check myself twice! Strange then that I clearly recall, as a toddler, being in my wooden cot in my bedroom, with my stuffed animals and wicker basket containing creams and cloth nappies (it was the 70s), on the day I was visited by something in red and silver, which appeared to shimmer at the end of my cot, and spoke my name. It seemed to me there was an energy about this 'Being'. I must have been scared as hell. I remember screaming and my grandad coming into the room to check on me. Years later, I can still 'see' this image of a strange Being as if it were yesterday. But I still struggle to make any sense of what this was – I disconnected my rational mind from this experience because I was too scared.

As a four-year-old, I had an 'imaginary friend', Eddie Currant. Most people in my family remember Eddie and how he was always around. No one thought it was odd that a four-year-old girl would have a friend called Eddie Currant. They just thought I had an over-active imagination. Later in my adult life, of course, I recognised the name 'eddy current'. I discovered it was/is a swirling current set up in a conductor in response to a changing magnetic field. By Lenz's law, the current swirls in such a way as to create a magnetic field opposing the change. It would seem that my child-like innocent self was acutely aware of 'energy' flux – I had even found the scientific name for it! Of course, I had no idea back then how this would lead to where I am now...

Now I'm writing these words, so much seems obvious to me: the frequent electric shocks I get from metal stairs and museum display boxes (York Railway Museum was a nightmare to me); the ache in my knees before a storm; the many watches that just stop within weeks of purchase with no explanation; the look on the science teacher's face when I touched the Vandegraph Generator in a science lesson and my straight, shoulder-length hair stood on end; the apologies I have to give when I shake hands with folk and I inadvertently 'shock them'; not to mention the several computers I've had that seemed to have a life of their own; and I seldom get through airport security without setting off several alarms. It would seem I tend to carry a personal electric 'charge' of sorts around with me.

Once, when I went to stay with a German pen friend in a rural suburb of Bavaria, I was given a room in the eaves of the house. It was a lovely room with deep, wooden furniture and a large window. One night I awoke to a sense of great sadness and foreboding; I felt an energy shift of sorts pass through the room. The air felt very heavy and I sensed there was a storm coming. I must have drifted off as, sometime later, I was awoken by streaks of lightning, thunder and loud wailing cries echoing around the house. As I got up to see what was happening, I felt what I can only describe as another energy shift. Then there was a mighty crashing of glass outside my room. A full glass cabinet containing trophies and family photographs had completely shattered from ceiling to floor. The sobbing was from the family, who had just received a phone call to tell them their nephew had died that night in a motorbike accident. I was so overwhelmed by this event, I had to leave and come home, much to the annoyance of my parents, who thought I was just being 'flaky' and again, overly sensitive.

Although I was happy to be studying English, I hated my time at university. I spent so many days feeling 'disconnected' and unsettled. Needless to say, I distanced myself from crowds as much as possible. I didn't live on campus, choosing instead to live six miles away, and I took a little waitressing job in a small café to pay my bills. This was the 90s, a time of big raves, huge gatherings, wild parties and festivals. I stayed away from it all, preferring to remain in my room and read, visit art galleries, go to the cinema on my own, go running alone, or write poetry. Sadly, I'd drifted away from the spiritual side of myself and from the church I loved.

I didn't begin my teacher training until I was 29 years old (after having my first child). In all honesty, I felt like I'd found my calling. The school was a small, rural secondary school with around 400 children, most of whom were related to each other from small local villages. I loved teaching English Language and Literature; I felt 'at home' and at peace. Eventually, however, the 'powers that be' decided to amalgamate three schools into one and I decided to move on.

My next post was in a large North Yorkshire secondary school and I was eventually promoted to Head of Department as a special educational needs co-ordinator. With a team of 13 people, I was learning quickly that the energy required to lead with quality was immense. Add to this the pressure of Ofsted, my role as a special needs coordinator, my teacher governor role, my two small children and the fact my husband was working away, and it wasn't long before the cracks began to show.

In 2012, I started to experience a significant increase in stress. I struggled to juggle everything and took to extremes to try to manage my feelings: I went to the gym every day and pushed myself to the limits, yet my body and mind were not connected holistically. I was working in excess of 60 hours per week and finding that I couldn't be there for my own children as much as I wanted to be. Eventually things came to a head and in 2013, I was signed off by the doctor with work-related stress. I was in shock. How could this be? I was supposed to be the strong one; the person who had her life sorted, the person who knew where she was going in her career... To watch it all crash and burn before my eyes was heart-breaking.

I spent a few weeks in bed, crying, eating and feverishly searching Google for something, anything to help me. The doctor had put me forward for counselling and offered me anti-depressants. I was embarrassed; I didn't want counselling, I didn't want anti-depressants. I knew I needed some clarity in my life and I just wanted to feel better.

A chance conversation with a long-time friend led me to seek help of a more holistic kind. I decided to try hypnotherapy. All I can tell you is that the difference in my mind and body connection was so profound that I booked onto a course in Glasgow the same week! As it turned out, this was the best thing I could have done (and led me to undertake several more courses and certification). Whilst there, I 'stumbled across' an Angel Conference with a chap called Kyle Gray, who described himself as an 'Angel Whisperer', something I'd never heard of. As I entered the conference, I was given free choice of where to sit. Each chair had an Angel card face down on it. I was interested to turn over the card on my chair. You can imagine the shock on my face as I read the card and it said, 'Stress Management'! It was an odd moment of clarity, like a light from within; a small voice or certainty, a feeling of connection – I still have the card to this day. I thought at first that 'stress management' was about me managing my own stress. Later in the conference, I realised that I had been 'called' to learn how to support other people with their stress. The connection was complete: this was my learning journey. I was a teacher. Maybe I could be more than one kind of teacher? In 2013, I resigned from my job as Head of Department and opened my hypnotherapy business. As the clients appeared, I focussed on their energy and they began to report some extraordinary results.

What was odd was that in session, sometimes I too would go into a trance of sorts and my words felt as though they came from another part of my mind. I put this down to my training and the fact that I loved language; as a student of English and an English teacher, of course it would just be a natural part of my therapeutic skill set… or so I thought…

Working as an independent therapist can be isolating. I decided to find a new mentor; this is when I was guided to Alison Ward. The things Alison told me in the first session I worked with her were phenomenal. I was astounded at how she seemed to know so much about my abilities – more than I knew myself. In one session, she repeated almost word for word what I'd said to a client – how could she have known this? I was in North Yorkshire and she was in Birmingham at the time. As it happened, the results were not just down to my knowledge of the English language: I discovered, with Alison's support, that during sessions, I'd been making an energy connection with clients and channelling what I can only describe or understand as 'angelic energies'. The problem was that I was often left exhausted after sessions and I didn't understand why.

Over the months that followed, Alison taught me to recognise my boundaries and to recognise, nurture and protect my energy stores. I learnt that empty vessels serve no one. I learnt things that would have protected me so much during my teaching role… If only I'd known back then what I know now. That was the trigger. I realised that through my work, I could show other professionals how to take care of themselves, how to work cleanly, how to draw their boundaries and look after their own energy stores. I also learnt how to separate myself from people who have toxic energies and how to stay safely away from the drama of others, even if they are within your own family.

You've probably realised that, yes, I'm a natural introvert, although some people might be shocked at that disclosure. My truth is that I'm still not overly keen about drawing unnecessary attention to myself. However, I have learnt that 'it's not about me', it's about the energy I put out there into the world for others: a lighthouse doesn't jump into the sea to save ships… It shines its light to guide them safely through tricky weathers and rocks.

I've seen over 1000 clients in one-to-one sessions and workshops at the time of writing. I've also worked with the police, a national charity, a local housing corporation, local academies, care staff in residential homes, staff in colleges, and I've recently been asked by the NHS to provide therapeutic services and support to their cancer care co-ordinators on Teesside close to where I live.

Did I forget teaching? Well, no. During an Angel Conference with Alison Ward in October 2016, I was gifted a project… Her work helped to guide my intuition towards creating a new business. In addition to my therapeutic work, I have now set up a centre for children who are very sensitive towards school and find schools chaotic places. Students can access their learning with qualified teachers in a quiet, therapeutic environment. The name? Connect2Education. Connection is everything to me now. I had disconnected from myself all those years ago because I was scared. I'd pushed those feelings away because I thought that being sensitive was a bad thing. I'm so glad I was guided by Alison to reconnect that part of myself that meant I could follow my life path. I'm so pleased to say I reconnected to my spiritual self too and with my local church. I'm a member of the choir and I find their energy very therapeutic.

If you take anything away from my story, I'd say, please learn how to protect your energy. Hopefully you'll discover that it's ok to trust your instincts and seek your own path. It feels scary at first – however, if you're burnt out emotionally or spiritually and know deep down that you're destined for a more holistic life, then please do take some time to explore the possibilities. Invest in yourself, invest in your own personal discovery, because it's not just about you. We are so much more than other people say we are. Shed the labels, step up and reconnect with your life path. I promise it's there waiting for you.

www.juliephillips-therapeutic-coaching.co.uk
julie@juliephillips-therapeutic-coaching.co.uk
FACEBOOK: @juliephillipstc
TWITTER: @juliephillipstc

We carry on with the burnout issue with the lovely Leigh Campbell from Northern Ireland. Leigh has found her power and has stepped into it, finding her purpose along the way. Another Empath who could no longer work in the corporate world.

BECOMING A MIGHTY WOMAN

Leigh Campbell

If someone had told me 13 years ago I'd be sitting here as a hypnotherapist, psychotherapist, mindfulness teacher, and have been nominated for a Mighty Women Award for my work in healthcare this year, I would have laughed you out of the room.

I grew up during the troubles in Northern Ireland. Bomb scares were a daily occurrence and my dad had to check our car for bombs. Our neighbour was a policeman. My town was blown up three times, the last of which I drove past the place minutes before the explosion. Our cars and handbags were checked everywhere we went. I knew people who'd been shot or hurt by a bomb and, as a child, I never knew any different.

However, I look back on my childhood as a great childhood. I was very lucky to live by the sea, away from most of the terror and shootings, and typically had the cookie-cutter blueprint life: good primary school, then all-girls grammar school. But I hated the grammar with a passion as I was made to feel as if my achievements and goals were never good enough. I left there not feeling heard, with little or no sense of value in myself, and my dreams of owning my own business destroyed as it was all about the A-star grades and university places. There was no room at all for someone like me, who thought differently and wanted something so much more.

I buried my dreams and continued the 'usual' good career path into optics, then into managing Ireland for one of the largest make-up companies in the world.

I was high-functioning, had a great job, a company car, a nice house, but I was living with chronic anxiety – calm on the outside, but underneath my feet were paddling along really, really fast, and nobody could see that as I was very, very good at my job. I felt like I was drowning daily.

It's so easy to get stuck in the trap of doing something just because you're good at it, or because you've spent a lot of time being good at it and are afraid to let it go. That's exactly how I was living – in fear, working 60 hours or more a week. I was never home. I lived in hotels, which were very lovely, but in the end they all the look the same when you're beyond tired after driving 300 miles a day, with more work to do as you eat dinner. But I was scared to walk away as I had nothing to walk towards. It seems the more capable we are at something, the harder it is to walk away from it, especially if we seek approval, which I definitely did back then. I felt like the biggest people-pleaser ever!

I was beginning to realise that stress was becoming an issue. I remember thinking, 'I don't know how I'm ever going to get out of this stress.' Every time the Blackberry rang or the red light on it flashed, I literally jumped out of my skin.

So, what happened to change all this was not something I had a say in, but it did change the course of my life drastically. I flew to Gatwick airport and, as I was reaching for my case, a lady hit me in the eye by accident and I've never felt pain like it. I was in so much agony, I took myself off to Basildon A&E. They didn't even look at my eye properly and just told me to rest in the dark for 24 hours to reduce the inflammation. Well, a few days later it seemed to be ok.

But it wasn't ok. For the next six months of work, I would get what the doctors called 'cluster migraines'. Doing events, meetings and driving 400 miles daily, I would get a headache. My vision would be a bit blurry but next day it was gone. Until one day it didn't go away. It got worse and worse to the point where I was being sick, my eyeballs were twice the size they should be and I was in panic mode. I couldn't believe what was happening to me as I was losing my sight. I was exhausted, depleted and frightened.

I'd worked in optics for years in my twenties as a Dispensing Optician, and I had my eyes tested all the time, so I wasn't thinking eye issues at all. My new boyfriend of four weeks took me to the Emergency Room and I rewarded him for that by throwing up over him. I even remember laughing and saying he didn't have to stay. I was mortified but I couldn't see well and pain was taking over as I started losing my sight fast. It's probably the most life-changing, scariest thing that has ever happened to me. Three years previously, I'd hemorrhaged after a tonsillectomy and I nearly died, but this felt totally different because I was aware of what was going on. And when this cloudiness came over my eyes, I was in so much pain and I was so ill.

I was given morphine but was really sick again, and once more, I threw up over my boyfriend. But he stayed and made me laugh so much, which helped a lot as the doctors didn't really understand what was happening. My age of 31 and my symptoms together were incredibly unusual. Well, of course, they would be – it was me, after all. Nothing was ever simple with me. It was very much, 'Why me?'

The medics were trying to put a drip in me but I was allergic to some of the ingredients, which made things even worse, so my sight was deteriorating for two and a half hours. They then couldn't get a vent flow in me for a new drip and I ended up having ones hanging out of my arm. The doctor even put one in the wrong way, and I had one in my foot and was screaming in pain. I actually had to pull one out because they'd missed the vein and I remember screaming at everyone to just get the hell away from me. My eyesight was getting worse and nobody was helping me, so they got a nurse and a podiatrist to come up and put a vent flow in my foot, as my veins had collapsed. It was painful but it worked.

Little did I know, but my eye pressure was 60 and when it's that high, you're a very ill person. Eye pressure should be about 15. At 60, you should be blind. There's no real going back from that, or so I thought, and I remember the A&E doctor shining a light in my eye. He said my pupil wouldn't react to the light and I immediately knew it was glaucoma of some sort. He didn't realise that I knew all about that, and that's when I really started to panic. I felt as if I had absolutely no coping mechanism for this. After all, it was a 'disease of the elderly' so they kept telling me. That didn't help at all.

I was distraught and started thinking about my job and my house, as I didn't get sick pay even though it was a huge, multi-national make-up company, and I was terrified. So, while I was lying there in hospital, I knew I'd have to beg my boss to get paid so that in the meantime I could at least pay my bills as I was going to be off for a while. But I had no answer so I was trying to work with bad eyes, still answering my Blackberry in hospital. My stress levels were really high. I was so frightened, exhausted, alone, and when I looked into the mirror one day in the hospital, I could see that my left eye was particularly bad. It was twice the size it should be. I felt I looked so ugly. My eye colour had turned black from green as my pupil was damaged. My right eye was fine again, but I was scared of losing my sight as my eyes wouldn't stay stable.

The pressure eventually came down but it was very difficult to keep it down as my glaucoma is an extremely rare, acute form. It's incurable and is called 'plateau iris syndrome'. Laser was the next course of treatment, which either works or makes it worse. I had machines on my eyes 20 times a day. It seemed to help at first and I was able to leave the hospital.

But a week later, I could feel bad pressure, so I drove myself to the Royal Belfast hospital. They admitted me straightaway as my pressure was even higher than before, at 66, and I was being violently sick again. I was devastated.

For the next nine months, I was in and out of hospital. I lost my eyesight again and got it back again, but unfortunately I'd lost my near vision, which affects reading. It could have been so much worse, though. All this, while trying to maintain my career. I even had letters to give to any doctor in the country while I travelled to meetings, and a 'do not dilate my eyes' wrist band in case I had a car accident or passed out.

I then had surgery on my left eye to replace the lens, all while still trying to work and pay the bills. It was a new treatment and I was willing to try anything!

I remember having a big patch on my eye afterwards. I was in agony after taking it off. Then I tried to walk down the stairs and the stairs looked very different now, as my vision was all over the place. I couldn't drive for a few weeks and my patience, my emotions were everywhere. Work were still not paying me, even while having my eye surgery, but my boyfriend at the time was great. That was the thing that kept me going – I'd finally met a good guy!

I moved in with him, very much in love. We were planning a future, or so I thought. But one night, a few months later, he returned home from a party very drunk and, with great delight, showed me messages from the woman he'd been seeing behind my back, plus around seven others, and my heart really was truly broken. I thought we'd get married and spend our lives together. I was distraught and I left straightaway. Outside the house, I threw up. I was a broken woman. My intuition had failed me; I was stupid; I was to blame. If I hadn't been ill, if I hadn't been so distracted and stressed, blah blah blah, then all would have been well. The full self-blame part of me took over. I felt destroyed and the man I adored was not the man I thought he was.

Not long after I left, I was driving to Galway for meetings. They'd just built a very long, new motorway, with a decorative central reservation, and I remember thinking that if I drove into that, it would take all the pain away; the heartbreak; the fact my eyes were damaged; I was damaged, not perfect. It would take me away from this job that was adding to the stress. I wasn't listening to my whispers, the callings to something else, I was ignoring every good thing about me and my life.

I didn't try to kill myself that day because there was something in me that said, 'Don't you bloody dare!' And I listened, for the first time in years. I kept hearing, 'Life is worth living, life is precious, and you're here to do something special'. I didn't know what at that point and I couldn't see why all this horrible, painful stuff was happening to me, so I moved to a lovely house down the coast and I loved living there for a time.

My work was changing. It was growing massively and it never stopped, my phone never stopped, and I was busy, busy, burying all the emotions of the eye issues, losing my sight and the months of pain, learning to live with all the changes in my vision. It was good for distance and the vision in my right eye was brilliant so I got on with it; still ignoring my path, still ignoring my heart, my passions. I'd shut down all that for fear of getting hurt.

Then I met someone else, and I thought he was my knight in shining armour. But unfortunately, over the next four and a half years, I became more sad, fatter, very stressed, and a very unhappy version of me.

In his eyes, I was always wrong. If I saw my girlfriends for a coffee, it'd probably be two days of rows. If I went out with my friends more than two or three times a month, I was a bad partner. He believed that, when you're in a relationship with someone, you should be with that person 24/7. If I wore something nice, he'd tear me down. 'Are you going out like that?' was a favourite phrase. Everything I did was questioned.

If didn't eat the same food as him, it was a row; if I went for a walk on my own, I was shouted at, and I'm a strong woman, I really am. But it was easier not to say anything. I didn't see my friends for months. I couldn't believe I was in an emotionally abusive relationship, but I didn't have the strength to walk away then.

I found myself throughout this time shrinking into nothing. I remember feeling very caged and deeply unhappy; my self-worth was on the floor. I questioned myself daily. My work and life were busier than I thought possible and it was painful. I was crying daily at this point but still holding all the stuck emotion in my body, which is never a good thing.

I kept thinking, how can I get out of this? Where is my path out of here? I was so angry and frustrated at this point too. I was literally screaming out to the Universe, 'Where is it? Where is my escape route?' I couldn't see a way out.

Well, I must have screamed loudly enough, because not long after, my friend, Lee took me to do my Reiki I energy healing. I recall sitting in the room and thinking, 'WTF am I doing?' I enjoyed it, but then went on with my work without giving it much thought. Oh boy, was I in for a ride!

Not long after, I was in Cork. I'd been working away all week and I literally threw my phone at the wall, it was so stressful. Head office changes had meant lots of angry stores and customers.

I was driving home (it was about eight hours to drive home that day from Cork) when I felt a pain in my left arm; a heart pain I called it. I couldn't breathe well so I drove to the hospital about an hour from home and was admitted with a suspected heart attack. But all was well that way. The surgeon who looked at me said I was a fit, healthy, smart young woman but I needed to heal deep hurt and he pointed to my heart. Yet I had a hole in my oesophagus; my solar plexus was literally on fire and burning a hole in my body. It was a huge wake-up call. His words stuck with me, and they're not normally words a surgeon would say. It really hit me that he was right.

In distress, I got home, but when I went to make some food, I couldn't even figure out how to switch my oven on; I couldn't figure out how to cook a basic dinner, or even open the back door. I was sitting on the floor crying, moving back and forth trying to soothe my weary soul.

I thought my partner would understand. But he looked at me on the floor and said, 'Get the fuck off the floor. You're pathetic.' And my heart sank even lower.

All I needed was kindness; for him to lift me up and carry me; to hold me and tell me everything would be all right. Everything I'd done for him and he didn't do any of that. In fact, he shouted at me for weeks as I took a year off sick – full pay this time, yet he wanted me back to work.

That was my broken moment. It was the moment I realised he would never be kind to me; would never care about me. And it was destroying me.

Deep down I knew I had to find a way to feel better, and I couldn't go back to work until I'd healed that hurt. I finally started listening to my inner voice; my inner wisdom.

This is when my life changed. I began to notice nice little synchronicities. A friend of a friend, whom I have met many times, had trained as a hypnotherapist. Then one of my best friends said, 'Why don't you go and see her? It might be worth a shot' – because I didn't want to go on antidepressants. I'd been on Seroxat, which is now banned, in my early twenties when my grandfather died, and I actually knew I hadn't processed those emotions properly, which I'll come to shortly.

I was still not functionally well so I went to see my hypnotherapist, and within two sessions I was human again. The difference to me was life-altering. It saved my life.

I started losing weight; I was becoming more confident again and could see things clearly, like I was my own observer in the room. I could see that my partner was abusing me, torturing me mentally; ignoring me all day, blaming me for everything. It was becoming harder and harder to live like that, as he hated the changes in me as I grew out of my despair. I was learning new techniques of thinking. I was changing my life.

Seeing a hypnotherapist had such a massive impact on my life that I knew I had to train in it. I just knew. I couldn't shake the feeling of 'this is for me', so my own hypnotherapist told me where she'd trained and it felt perfect; it just felt so good!

The practical courses were in Italy. I'd be with four other trainees and three tutors near the Italian lakes, in an amazing little hotel with the kindest people. I felt at home and so open to this learning, and I've never stopped learning since. I'm always listening and being guided by my soul and intuition. I made some amazing friends and experienced so much relief from my stress and my past.

I can't tell you the joy I felt during a training day, when we practised on each other and my anxiety relief resulted in me laughing for three days. I'd never felt such joy in years, or perhaps ever! I was surrounded by people I felt at home with, who accepted me for me.

It was amazing for me. I can look back and truly say I felt I was guided to my hypnotherapist, as my friend had lived beside her years before when she was in a different career, and I wouldn't have met her otherwise.

After my six sessions or so with her, I decided to go back to work, about ten months after I'd broken down. I really didn't want to go back, and I had this niggling, annoying feeling that I wouldn't stay long. I'd changed so much; I'd learnt so much about myself that I knew deep down I had to start my own practice. But I wanted more money in the bank before I did that. Looking back, I wish I'd just left work and started it, but I chose to carry a little of my old self with me for a bit longer.

I'd only been back for a couple of months when in the January, a car hit me really hard from behind into a dual carriageway. Luckily, there were no other cars involved, but I was hurt and was put on a spinal board and taken to hospital. My then new boss was trying to get a report out of me in hospital. She phoned me and asked me to compile it. Well, I discovered I had no fear that day, and I told her to shove that idea where the sun don't shine!

I knew then that I would leave. I'd damaged my shoulder and I couldn't drive for 12 weeks. Again, I had to take time off sick, and I never went back…

Six months later, I returned my company car and that was it. I never looked back and I started building my hypnotherapy practice. This became harder and harder as my partner 'banned' me from seeing male clients – seriously eye-rolling stuff, but that was his stuff. I could see it wasn't my fault and I'd finally stopped justifying myself to him. At last I was on a path of helping others and creating my dream life. And I was happy. But he was just getting more and more angry that I was changing, so I became more of a caged animal within the relationship and he was just so cruel.

The final straw for me was when I was editing up my website and social media pages. He wrestled me to the floor to see my phone. I left that day. I called my dad and I left everything behind – my clothes, my stuff, my car, everything – and I never looked back. That was six years ago.

It taught me that when something never feels right, it never will be. I spent years ignoring those niggles, embracing my stubbornness to make things work, numbing things out. It's bloody exhausting!

The day I woke up without my partner there and with that feeling of freedom was one of the happiest days of my life. I had changed careers, had left someone who was hurting me and was living my life on my terms. And I was on a path to something for me that would help me change others' lives too, and not just my own.

The week I left, my hypnotherapist was running meditation classes by her friend who had come over from England, and she was doing a channelling from the Egyptian god Tehuti, something I didn't really understand a lot about, but was drawn to and felt I needed so as to experience more peace. Plus, I have a huge affinity with Egypt, having visited a few times.

There were a few of us in this beautiful, calm room and I was just so tired, having left my home and relationship. I felt free, yes, but I was tired and was looking forward to meditation time.

A beautiful meditation was followed by this fabulous soul going into trance, and her normal voice became a deep, different voice. I was very fidgety and itchy throughout the whole thing, and at the end, everyone could ask Tehuti a question, which they all did, but for some reason I didn't.

Then the channelled voice said, 'Someone hasn't spoken yet and it's important that I speak to her.' Well, that someone was me. I got goosebumps like mad and the energy in the room really changed.

What was spoken next blew me away and made more sense than anything that had happened to me over the previous years.

'Leigh, your trauma is now over,' was said about ten times, and the tears flowed big time. The voice said they'd been waiting for me to wake up and all these things I'd endured were for the greater good. Well, fuck me, I was blown away with the things being channelled just for me!

I had been a high priestess, a powerful healer and a leader in a previous life. The voice described a wealthy, powerful island, ships, houses and beautiful buildings, and explained that I had lost that part of me but it was now found again. And I was never to forget my power.

Again, 'Your trauma is now over' was repeated, and other things were said they couldn't possibly have known. I felt, in that blow-your-mind moment, that I had absolutely made the right decision to leave my job, my home, my relationship, and start life again as the Leigh I'd always wanted to be, free and happy. It was ok to be me! I felt validated for the first time in my life. I was being called to serve and create a path for others to feel good and heal.

I had finally woken up to my power and I wasn't going to be anyone else but the real me. I had awakened the part of me that knows the answers, my purpose, the direction I want to move in. I had ignored that part for so long but it was always there; I just couldn't always feel it or see it, but now everything was clear... I was ready!

I realised what the heart and soul want doesn't always make sense, and it doesn't have to. I knew I had to leap and take chances; I wasn't living in fear anymore, I was excited!

In knowing myself better, I realised my big word in life is 'freedom'. Freedom to live and create a life I love. I've been self-employed for eight years now as a hypnotherapist and psychotherapist, specialising in anxiety and trauma. I speak in different venues and last year, I was a finalist for a Mighty Women Award for my work in healthcare. All the work had paid off and I have the best job in the world.

I had reclaimed me: I took the plunge, I leapt into my wholeness, my imperfections, fabulousness, quirkiness and all.

I now look back on all the deeply painful events. I've only mentioned the life-changing ones here. But there were other difficult, hurtful times and I'm grateful for all of them, no matter how messy they were at the time, because all those things shaped me. They've allowed me to find my purpose; to find the Leigh I genuinely am, which is a truly powerful woman with a purpose.

I lost a few friends along the way but they weren't really friends in the first place, and now I have amazingly talented people around me online and in person – my tribe. And that's what you will get too, if you take that leap into your uniqueness and what lights you up.

I now choose to live my life with love, compassion and determination. My eyes are stable and, although it's called 'incurable', I live my life as if I don't have glaucoma. I focus on my eyes' health and healing every day and I've not had any problems in ten years. If losing my sight happened to allow me to 'see' better, I'm very grateful for it now my eyes are stable and healthy enough. I may have an incurable disease but I don't live my life believing that. I live my life as if I don't have it. Sometimes the worst things that happen are the best things that can happen, because we get to see life in a clear and better way.

I will finish my story with this: follow your intuition even when it doesn't make sense. Keep listening to your whispers, the inner wisdom. These things lead you to what lights you up. If you keep waiting or ignoring them, you may never find your path and the bliss that it brings.

www.leighcampbellcoaching.com
hello@leighcampbellcoaching.com
FACEBOOK: @leighcampbellco
INSTAGRAM: @leighcampbellcoaching

Now, get the tissues ready. This is a tragic story of Keiley and her ectopic pregnancy. The world nearly lost Keiley, but God had other plans for her. You will be warmed by her heart-wrenching story of loss and great inner strength. I asked dear Keiley if she would share her story, as she wanted it to be put to good use and inspire other mums who have lost their baby in this way. As I write this, we are soon to celebrate Keiley's 40th birthday. Bless you, beautiful Keiley.

BRINGING ME BACK TO ME

Keiley Pegler

It was Wednesday 9th January, 2019. I was 38. And I'd just discovered that I was pregnant. I was over the moon. Sadly, this happiness was not to last long. The following day, I suffered an ectopic pregnancy. I lost my baby and almost lost my life, but it was my Awakening.

Let's rewind a little and I'll build the picture for you. It all started in September 2018. I would see figures in my vision. I wasn't scared by them; they were like a dream and as soon as I blinked they were gone. There was always one man, who wore an old-fashioned brown suede jacket with black trousers. I first spotted him as I went to shut the front door and took a double take when I saw this man at the end of the path. As I looked back, he was gone. I know it sounds mad but I wasn't scared, as I knew there wasn't an actual person there.

This guy would then start to appear whenever I felt worried or scared, which sadly at that time was quite often. I would just get a glimpse of him, almost like he was reassuring me that I was going to be ok, but also warning me that things weren't quite right and that's why he was there.

One Saturday night I had a nightmare; the type that wakes you, sweating and panicky. This dream was so vivid. I walked into the bathroom and saw myself sitting with my head over the toilet, like I was being sick. I walked over to myself, almost laughing, because I couldn't understand how I was sitting there. I was even wearing the pyjamas that I had on that night. As I went to touch the figure, I pulled on my shoulder, my head fell and my eyes rolled back:

I was DEAD. It was awful and really frightened me, but now I realise that all these were warning signs.

On the day of my ectopic pregnancy, I woke feeling a little off colour but put it down to morning sickness. Whilst in the bathroom, I was sick and started to get sharp stomach pains. The stomach pains began to get so bad that I knew something was seriously wrong, and I was taken back to the nightmare. I knew I had to get out of the bathroom but I couldn't stand without feeling like I was going to pass out.

I managed to crawl to the bedroom and phoned 111. I explained my symptoms to the call handler and she deemed it an emergency and sent an ambulance. Luckily, my husband arrived home at the same time as the paramedics.

On arrival, the paramedics asked me a number of questions, but it didn't take a lot to realise that I was in a bad way. As they took my blood pressure, I could see the worried looks they shot each other. I would later discover that my right fallopian tube had burst, causing severe internal bleeding, which was why I had such low blood pressure. After a number of failed attempts to bring my blood pressure up, it was decided that I should be taken to hospital. But when they tried to move me, it didn't end well. As they sat me up, I must have pressed everything onto the burst tube. The pain was so bad that I passed out. I'm not sure how long I was 'out' for, but I had the most bizarre experience: I felt like I was in a video game. It was orange and brown with lots of characters. When I came round, I couldn't work out what was real, the video game or this.

It took three hours, five paramedics and three ambulances to get me out of the house. The friendly chat with the paramedics on their arrival had now developed into a life-saving journey but, even though we all knew this and the pain was horrific, I felt a sense of calm. I knew that I was going to be fine.

After three hours in emergency surgery, I was taken to intensive care. The first thing I heard as I came round from the anaesthetic was the soft, gentle voice of the nurse. She introduced herself as 'Christina'. That was my nan's name and it had been her birthday the day before. I instantly felt safe and knew that my late grandmother had an awful lot to do with me surviving such a terrible ordeal.

A few hours later, I was taken to the high dependency ward. Christina didn't leave my side even though she wasn't meant to leave ICU. She even came with me when they wheeled me back to the ward, taking one final look to make sure I was fine. The on-call surgeon then came round to reassure me that he would be there throughout the night. I remember him talking about lots of things and not really taking them in, but simply asking, 'What happened?' He explained in great detail (too much detail really to someone who had gallons of morphine running through them) and confirmed that I was very lucky to be alive due to the amount of blood I'd lost. His closing line was, 'If we hadn't operated, you'd have been dead in 15 minutes.'

When you come that close to death, it makes you realise how precious life is. We take for granted waking up each morning; it's not a given and it won't always come. I realised that I had been unhappy and had to make changes to make myself happy again. I needed time to heal. To grieve. To become ME.

The days and weeks that followed were filled with hospital and doctors' appointments. My body still thought I was pregnant and each week, I'd have to go back to the same hospital ward where I'd lost my baby, to be greeted with the sight of excited ladies going for their scans and check-ups, whilst I sat there waiting to have my weekly blood test to show my pregnancy levels dropping. Each week, I'd pray that they were wrong and that I'd be told there had been a big mistake. But I knew that wasn't the case. It took seven weeks of visiting the hospital to be told finally that I was no longer officially pregnant, and for some reason it hit me like a ton of bricks. I'd lost my baby on the 10th January but this seemed so final. I'd never experienced heartbreak but losing my baby made me feel like my heart was literally broken. It was pain that I didn't know was possible to feel; it was raw, it hurt like crazy. I remember questioning if I would ever smile, laugh, or actually find anything funny again.

I was lucky enough to be offered counselling after my ectopic pregnancy and they diagnosed me with PTSD, which came as no surprise given the ordeal I'd been through. My counsellor was amazing. It was great to be able to talk freely without her trying to fix me or make me feel better, like your loved ones try to do. She just let me talk and after each session, I felt better and stronger. I really looked forward to sessions as my confidence began to grow again.

I also tried Reiki for the first time and it was incredible! I was in there for almost three hours! The therapist, a beautiful lady called Elizabeth, started by clearing my chakras. She said that I'd been holding on to so much grief and sadness and it was time to let go. I felt like I floated home and after each session, I was lighter with the feelings that I was letting go.

I was also lucky enough to discover a lady who literally lives around the corner to me, who had just qualified in reflexology. I was still getting pain in my tummy from where I'd lost my right fallopian tube. She believed that the pain was due to scar tissue and worked to break this down at each appointment. After a few treatments, I stopped getting the pain and again floated home!

Along my journey, I also discovered a local group of women in Essex, led by two inspiring, strong women. They ran a course called 'Awakening the Soul' and it did exactly that! As I walked into the room full of all women, I wanted to run straight out. I don't like meeting new people at the best of times, let alone when I was feeling so low, but I shouldn't have worried as they were all feeling the same. Within a few hours of being together, I felt comfortable enough to share my story. There were tears, other experiences shared and I realised that I wasn't on my own. As the day came to an end, I felt liberated. I'd pushed myself out of my comfort zone and felt like I could take on the world.

I believe that all these people were brought into my life for a reason and each one of them played a huge part in bringing me back to ME. My family and friends were amazing throughout; they would visit, Facetime, call. They would listen, cuddle me and I could actually feel the love. My mum didn't leave my side for months. I knew that her heart was broken too but she would (and still does) reassure me that everything would work out exactly the way it should. My job became a huge comfort to me too. I realised how important it is to have structure in your life, whatever form that comes in.

Fast-forward a few months, and I visited Italy with my family in July 2019. We visited Andrea Bocelli's hometown and the stunning Teatro del Silenzio. On the approach, my uncle played Andrea's classic hit, 'Time to say Goodbye', and I realised at that point how far I'd come and how it was time to say goodbye to the hurt, sadness and disappointment. I still have sad times – Mother's Day, birthdays, anniversaries – but I have the tools to deal with them. I also realised that the Universe had to create something so life-changing for me to actually change my life.

On that holiday, I started to laugh again; to smile again; to find things funny again and, most importantly, TO BE ME AGAIN. And so the journey continues...

misspdesigns@hotmail.co.uk
FACEBOOK: @keiley.pegler
INSTAGRAM: @pegs444

Read Neshla's story as she struggled to understand why her natural psychic gifts weren't accepted by family and friends. Then she discovers psychic cafés and fayres. Eventually Neshla finds a healing modality that she naturally resonates with. Since coming across Rahanni Celestial Healing, she is now at the forefront of its development and, of creating awareness.

FINDING MY PATH

Neshla Avey

I always knew things, strange things that happened but I didn't know why. Mum used to pull a face when I knew who it was on the other end of the phone before she answered. She would roll her eyes and say I was a lucky guesser. However, there were some things she couldn't explain; couldn't put down to my 'overactive imagination'.

I thought everyone was like me, but when I realised I was different, I didn't want to be. I just wanted to fit in and be like the other girls at school. It was difficult enough being half foreign, as my father was from Cyprus and, in the 1960s, most people were very British and all had simple names like Jane or Susan. The last thing I wanted people to think was that I was weird too. I was extremely shy and certainly didn't want to stand out. So I suppressed it all, switched off my psychic instinct and carried on life to fit in with the crowd. Oh, if only I'd known then what I know now, perhaps I wouldn't have suffered with severe migraines, labyrinthitis and sinus problems – all linked to shutting the third eye!

I met my husband, Simon when I was 20, got married, and when I was pregnant with my first child, it all came flooding back. I couldn't avoid the signs. I kept noticing things; they would pop into my head. I then bought a few spiritual books and they resonated with me. Simon wasn't really into spirituality and didn't understand it.

One day I saw an advert in the local magazine to learn tarot. I decided I really wanted to do this and was determined I would. I went to my first class and took to it like a duck to water. I had no trouble tuning in to the cards. The teacher, at the end of the first class, picked a few cards out and asked the group what they thought this would mean for her. Everyone started joining in and saying what they thought but I kept quiet as I couldn't see what they were meaning. At the end of the class, the teacher called me back and asked why I was quiet and hadn't joined in with the group reading. I told her I didn't see what they meant as I'd got a completely different answer. She asked me what it was and when I told her, she said I was totally spot on and she could see I didn't really need to be in the class as I was a natural. That really boosted my confidence but I attended the rest of the classes anyway. I then went on to learn astrology and felt it made perfect sense. Funnily enough, it was around that time that my migraines stopped appearing.

I practised with friends who were open and people said how accurate I was. Simon could see there was something in it but was a bit worried as I think he thought I'd bring evil spirits into the house. However, after a while he got used to me giving readings for friends and family.

I eventually went back to work after six months of maternity leave and life got back to being busy, so I didn't have a lot of time for readings, but I did still do the odd one or two. I never charged for them. I just enjoyed doing them and I often surprised myself. I loved having the feedback that I'd helped people with decisions etc.

A couple of years later, the daughter of one of our neighbours was involved in a bad car accident and, as a result, lost a leg. She was 18 and training to be a ballerina. She had a prosthetic leg given by the NHS but she wanted a special one so she could dance, which was only available in the USA and very expensive, as you can imagine. Her mother decided to do a fund-raiser at our local pub and asked me if I'd give readings to raise some money. At first I was reluctant as I'd never done readings for strangers, only friends and family. However, Simon, by this time my number one fan, pushed me to believe in myself and said, 'What's the worst that could happen? It's for charity, you'll be fine.'

I eventually gave in and very nervously went to the pub the following week, with both my husband and daughter by my side. I did readings for £5 each, which were a great success, and I actually found it easier to read for complete strangers as I knew nothing about them so had to rely totally on my psychic insight. The feedback I got was amazing and I was so proud of myself. I was on a high and it was great to have had the opportunity to help raise some money. I have a letter of thanks from my neighbour and I'll always treasure it. After all, it was the first time I'd done readings for the public.

Life took over again and the readings were few and far between but I always kept my hand in. I had my second child five years later and had even less time for readings, especially as I went back to work again after he was six months old. I still read spiritual books though and attended mind, body and spirit fayres when I had the time to do so.

When my youngest was six, we moved to Southampton for my husband's job and I decided to give up my job to go freelance, as I couldn't commute myself. I was in medical publishing as a production line manager and I loved it. However, my manager had other ideas. He didn't want to lose me so I started working from home, only going into the office once a week. I knew nobody in Southampton, which felt a little strange, and I didn't do any psychic readings on the side, although I'd grown to enjoy doing them. They'd become part of me, part of who I am. I missed them and the comfort they gave me, an outlet for my psychic side. There was nothing much in this area psychically that I could find and I missed being around people, especially those who were into the same stuff as I was.

One day, I was reading a spiritual magazine and I saw an advert for Psychic Café, where people could set up their own psychic cafés and teach others. It really sang to me and I mentioned it to Simon. He smiled and said he was surprised I'd thought about it as I was shy and would have to stand up and teach in front of groups. I knew it would be coming out of my comfort zone but thought it would be a good way of meeting like-minded people and perhaps making a few new friends. I also felt that, having read so many spiritual books, I had a lot of knowledge to share. So I paid the franchise money and set up the classes in our local community centre. I was so nervous before the first one, but only two people turned up so I was grateful in a way, although it actually cost me to run the class!

After a few months, more and more people came and I got more and more confident. I got them all interacting with each other and each month, I taught a different subject, each time gaining more and more knowledge myself. I'm still running these workshops years on and look forward to them every month. I'd never taught anything before but found it natural and I enjoyed it.

It was in class that somebody mentioned a new psychic fair starting about half an hour away, and I decided I should be brave and do some readings there if I could. I contacted the lady, who was happy for me to join them. When the day came, I was so nervous – ridiculous as I'd been running my classes – but it was a long time since I'd done many readings and this was to the paying public.

On the day, I was shown to my table and I set it up ready. I was told the person next to me would be selling wood crafts, so you can imagine my surprise when a lady arrived and started setting up her table for readings. She was very friendly and told me her son was due to do the wood crafts but wasn't well and, rather than waste the table, she would do readings. She said she'd stopped doing readings at fayres years ago but it was nice to be out again. Although she was so friendly, it made me even more nervous being next to a pro! She had a sheet on her table for bookings and so many people came up to her and said hello, and put their name down. Little me next door was totally overlooked and I panicked a bit but just thought, 'I'm here now, I'll do what I'm meant to do.' However, I didn't need to worry. When the doors opened to the public, people started drifting my way. Before long I was totally into doing the readings and I didn't have time to think about the lady next to me.

At the end of the day, she came over to me and said she had a message from Archangel Michael. She said he'd told her he was proud of me as, instead of dimming my vibration and hiding, I'd raised it and had accepted things were as they were meant to be, and that was what had drawn people towards me. That meant a lot to me and I'll always remember this.

After that, I kept getting asked for readings from the people in my classes, so I started charging for them; only donations but it was something in exchange for my time. A couple of ladies even asked me to go to their houses and do a tarot party for them and their friends. After a while, a few people in my class had asked if I taught tarot and I'd always said no. However, once I had quite a number asking, I thought it was perhaps something I should do. It felt right and I spent time devising a structure as to how I could teach. Simon was encouraging and said I should do what I loved doing. I taught six people to start with and they all really enjoyed the class. Over the years, I ran a few of these classes and each time perfected the way I taught and the notes I handed out. I learnt as much from my students as they did from me.

One day, I found that, locally, they were running a spiritual fair but, rather than doing readings, I decided I would go along as a customer. Simon looked after the children and I went on my own – oh, to have some me time in an environment I felt so comfortable in! I had a great morning out and bought many spiritual goodies to take home.

It was on my way out that I spotted a lady in the corner with a couch, doing some form of healing. I'd never been drawn to healing but something told me to go over to her stand. I went to her and we started chatting. She was a lovely warm soul, who has since become a good friend. I said I'd have a go and got on her couch. Wow, the colours I could see; the energy I felt! It was amazing and most of all, it felt wonderful. I told her about the experience I'd had and she said I was a natural healer myself. I was surprised as I hadn't even thought about it. However, after chatting for a while, she told me she was learning to become a Reiki teacher and I said I'd be her first student. On the way home, I wondered why I'd said that but trusted it was meant to be. Three months later, I learnt Reiki I, followed by Reiki II six months after that. I did enjoy working with energies but didn't really feel it was my calling.

A while after, I went to the Mind, Body & Spirit fair in London with my daughter, who was also getting into her spiritual side, and, while waiting for her to have a reading, I browsed at some other stalls. There was a stall with Theta Healing and I had a look. The lady started chatting to me about this form of healing and said there was a competition to win a weekend to learn to become a practitioner. I remember looking at the huge Perspex box and asking her if it was one prize per day or over the whole weekend. She told me it was over the whole weekend and, although I wasn't really bothered about the prize, I thought I may as well join in. Two weeks later, imagine my surprise when I received an email telling me I'd won the course, which was set up for a couple of months' time in London. I went along and really enjoyed it, and I met some lovely people that weekend. However, what put me off was that there were so many other courses to do for it, which would cost a lot of money, so once again I let it slip.

A couple of years later, I bought a pack of Ascended Masters cards and kept picking Lord Melchizedek, Spiritual Law of Attraction. I had no idea what he was trying to tell me until I went to London for a meeting at work and forgot my book to read on the train. I bought a copy of a new magazine, *High Spirit*, which has unfortunately now gone out of business. It had an article about Rahanni Celestial Healing, and this really resonated with me, especially when I read it was channelled by Lord Melchizedek himself. I had goose bumps all down my arms and knew then I had to learn this new healing modality. I phoned the lady who channelled it and found she was in Essex and the only teacher. Therefore I had to travel the three and a half hours' drive to learn this, but I knew it was meant to be. And it was amazing; so heart-centred, gentle yet powerful. So much so in fact that I knew I had to become a teacher, and I went back six months later to learn it. It's the only healing I've felt I needed to teach, and I started doing healing on others as well as my readings, as a sideline.

Meanwhile, work had moved to central London, which was a little far to go each week with a family and home to look after so, once again, I handed in my notice. And once again my boss didn't want to lose me, so I agreed to continue working from home and only go in for some meetings, with the rest on Webex. I really missed being with people though, so started travelling a little further afield to attend psychic fayres as a reader, which I thoroughly enjoyed, and I loved the feeling of being able to help others. It got to the stage where I was actually doing quite a few readings in the evenings, teaching my classes and, at weekends, doing the fayres, and I realised I couldn't do it all. My family were growing up so didn't need me as much, as they were doing their own thing, and my husband often worked weekends so it wasn't bad in that way. It's just that I was getting exhausted.

It was December 2014 – and now or never. I'd thought about it before. It was a brave step but I knew I was getting so much more satisfaction out of helping others than making a big company even richer. My husband was reluctant at first but I reminded him that I could always go freelance if I couldn't make any money out of it. I knew in my heart it was totally the right thing to do and never doubted that it would work. I picked up the phone and, when my boss asked, 'How much can I offer you to get you to change your mind this time?', I told him that I wouldn't be changing it so no need to discuss figures.

So, in January 2015, I started on my new journey doing psychic readings, healings and teaching. I got a website designed and things took off bit by bit. There were times when I waited for the phone to ring as things were quiet but I needn't have worried as, before long, I was extremely busy. Simon even said to me he thought I would have to go freelance, but he was very proud of me and was getting quite spiritual himself. Mum has come to believe in me and my abilities, but my siblings and my dad still think of it as a bit of a joke and don't understand it. I remember once going to my niece's sixth birthday party. Someone had given her a magic wand, which you shook and it made a tingling sound and glitter floated about. Dad picked it up, handed it to me and said, 'This'd be good for your job.' Everyone laughed but this time, instead of reacting, I just thought I'd let it go. I knew what I was doing was right and there was no point arguing my point anymore as it fell on deaf ears.

I was still running my monthly workshops but expanded and, as well as teaching tarot, started doing psychic development classes and teaching my healing. I've taught many people tarot, psychic development and Rahanni healing. I've also been brave enough to do talks at various fayres and have overcome my shyness and really come out of my comfort zone. Simon and I now regularly travel to fayres across the country and, while I'm doing my readings, he does a bit of photography, which is his passion. We both enjoy travelling to different places and often add a couple of days after the fair to look around the area. Now the kids have left home and Simon doesn't work weekends, it's given us the freedom to do this.

It wasn't long after that Carol, the lady who channelled Rahanni Celestial Healing, asked me if I'd take it over from her when she left this planet, as she was 75 at the time and her health wasn't very good. I was honoured to say yes and was amazed she'd picked me, but she told me that as soon as I walked into her room she knew I'd be the one to take it over. I put down the phone and remember thinking, wow, what a big responsibility that is, but I knew it felt right. I've now taught over 400 pupils and 50 teachers, so I'm proud to be getting it out there and know it's part of my job. I travelled to many places such as North Wales, Devon, Somerset, Kent and Bristol to get Rahanni out there, as there were no teachers in those areas. Now there are quite a few and this healing modality is spreading where it is meant to. I still travel a bit but not as much as I did in the early days when nobody had heard of it.

While in Cyprus on holiday with my husband Simon, I started getting images in my head and came to realise these were tarot card images. We bought a notepad and, as they came into my head, I would describe them to Simon and he would draw them on the pad. Before long, I'd created my own tarot deck, which I called the Learner Tarot, as the designs are so simple and there had never been a deck like this before. I use these for my teaching now and sell them on Amazon. I even appeared in *Spirit & Destiny* magazine with an article about me and the cards, something I'd never dreamed would happen.

I'm proud to say that from humble beginnings I've now done TV and radio interviews, and been in the local paper about my tarot cards, as well as in some magazines, and I love my work. I've expanded greatly, doing Skype readings all over the world, and will never look back. I know I'm psychic but I never envisaged doing all this and if someone had told me that I would be, I'd never have believed them. Every day is different, everyone has their own different needs and I tune in and help that person as an individual. Not a day goes by without me feeling how grateful and lucky I am to be doing what I love. There is nothing more satisfying than being able to help others, and seeing people change for the better and become happier makes it all worthwhile. In fact, I enjoy it so much it doesn't even feel like work. I never realised how stressed I was in my publishing job until I left it, and I certainly needed the few weeks off between leaving and starting up my own business. I won't deny I did worry a bit and spent far too much on advertising in the first few months. However, I soon learnt that advertising doesn't bring in business. It's always word of mouth so the psychic fayres were a great start. These days I don't do so many of the smaller fayres but I do the larger fayres, which have a wonderful buzz, and I've met so many other stallholders who feel like family. We always look forward to catching up at other events.

For those of you out there who have an ability you've denied or aren't sure what to do with, don't leave it as late as I did, but explore and find out what you're really here to do. There is so much more information out there now and the internet has really helped people get their message across. It's also far more acceptable than when I was younger, when people hushed the psychic world. People are so much more interested now. I can't hide anymore behind my publishing job when people ask me what I do for a living, and I get a far more positive reaction these days. A lot of people ask more questions and find it fascinating rather than avoiding you. What I've really learnt is that I should have believed in myself sooner, done something about it and helped more people along the way. It's so satisfying being able to help others on their path; something that money can't buy. Life's not about making money but enjoying what you do.

www.neshlaavey.com
FACEBOOK: @neshlaavey
INSTAGRAM: @neshla111
TWITTER: @neshlaavey

Realising her natural gifts, Debbie accepted and developed them, but was in for a shock when her local church rejected her and 'asked' her to leave. Debbie has since further developed and set up Mind Body Spirit Fairs in Scotland.

FROM CHURCH TO CORPORATE TO DINOSAUR

Debbie Bolton

I grew up in a deeply religious, born-again Christian family, with my father being a preacher at a local church. From as young as I can remember, I'd always been taken to church twice on a Sunday, and to various Christian groups for children during the week. I felt as if I was 'brainwashed' by the church, to the point where I even attended in my twenties, was baptised and became a church member. At that age, I lived 450 miles away from my parents, who still influenced me to attend.

Then, at one point, I felt as if I was living a lie. I was attending church, but I didn't believe what was written in the Bible, purely because the congregation in the church didn't live what was being preached. There was no brotherly or sisterly love towards each other even though they said there was. In reality, there wasn't. At one members' meeting, the members were told to invite single and older people around for lunch after the service on a Sunday morning. I wasn't invited once to anyone's house in two months in an 80-strong membership. I mentioned this to the minister, who made a point of telling the members again during the next meeting. I was still not invited around in a six-month period. That's when I made the decision to stop going to church. I couldn't go along to a place where people weren't looking after each other, when the person we were supposed to be worshipping told us to do it.

I shared a house with my brother and he consistently came back from services and meetings saying, 'So-and-so says they miss you,' and this went on for months. This was also a classic line that's said to people around the churches to tell them their non-attendance is disapproved of. At no point did the minister or any of the elders of the church contact me to ask me why I'd stopped attending.

Over this time, I met a man and got engaged to him. We got married and moved to a nearby town, which was closer to both of our respective workplaces.

Soon after, the phone calls from the elders started to come in on a weekly basis. They wanted me to write a letter of resignation of my membership, which I didn't do. This went on for several months. Eventually, they started to relay messages through my brother and, again, I didn't write my resignation letter. There was a part of the constitution that said if communion wasn't taken twice in a row or if a person hadn't attended for two months, with no contact, then their membership would be revoked. But the church evidently didn't want to go down that route. This was six months since I'd stopped going there.

Eventually, I wrote my resignation letter and sent it to them. One of the answerphone messages they left told me exactly what I should write! They were desperate not to have a blot on their record.

After leaving the church, I worked, made friends, and went on many holidays with my husband.

Four years later, a friend's mother died. My friend had serious depression, was grieving, and was looking for something to help her through it. She attended a local meditation group and, the following day, she was more positive. With my curious attitude of trying anything once (and if I don't like it, I'll never do it again), I went along with her the following week.

This was the start of a three-week journey that completely changed my life.

My first meditation experience nearly turned into a disaster. I was told at the start to 'just go with it' and allow my mind to picture what was being said. So, that's what I did. The meditation was about connecting to others throughout the Earth. I was in the middle of several circles. The next from me was my husband and loved ones, the next was my friends and other family, the next my colleagues, the next was other people I knew, the next was everyone else in the world and the final circle was of all the animals.

The circle of animals let my mind go places, but I just went with it. There was a hamster next to a shark, a monkey next to fish, a cat next to an elephant, but I kept going with the instruction to 'just go with it' instead of questioning it. Then we were told that the circle of animals had merged with the circle of everyone else in the world, and all the circles were merging and coming towards me. This began to happen but what I wasn't prepared for was for a dinosaur to come trampling through everything and take my husband's head off and eat it!

Needless to say, that was an unusual experience and one I nearly didn't recover from. I thought about it for a few days, but despite the scare, I went back the following week. Again, this dinosaur turned up in my meditation. This time the leader said that perhaps I wasn't protected enough, so she said we'd work on that more the following week. We did, but the dinosaur continued to turn up and did so on a weekly basis for nine months. We'll come back to the dinosaur.

Two weeks after my first meditation experience, the leader sent out an email to ask me if I'd like to attend a Reiki I course. I worked in a corporate environment and was achieving in my job. I made the decision to attend the Reiki I course with my corporate brain, as I was to receive a certificate at the end of it. Corporate brains see that as a valuable commodity to put on their CV. So, I attended the course and followed the instructions of what to do for the two weeks prior.

What happened next is best described as phenomenal. I was eager to learn just for that certificate and, right before the first break of the day, the leader wanted to open us up to Reiki. At this point, I must say that I had a contempt for Angels. I didn't believe in them and thought they were a joke; part of my religious upbringing. During this opening up, I was given a gift from the Universe of a feather, which symbolises an Angel. I became a little more open-minded and made the decision to get an Angel reading from the leader. If an Angel was bothering to contact me, then I might as well find out who it was.

I don't know exactly where the shift happened throughout this weekend, but, by the end of it, Reiki had changed my heart. I tell people that I made the decision with my corporate head, but Reiki changed my heart. I felt peace for the first time in my life; I felt calmness and a stillness that I can't explain in words, and I received a beautiful experience during my attunement whilst I felt the energy and love of the Reiki Masters.

So, three weeks after my first meditation experience, I was changing in a way I never had before. The day after the Reiki course, I was back into the corporate world and I wasn't enjoying it.

I attended the meditation classes on a weekly basis, and they were a small oasis from the corporate life that was my career. Every week this dinosaur turned up and was a regular feature of the post-meditation discussion. This carried on for months and people discussed many different meanings. In the early days, others' theories were that it meant something deep-rooted. In the end, I came to the realisation that the dinosaur represented my remaining beliefs that had been instilled by the church.

Below is a poem I wrote after the dinosaur left my meditations. And just for everyone's information, the dinosaur has never reappeared again!

One of the principles of Reiki is, 'Just for today, do not be angry'. I started to take that mantra to work with me. If I thought I was going to explode, I would put a high-vis vest on and march up and down the warehouse muttering to myself, 'Just for today, do not be angry.' I found it challenging but eventually, I chilled out and relaxed into my life.

Due to meditation and Reiki, I now regularly attain the peace and stillness of my soul that I experienced many years ago, blocking out the worries of the superhighway of thoughts in my mind.

To the Death of My Dinosaur and What It Means to Me

We met on a Wednesday in a room in my head
You embraced my loved ones and I watched them bleed
Many times, you showed yourself to me
And the burden of you did not make me feel free

My mind's eye makes you into a dinosaur
Something deep-rooted and old
You never told me who you were
Or what you resembled to me

At first you made me think this was all a joke
You nearly ruined everything
My spiritual journey was just beginning
And you were tagging along for the ride
Every week you would appear and scare me
Your face right in mine, taking me by surprise
I can see your lumpy scales, skin, and eye
Staring right at me, waiting for me to make my next move

Sometimes you were just behind me, breathing down my neck
Making me uneasy as if I should not be here
But I did want to try, and I felt every benefit
So why would you try to interfere?

One beautiful evening we opened our hearts
Mine was a sensational rose, opening each petal in turn
The tranquil serenity of the moment
Then like every watchful predator, you appeared and ate it in one gulp

Why did you ruin something so pure?
Why did you appear out of nowhere?
You were not invited, you were certainly not needed
But my inner strength carried on

An Earth meditation sitting outside
I created a bubble of protection
There you were from the outside looking in
Staying a distance away from me

The next time we met, it was not a surprise
But I got brave and talked to you
I told you to go if you were to be a problem
You watched and just stood and stared

I could hear your breath but could not feel it
I could reach out and touch, but I did not dare
I was intrigued by your presence
I wanted to know who you are

One evening I confronted you, an annoyance you had become
As normal, I confronted your intentions
You turned and left, I could see your tail
Seven times you turned away until finally I was prepared

We approached each other head-on
And you let me know loud and clear
I need to spend more time for myself
Then you voluntarily turned and walked away

I felt a little sad, I thought this was the end
I followed what you said
But the next week you appeared again
Your presence became our group's in-house joke

Time passed; our group changed
But you were the constant I came to expect
You still appeared watching me silently
As if I were your prey you knew you could not catch

One fateful evening I came to meditate
Tonight, it was about our Angels
I met Sam in a cave, and you were at the door
Our auras kept you there

We walked out of the cave hand in hand
Our auras pushing the way ahead
They pushed you off the path
You fell down the side of a cliff

We walked right past you as if you lacked importance
We walked up to the top of the mountain
Looking across I could see you on your side
Your passing was obvious to all

You too are also invited to ponder
Why was he here?
Will he appear again?
Were my beliefs so deep-rooting my dinosaur represented them?

Its significance now appears to be gone
But I will remember
The death of my dinosaur
And what he means to me

www.loveandabove.co.uk
Indigoangel444@outlook.com
FACEBOOK: @loveandabovegroupstherapiestraining
INSTAGRAM: @debbieindigoangel

An interest in Buddhism led 'Diamond Di', as I call her, to study counselling, which then naturally took her into the spiritual realms. Di's book, The Sacred Order of The Magi *was born in 2010 and is to be made into a film for us to see what actually happened to the three wise men.*

MY SACRED JOURNEY TO THE MAGI

Dianne Pegler

The title of the wonderful book you are holding describes my own spiritual journey perfectly. Perhaps mine could also be labelled *Rabbit Caught in the Headlight Psychic*!

My spiritual Awakening began when I encountered a rather bad-tempered Buddhist. It was 1996 and I had just started working for Social Services in East London.

An angry Buddhist is the antithesis of what you may imagine so perhaps it is kinder to say that Caroline (not her real name) was very definite in her views and opinions… and not afraid to voice them.

For some reason, Caroline liked me and we would join one another for lunch, which is where, one memorable lunch hour, I discovered that she was a member of the Soka-Gakkai form of Buddhism, founded in the 13th century by Nichiren Daishonin in Japan.

I have always been interested in Buddhism. My religious project at school was about the Buddhist doctrine, which wasn't very well received at my Catholic convent grammar school at the time, I recall. So, I was an avid listener to Caroline as she discussed her Buddhist spiritual doctrine.

On reflection, I realise that I was at one of those crossroads in life. It was my time to 'awaken' even if I didn't know this myself.

Caroline told me those who wished to know more about the wonders of this religion were asked to chant the Soka-Gakkai mantra for 100 days to experience it for themselves. Caroline explained that chanting the Nam Myoho

Renge Kyo mantra activated the Lotus Flower within to blossom, allowing Universal Enlightenment. It's often known as The Miracle Chant.

Nam, I bow to the divinity within you. It holds the same base origin as the familiar Sanskrit greeting, 'Namaste'.

Myoho relates to the Wonderful Law or Mystical Law of the Universe, which is the doctrine of cause and effect considered by Buddhists to be the ultimate Law of the Universe.

Renge translates to the Lotus Flower. The Lotus Flower seeds and blooms at the same time, representing the concept that cause and effect are 'sewn' at the same time, although effect may not manifest until later in time. The analogy of the Lotus Flower blooming in the murkiest of ponds emphasises that we also hold the potential to bloom whatever our circumstances.

Kyo translates to 'the voice' of the Buddha.

Being the same person inside, although somehow life had got in my way, who was so attracted to the ideals of the Love, Peace and Harmony of the 60s' hippie movement, this all sounded so magical. It was music to my ears and I couldn't wait to go home and to begin chanting, although the raised eyebrow by my husband makes me chuckle to this day. The memory also makes me smile because those initial 100 days of chanting sparked off a 'Magical Mystery Tour', to borrow a phrase, which I could never have imagined in my wildest dreams.

By the following June, I had completed a BSc Certificate in Counselling and embarked upon teacher training in Louise Hay's 'Heal Your Life'. On arrival at the training college in Birmingham, my newly discovered confidence seemed to disappear. I was a proverbial 'rabbit in the headlights'. I felt completely out of my comfort zone and seriously questioned what had possessed me to do such a thing. It was however one of the best things I have ever done, but at the introductory session of the first evening, it took all my courage to even find my voice.

What a year 1997 was.

Diana, Princess of Wales, passed away in late August. For those of you who remember it, you will recall the heightened energies of that week as though the sights and sounds had been transformed into 3D.

In September 1997, I attended the enrolment evening at a local adult evening college that had hesitantly agreed to my request to teach 'Heal Your Life' classes over a ten-week period. I recollect that the college administrators had said, 'We're not sure how much demand there will be for the course. Please don't worry if no one registers.'

During the evening of enrolment, such was the clamour to enrol that a subsequent ten-week course commencing the following January was quickly arranged. I was delighted for myself and that I'd also justified the 'leap of faith' the kindly administrators had placed in me.

As well as presenting the ten-week adult course based on Louise Hay's bestselling book, *You Can Heal Your Life*, I was passionate about taking her philosophy and life skills to children. If children learnt to appreciate the beauty within themselves and realised that they held gifts and talents unique to themselves then they would flourish in the world. I reasoned that the children would grow up knowing this within themselves, rather than feeling the need to attend adult night classes and personal development courses later in life.

That was the spark that ignited within me during the 'Heal Your Life' training. I was on a mission. I had never been so determined in my life.

Together with a friend I'd met on the course, we developed Hay4Kids. Hay4Kids comprised of a teacher training play course, a board game and positive affirmations cards all based on a Treasure Hunt Quest for the children to discover the hidden gems on a mysterious island. The aim was, of course, that the children realised that they held the hidden jewels within themselves all along.

My friend and I presented the Hay4Kids programme to Louise Hay herself at her home in San Diego in October 1997. We sat on Louise's bed while she watched a video of children playing the games at the Treasure Hunt play day. We played the Treasure Hunt board game with her at her dining room table. Surreal moments, which always make me smile. Not many can say they have sat on Louise Hay's bed.

All this happened just one year after I began to chant.

We presented Hay4Kids at the Louise Hay Advanced Teacher Training course in Virginia Beach, VA the following year. It was successful within the Louise Hay teaching foundation but never achieved the success we had hoped for outside that arena. Various factors were involved. However, I console myself with the knowledge that a good many children's lives were enhanced with the life skills and personal development tools found within the Hay4Kids programme. Hay4Kids manuals were sent to Louise Hay teachers in the UK, the States, Canada, Europe, South Africa, Australia and New Zealand.

We decided that we had to call a halt to the path of Hay4Kids in the early 2000s, although I have never fully given up hope of resurrecting it one day. This left a gaping hole inside me. I was secretly devastated that I had not fulfilled my dream for the children.

The Beautiful Beings who came to my rescue at that time were Angels. I had *stumbled* across them while running the 'Heal Your Life' adult classes. A group of the ladies begged me to teach them about Angels which, at the time, was probably as much as they knew themselves. However, they proceeded to hire a room close by where they all lived and once a week on a separate night to the 'Heal Your Life' classes, we helped one another discover our love for Angels.

On the first evening, we made a circle of chairs. I led everyone in a guided meditation to meet their Guardian Angel, asking their Angel's name. The excitement built as everyone revealed their own beautiful Angel name, some of which were rather exotic. We were all thrilled by the success of the evening. There was animated conversation as we put the chairs back to where we had found them, until it all went so quiet that you could have heard a pin drop. Behind one of the chairs lay a perfect, curled, white feather where there had been no sign of one before. I shall never forget the sense of joy and the peace the sight of that feather brought to everyone that evening.

Angels were my salvation after the cessation of Hay4Kids and have continued to be so to this day. I don't know where I would be without them.

I trained in Angel Therapy with Doreen Virtue in Glastonbury in 2005, which, strange to say, is where my path crossed with Alison. It would, however, be a decade later before we discovered that we had been on the course together. I'm sure the Angels had a little smile when the 'penny finally dropped'. I know Alison and I did. We were astounded.

I know that Doreen's path has taken her in another direction now; however, I will always remember the times I spent with her with great joy. I acknowledge with great appreciation everything Doreen taught me. I wish her only joy and peace on her journey.

I have always had a seeking mind and am never happier than when I'm in the throes of a project. In 2008, I began to research whether Jesus had visited England. I tend to think that we accept that now but it was not the case then.

While most people would have begun their search in Glastonbury, the acknowledged spiritual magnet for many spiritual truth seekers, my inner guidance told me I needed to seek Jesus in Cornwall. The following year I came across the book, *The Missing Years of Jesus* by Dennis Price, where he writes about the 18 unaccounted for years of Jesus in the Bible, from when he was 12 years old until his sudden reappearance aged 30. It's a fascinating book.

Within the book, Dennis presents compelling evidence that Jesus did visit England, accompanying his uncle, Joseph of Arimathea. Joseph traded tin in Cornwall and silver in North Devon. Confirmation of my inner knowing.

We live in Essex so holidayed in Cornwall several times within those years. It's a beautiful county, rugged and wild. We love it, as a family. All the while, I was seeking that special connection to Jesus that I knew I would feel when I had found it. We visited St Michael's Mount off the coast of Penzance, which lies on the same Archangel Michael ley line as Mont St Michel in Brittany. I climbed to the top of the mount to sit in the chapel. That 'special feeling' wasn't there although it is magnificent.

We visited Tintagel, the home of my guide, Merlin. The view from the ridge overlooking Merlin's Cave is breathtaking. But I didn't feel any connection to Jesus there either, unfortunately.

Then I discovered the Roseland Peninsula of Cornwall. The Roseland is a hidden gem and reportedly gets its name from the Cornish word for 'jutting point', but I knew it was the Rose Line of Jesus and Mary. It had to be. I knew I was close to finding Jesus in England. I could feel it even before we visited.

You know how it is when you haven't heard of something and then everyone seems to be talking about it? That's how it was with the Roseland. A friend said to me, 'You must visit St Just in Roseland church. It's the most beautiful church in England.' I took this with a pinch of salt. That is until we visited the church in September 2010. It is stunning. I knew immediately I had found the essence of Jesus. With every fibre of my being, I knew he had been there 2000 years ago.

The 13th-century church of St Just hugs the bank of the River Percuil opposite the Sacred Well of St Just. Whatever the season, it's beautiful, with a pervading ambience of grace and solitude.

Just before Christmas 2010, I received a message. Round and round it went in my mind:

'There Is A Band of Brothers Called The Magi.' That first sentence led to 21 messages revealing the 'hidden' story of the role the Three Wise Men had played in the life of Jesus.

It was Melchior, the youngest Magi, born in St Just in Roseland, who had patiently waited for 2000 years to tell their amazing, secret story.

Melchior's 21 beautiful messages are to be found within my book, *The Sacred Order of The Magi,* which was published in May 2013.

In early 2014, Melchior told me in a further message that I was to make a film based upon The Magis' role of Spiritual Security Force to Jesus. The film was to be set in the present day.

I have no involvement with the film world. I had however learnt to trust in the messages I received from Melchior. I wasn't dismayed at all. I just set out to do what I had to do, even though I may not have known the 'how'.

As I write this piece about my spiritual journey, on the first day of May 2020, we stand on the brink of making this spectacular film.

As with the *Reluctantly Psychic* book, the journey towards making The Magi film has been one of collaboration and support. I believe that to be the only way.

Oh, and by the way, I'm not quite so much a 'rabbit caught in the headlights' these days.

Dianne Pegler is author of The Sacred Order of The Magi *which can be found on Amazon.*

Dianne.pegler@icloud.com
FACEBOOK: @dianne pegler
INSTAGRAM: @diannepegler

Justin 'saw' his gifts from the age of four but kept it a secret when he entered a world of teaching by his guides. He eventually came out of the spiritual closet and actively works as a medium now.

JUSTIN SAGEN'S STORY

Justin Sagen

My name is Justin Sagen, and I'm a psychic medium and spiritual healer based in London, UK. This is my story.

I kept my gift secret for most of my life, trying to make sense of it and learning to live with it. At school, the teachers thought I was getting distracted but I was communicating with the spirit world. To my friends, I was described as always being in another world and they would call me 'Spacey' for many years. I wasn't trying to be spaced out, it was just that it was like having a phone in my head that rings and takes calls. I was talking to my spirit guides and although I didn't know who I was speaking with at the time, later I realised that it was in fact a gift.

I could feel energy or the presence of Spirit around me as far back as when I was eight to nine years old. Communicating with them was normal. I didn't think it was important or anything special. I just wanted to have a normal life but that would never make me happy. When I was 16, I read my first book about Buddhism. It ignited a fire of curiosity and intrigue inside me. I was fascinated with meditation, monks and the search for enlightenment. The meditation helped me to calm my mind and to process the turbulent emotions I was experiencing from my home life. I wanted to learn more about myself and expand my mind.

I was shown a path to self-discovery by my spirit guides and a path to living with higher states of consciousness. I read books about positive thinking, Neuro Linguistic Programming (NLP), spirituality, Zen and a host of topics that I still research today. I gravitated towards spiritual people and made some really good friends, who would help me to understand the shift that was happening within me. There were times when I thought my mind was going to explode. I could also drift into a blissful state quite easily. I now recognise that what was occurring was a massive shift in my ego to make way for a deep connection with Spirit.

During this time, I experienced a lot of strange coincidences. I was discovering how I could use my mind to make positive things happen. In my twenties, I experienced very intense psychic experiences: suddenly, a psychic download would flash through my mind lightning fast. I would try to remember it, like a good dream, or grab a pen to jot it down, but often it slipped away. These were very abstract spiritual concepts that made a lot of sense to me at the time. Now I understand that my mind was picking up signals from the spirit world. A good analogy for mediumship is a radio: the medium uses his/her mind like a radio. He/she then attunes their mind to the right frequency to pick up the station where the spirits who want to communicate reside.

As time went on, the door to the psychic world kept on knocking and the more I ignored it, the louder it became. I was drowning in spiritual awareness because I wasn't using it. It was only when I began offering readings to friends that I felt like a massive block in my energy system had moved. I felt wonderful; a shift in me had taken place. This helped to build my confidence and I started offering professional psychic readings.

As I accepted my sixth sense more, I realised that my spirit family had assisted with many transitions in my life, which could only be described as destiny or fate. Some of the decisions I had made when I'd trusted my intuition turned out to be the best decisions I'd ever made, and this strengthened my trust.

My father introduced me to breath-work and meditation. I didn't live with him but I used to spend my summer holiday with him in Canada when I was a teenager. He helped to accelerate my psychic and spiritual growth. He took so much pride in spiritual development and meditation. After spending a year with an enlightened mystic in India during the 1980s, he experienced his own epiphanies. I've practised breath-work and meditation since then. Breath-work became my drug. The more I did, the more my consciousness expanded and the more aware I became.

Although I had this input in my early adult years, it was only when I was in my late twenties that I really started to accept that I could be a psychic medium.

It was mainly through psychic experiences and the realisation that I could actually help people. My job wasn't fulfilling me and I longed to be working with Spirit and enjoying the connection to higher states of consciousness. I knew this was something I should embark on, but it was still a few years later before I began to listen in.

In my life, I've had a mixture of positive and negative psychic experiences. Having conversations with loved ones who have passed over is always pleasant. Experiencing altered states of consciousness during breath-work is always amazing. I've also had some pretty wacky psychic adventures, including being abducted by aliens and meeting strange beings from other dimensions. This happened consistently throughout the ages of around 10 to 18. I remember waking up and feeling like I'd been somewhere else. After meditating on the experience, I realised that these beings had managed to abduct my soul from my body before travelling in my Astral body to the other side. When I awoke, I didn't recall much but I knew I'd been somewhere else.

Although I've had some unpleasant experiences, I believe they did open up my psychic abilities and they were very valuable to my development in this field. Without them, I would certainly not be doing the work I am today. Other factors that have assisted my development would be my diet. I've always had a healthy diet, abstaining from excessive amounts of alcohol, meat, refined sugar, white flour and processed foods, and I believe this does keep the psychic pathways clear. The pineal gland is the gateway for the soul when it enters into the Astral plane, and ingesting toxic substances can calcify the pineal gland and shut down psychic faculties.

The psychic world can be strange and can offer a lot of bizarre experiences, and making sense of them can be difficult. I've found dream analysis books to be most helpful. Sometimes, it's a bit like being awake in a dream and you don't know what will happen next. It can be scary to see things you don't understand, and have thoughts that you question the origin of. You can always call upon your guides and teachers in spirit for guidance or protection if you ever feel lost, as I have done countless times. They are there to ground you and help you understand your experience. This has helped me to grasp what is real and what is imaginary. The truth remains when everything else falls away, meaning if a thought or feeling stays with you then this might be a message for you from Spirit.

Of course, everything has a reason for appearing in the mind, but like a dream we may remember upon awakening, it doesn't prevent us from getting on with our day. If I were to say to you, 'Don't think of an elephant', most likely an elephant would pop up in your mind. That's how creative the mind is. It's the most powerful computer you can imagine.

Taking control of the psychic faculty can be challenging in today's busy world. I've never been forced to completely close it because I've always had jobs where I've used my intuition. But there have been times when I've wanted to totally shut it down because I felt I was receiving too much information. I've found physical exercise to help with this, and grounding my body by walking barefoot outside directly on the earth. It took some time to learn to control this faculty, but with the right techniques I did. A lot of people suffer from hypersensitivity where they pick up too much from their environment. This can be healed and I suggest meditation and a healthy diet.

Remaining in the 'real world' and the spiritual world is definitely a crucial skill, not just for readings but for general life. It's important to close your faculty if you're in a busy environment or just need to focus on something. Opening your faculty can also be useful for creative projects, inspiration, healing, psychic readings and meditation. At times, I've felt that my sixth sense has completely gone and I won't be able to regain it, but luckily that has never happened (even after a few beers).

Meditation practice has helped me to really gain control of my sixth sense. I completed my first ten-day silent vipassana meditation course when I was 17 years old – I was the youngest person they had ever accepted. It gave me a solid foundation for spiritual growth. My meditation practice has offered me the tools to quiet my mind, and clarity when tuning in to the spirit world. The psychic medium is a messenger from the spirit world to this world. Their role is to simply pass on information. I've found that the clearer my mind is, the more accurate the reading will be because I'm not allowing my mind to filter or interfere with the information being communicated. This is the secret to a successful reading.

Before I perform a reading for a client, I always meditate and make the intention to communicate with the client's spirit guides and Angels. I've found that setting an intention of how you would like the reading to go is incredibly powerful and shouldn't be underestimated. Spirit communicates with me in different ways at different times. There have been times when my spirit guides have really wanted to get my attention. Once, I started to write a letter and my hands froze. I couldn't type. My fingers could not touch the keys. I was writing a resignation email to my boss. A few days later, I received an email to say that my salary was going to be increased. So I was very glad I didn't write that letter! Now if I get the nudge to stop writing or my fingers freeze, I always take it seriously. Another time, my body became frozen and I couldn't move for about 15 minutes. It was like someone had just glued my feet to the ground. I learnt that there was a message coming through from the spirit world I needed to listen to, and when I'd grasped that message, I became able to move again.

After working with hundreds of clients, I've noticed some important trends: often what a client wants to hear and what Spirit is conveying to them are two different things. It can be frustrating to understand the spirit guides' perspective. They can see the bigger picture for us and are committed to keeping us in line with our destiny. Their job is to keep us on track in life and to make sure that we're protected from dangerous accidents. We can form a relationship with them and they can help with all kinds of human issues.

When I perform a reading, the messages are presented to me usually through images. I can see loved ones who have passed over, in my mind. I can then ask to open up a conversation with them. I would describe it to be similar to reading a book; hearing the words in my mind and seeing the images. As soon as the connection is made, then I can communicate like I would in real life. However, it's important to know that the medium cannot perform a reading or gather psychic information about someone without their permission.

One of my favourite examples: a family came to visit me and they said they wanted to hear from the father's mother, who had passed over. I requested to speak with her and she came through loud and clear. She said that she would like the father's son to go to a school she had in mind. I described the image of the school and the father immediately recognised it as the one not far from where they lived. They'd been considering sending him there.

Another example is when a man once came to see me and had no questions. He just wanted a general reading. I could see there were Spiritual Beings from high levels of consciousness trying to communicate with him. They gave him a gift, which was a paint brush and a camera. He then told me at the end of the sitting that he was in fact an artist and a photographer. The spirits told me they wanted to be channelled through into his art.

Common questions I may get asked are, 'Will I be rich and successful?' and, 'Will I find my soulmate?'. Often, what may happen is spirit guides may not answer the question directly how we may like, but instead they help us to understand our life from a spiritually aware perspective. They tell me there is destiny and free will; there's a balance of the two, which complement each other. Ultimately, we're free, and nothing can come in the way of that. We can choose to do whatever we want in this life but there is also a plan for us: this plan we have designed with our spirit family before we came here. It will have the most important things mapped out, such as our parents, home life, school, jobs, and our most cherished relationships. We'll have goals of what we want to achieve at various stages of our lives. Most of us have chosen a higher purpose to life, where we can ascend spiritually.

Being in alignment with our original life path is linked to our level of happiness, so the more aligned we are then the happier we will become. The spirit guides want to get us on track with our destiny so we can be happy. The happiness we can gain from doing something on our path will be greater than the happiness from, for example, doing a job that just brings us wealth and has no other significant purpose. The guides encourage us to see beyond a mundane life and to look to the higher meaning of why we're here. In the realms of higher consciousness, living life for simple pleasures or just to accumulate wealth and not use it wisely means very little. We are all born with an ego that wants, needs and desires, that's normal. But if we live to serve our ego then we are missing out on spiritual development and accessing dimensions of higher consciousness. These realms are open to us, not just when we die but now, in life, if we follow spiritual principles. Some of these principles include developing compassion for all beings and abstaining from negative action towards others and nature, and from self-hate, neglect and abuse.

The spirit guides are pushing us to achieve and develop all the time, especially when we are in circumstances that are unhealthy for personal growth. Often, people who have struggled in life and have not had supportive parents or loved ones are closer to Spirit. Their experiences have pushed them to use their intuition and learn how to interpret Spirit's messages. They have had to have the courage to reach out their hand to the unseen world and ask for guidance. The mind can often label these experiences as delusions, or some kind of mental illness, but these are just beliefs about a hidden world we know little about. Psychic mediums have been accurate for many years and have even worked with police detectives to solve crimes, such as in the TV series, *Psychic Detectives* or *Sensing Murder*. There have also been remote viewers like Ingo Swann, who have worked on the government programme, Operation Stargate.

Life is our journey of discovery and learning spiritual principles can take lifetimes. We have to make the decisions in life that align us with our life path and the spirit guides cannot make them for us. Their job is to guide and protect. When we are on our life path, everything falls into place: the right people, relationships, jobs, or business opportunities present themselves. Having a practice like meditation will help to keep us focused.

Most people are very ambitious when planning their life path – there is so much to do and so little time. Part of the human experience is to experiment, push yourself and have fun. Many people take life too seriously and have forgotten how to laugh. My spirit guides constantly tell me that we need to have more fun, and if things don't work out the way we planned, there are always more opportunities. Your spirit guides will suggest things to you and it's up to you if you want to pursue them or not. They're just like real friends who know you, except they don't have bodies.

Spirit has its own way of working in life. Often things will just pop out at me and catch my attention. For example, I may be walking down the street and hear some people talking about something that I was thinking, or the TV or radio plays exactly what I needed to hear at exactly the right time. Or I discover the right tool to complete my project when I need it. These things tell me that there is so much to life that we cannot perceive through our five senses. Opening psychic perception is a way to understand how life is very much intertwined with the spirit world. It is this hidden force that is ushering in creative thoughts, ideas and inspiration. It's guiding us to meet certain key people and sending us positive energy when we feel down.

Spiritual growth comes through experiencing real life. Not all spiritual people meditate, practise yoga or have converted to a vegan diet. People learn through suffering and this changes their perception on the purpose of life. People learn, through overcoming tremendous adversity, how powerful they really are. The best teacher is your own experience: what it has shown you and what you can learn and apply from it. Experiences in life can play out over and over, like a TV series on repeat, unless we can press pause and work out the meaning of them. When we do, the journey begins.

www.justinsagen.com

Prophetic dreams, born with a psychic gift, a natural animal communicator, it took Lady Ann a nursing career to discover complementary therapies and her new path. Thank God Ann woke up to her gifts; I have been blessed to have received many treatments from her.

THE RELUCTANT PSYCHIC

Lady Ann Collingwood

I was never aware of my psychic abilities as a child even though my grandmother, known to us as 'Supergran', was a top-notch tea-leaf reader! I did have prophetic dreams, which were very frightening, and I also had Brer Rabbit, Brer Fox and Brer Bear hiding in my wardrobe, only to come out at night to terrify me!

I had a way of conversing with animals too. Injured animals and birds would find their way to me – to be brought indoors for a safe place and for healing – much to my mother's dismay. It was too much for her when an injured hedgehog was brought indoors in a dirty old sieve. I remember her shouting, 'Take that outside NOW!' So safe shelter was built and made for this animal in the back garden. I was only very young at the time. I don't think I'd even got to primary school age. Most of these animals found their way back out into nature, including a blind thrush, which had been injured because of its sight loss.

This, however, was the extent of my psychic abilities at that time.

In 1975, when I was 18, I trained as a State Registered Nurse at UCH in London and started to become aware of a very compassionate side to my nature and also a fascination with death! I began to notice energy – sometimes good-feeling energy, sometimes heavy; sensing atmospheric pressure, which changed when the weather changed, but nothing unusual or pointing to psychic ability. I never had any interest in psychic phenomena and actually felt very afraid of it.

I had my first of two daughters, Victoria, in 1985, who told me all about her Protector when she was only two years old! His name was John and he showed himself as a light and was always with her. He was very obvious, even to me, on the ceiling in the corner of her bedroom at night-time. This made me concerned and on researching, I was drawn to Angels and Guardian Angels to keep us protected. I was then guided to my very first spiritual book, *Messengers of Light*, by Terry Lynn Taylor, a wonderful book that enabled me to understand and support my daughter's psychic side. John stayed with us for many years.

However, I still pushed my psychic side away. It was through fear and not really knowing how to deal with it.

In 1988, my second daughter, Samm, was born, and she was totally fascinated by music and sound, even as a very young baby. It was easy to get her to sleep; just put some music on and she was away with the faeries! She was a real Faery baby: very sensitive, very loving, and she triggered this amazing feeling of wanting to protect her in everyone who came in contact with her. I noticed that she mirrored my feelings. If I felt happy then so did she; if I felt sad, so did she. If I was in a bad mood, then God help us all, LOL, for she changed from Faery to demon child!

In 1989, I was given the chance to do a reflexology weekend course with my sister – this literally changed my life. I was so affected by it that I went straight on to train as a reflexologist. In 1992, I started working with my new skill from a room I'd set up at home, and gave up my nursing career.

As I worked with reflexology, I started to see people's auras (the energy field we each have around us, which reflects colours and shows the health of a person, their vitality, plus their emotional, mental and spiritual health), which helped me to know where I needed to work whilst giving reflexology to bring that person back into health. It gave miraculous results. So I was now starting to accept my psychic side.

I had an incredible, and very psychic, reflexology tutor, who also introduced me to tarot cards and working with Spirit during my training. I felt much more comfortable now with the process as I had support that I trusted. As I started to open more to the spirit world, my life began to change dramatically and I have to say, not always in good ways – but this was all part of my healing process. As I was helping others to heal, I was also healing myself.

I then trained in different healing modalities and have continued to work as a complementary/natural health therapist and international tarot reader ever since (over 30 years now).

My two daughters, Vicky and Samm, both developed their psychic abilities. Vicky seems to also have animal-whispering abilities and is now a vet, plus is very clairaudient (hears Spirit). Samm works in finance and is clairvoyant (sees Spirit) and empathic, like myself (we feel what others are feeling).

Our lives haven't been easy, but it's much easier to have compassion for another by having been through difficult circumstances of all kinds oneself. I can honestly say that I truly love my life with all its very strange twists and turns, and I give grateful thanks to all my wonderful spirit guides, Dr Usui, Ascended Masters, Angels and Archangels, High Beings of light, Merlin and the wonderful Magi, who have patiently stood by my side. I love you all so much.

As I write this, I am now being guided to step into another role as a wedding and funeral celebrant. I am truly ready for this new adventure.

With love, joy and miracles. Never fear.

www.enigmahealing.co.uk
anncollingwood@me.com
FACEBOOK: @anncollingwoodtherapy
INSTAGRAM: @ann.collingwood.3

As we further explore people finding their soul purpose, we read about Lara finding her gifts within Angel cards. I'm excited to see where this will lead her.

MY GIFT

Lara Whatley

I fell in love in my twenties – with Angel cards. How they came to me was strange. I was speaking to a girl I worked with about her psychic ability. I'd always been interested in any form of spirituality so she brought in a pack of Angel cards to work for me to look at. I fell in love with them. I'd never seen anything so beautiful. I'd had tarot readings but never felt attracted. So I bought some Angel cards and started using them. This has been my journey since 23 years old and I've used them throughout all situations: relationship break-ups, my own worries, being homeless, work, family. They've brought a lot of comfort and guidance to me. I've learnt that these are one of my tools I use with my gift.

I started doing readings for family and friends. People got to know about my readings so I began doing them for other people too, and I haven't looked back. My gift gets stronger the older I get and I hear things from the other side. I've had to learn to ground myself as I do absorb energy. I even started receiving messages during treatments. Whenever I touched a client, I would get things come to me, and sometimes Spirit in the room. I've had to be very careful of who I approach. When I worked at a spa, I had to use my manager's watch during a treatment, and I got a message from her grandad. I told her and it did upset her a little, but it also brought comfort. I've had many experiences like that and, through working in the beauty industry, with people from all walks of life.

But let's go back…

I always felt I never fitted in and I didn't have many friends. A lot of girls weren't very nice to me in school. I even went through a stage of *trying* to fit in, especially with the boys. But I don't think, growing up, that I loved myself at all. I really struggled emotionally and felt very trapped.

When I was 15, I tried to commit suicide. I jumped out of a loft extension, went through the kitchen extension and fell onto a tiled floor. I just remember I couldn't move. The next thing I knew, I was in hospital with my dad looking over me, tears in his eyes. I'd never seen my dad cry. I had my cross necklace round my neck and I didn't feel alone. I was very lucky that night too and was told I didn't have any permanent damage.

Afterwards, I was living with my nan when, one night, I was in bed, and a big, beautiful, white light with an Angel within it came to see me. She said I'd be ok and I was safe. It was so warm and comforting. I told my nan and she said, 'Oh, that's so lovely. How lucky you are.'

There are a few family members who have said they have gifts too and it's so lovely to know I can speak about what we have. All of this, and the trials I've gone through, have always made me come back to my gift, and I have to use it in the best way possible to help myself. I'm still learning!

After I had my second child, I was asked to join a circle. It felt like being part of a family, with like-minded people, and I really enjoy belonging to it.

Channelled Message: *We all have to find our own way and paths. You are stronger than you realise as life is a gift.*

larawhatley@yahoo.co.uk
INSTAGRAM: @laraanne1985

We now have Liz Slade, who is learning and embracing to come out of the shadows. Liz talks about meeting Di Pegler, the Diamond Light Grid and how it has lit up her inner and outer world.

MY RELUCTANTLY PSYCHIC EXPERIENCE

Elizabeth Slade

I'm going to begin by sharing with you my most recent experience of the last four years, as this has had the most profound effect on my spiritual journey so far. I questioned throughout the first 11 months – why me? Is this really happening? Can I really do this? I'm not confident talking to groups of people or being in front of a camera. These last four years have really taken me out of my comfort zone. It would have been so easy to say to myself, 'Let's not bother', and to continue as I had been, but I know this experience has been totally guided and is part of my life path, so I've faced my challenges. I'm still working through some of them but I feel so empowered for doing this, and I realise I'm finally being true to myself as I'm following my soul plan.

Beginning with 2016: this has been the most exciting part of my spiritual journey. This is when I first met Dianne Pegler, who has since become a very close and valued friend. Dianne came to me for a treatment and, I have to say, my feet haven't touched the ground since!

Dianne contacted me after a holiday to ask if I ran meditation groups or if I'd be interested in meditating with her. I immediately said yes and we began meeting each week. Dianne spoke of her book, *The Sacred Order of The Magi*. She gave me a copy to take on holiday with me in the October. From the very first page, I couldn't put it down. When you read her book, you can feel Melchior with you, talking to you; it's so captivating and powerful, yet graceful and emotional. I have never been moved as much by any other book as I have been with this one. It's the kind of book you can read several times and each time you experience something different.

I was less than half way through reading when I received a message asking me to create a Diamond Light Grid in my therapy room. I was very surprised. I questioned, 'Can I? Is this possible?'

On my return to the UK, I spoke with Dianne and together we invoked the Diamond Light Grid in my therapy room. I followed guidance as to how the Grid was to be created. I was guided as to what crystals to place onto it and didn't realise at this point exactly how relevant they would be. I have to say, the whole experience was totally magical. A truly amazing experience for us both. As we invoked the Diamond Light Grid, we both saw it descending gently onto the floor. Inside the Grid, the intricacy of the pattern was similar to a huge snowflake. We didn't realise we'd both witnessed this until after the Diamond Light Grid was completed and we shared our experience.

The very next day, I received another message, asking me to work with them to form a new healing treatment. I was so surprised, I had to ask for confirmation several times as I never thought this would ever happen to me, only to others. After my initial shock, I felt very blessed and very excited to be embarking on what I realised very quickly was a mission for The Magi, mainly channelled by Melchior. I set to work immediately on the task in hand. At this point, I had no idea what a huge role this would be!

Dianne came over to my therapy room each week and patiently lay on my couch while I invoked the Higher Beings for guidance on this healing treatment. I remained very open and knew it was being channelled due to the way I was guided to complete The Ascended Masters Diamond Light, as it was totally different to how I normally complete a healing treatment. Each week I was given more information and guidance. It really has been one of the most exciting and moving experiences. As the weeks progressed, I realised how honoured and blessed I truly felt to be part of this. I now have the conviction of knowing that this is something I have to do as it's part of my mission and soul purpose.

This treatment has to reach as many people as possible because of the importance of what The Magi are asking of us all on a personal and planetary level.

When we invoked the Diamond Light Grid in my therapy room, Beings came forward to work on it – there were 24 of them! There were several I'd never connected with before, so it was exciting to connect and find out what they were about. To my amazement, each Being that came forward onto the Grid had the qualities needed to help on a planetary level, and on a personal level to raise people's vibration and, in turn, raise our Earth's vibration, bringing peace, unity and love to us all and our world.

I had wonderful confirmation about the Diamond Light Grid in my therapy room as clients came for their treatments. At this point, I hadn't shared my experience. When one client arrived, she asked me what was different about the room: it looked the same but felt different, like she'd just walked into a church. This feedback was very special to me as the lady isn't spiritual. So for her to feel this was fantastic. Another client said that, as soon as she stepped into the room, she felt like she'd lost two stone in weight. She felt so light!

This was all great confirmation that the Diamond Light Grid and the Beings vibrantly bless everyone and, on clients, departure, they take with them the beautiful Diamond Light vibration.

I now work with the Diamond Light Grid constantly. It has become an integral part of my daily life. I can honestly say to you that magic and miracles really do happen when you connect and align with the Grid.

The Diamond Light Grid is having a positive effect with the current world situation concerning COVID-19. This is all part of the grand plan of cleansing our world. People are beginning to enjoy the simpler things; there is a greater sense of community and caring for others. I'm part of a beautiful group called 'The Magi Sistas' from all parts of the country. We have been brought together divinely by The Magi, Dianne being used as the orchestrator of this. We have formed an incredible bond as we've grown to learn that we have all been together in a lifetime before. We work on the Grid together and also separately, sending out positive wishes and healing to worldwide situations. When working with the Grid, guidance is sometimes given in the form of messages, visions, feelings or just a knowing. Each time is so beautiful and unique; you feel a great connection to all that is and feel so very protected and loved.

As an example of how I'm working with the Diamond Light Grid, I personally send out healing for the corals within our seas to be replenished. Collectively, we send out healing for nationwide and world peace; for the darkness to be removed from the hearts and souls of those who wish to cause serious devastation to strangers, replacing it with love, peace and unity; for our police forces and divisions to be fully protected. These are serious situations that we work with. The Angels and Unicorns are sometimes perceived as 'fluffy' but, in reality, they are our strongest powerful guides and leaders, along with the Ascended Masters.

A great way I've worked with the Diamond Light Grid on a personal level is in regard to my daughter, Olivia. I was informed on the last day of Year 7 of secondary school that her class would be merging with another class for Year 8. Olivia was very unhappy with this due to there being a lot of disruption in the other class. She has dyslexia and was concerned this would affect her learning. I applied for another secondary school. It was over-subscribed and Olivia was placed on the waiting list. I contacted the school regularly and it was suggested I ask her current school if they would agree to a 'managed move'. Her school declined as she was a good pupil and they didn't want to lose her. This was also an unusual request as this option was only offered to pupils who were potentially facing exclusion.

Olivia's current school was not supporting her with her learning and there was too much disruption within the school as a whole. I applied to go to an appeal panel at the proposed school. I set up a Diamond Light Grid for this situation and worked on it daily. The date arrived for the appeal and I called the Beings to be with me during the meeting. The people on the appeal panel had no idea what position Olivia was on the waiting list, and I was given the opportunity to put my case across.

The governor of the school totally surprised the panel and myself. He too was surprised by the information he was about to share: there had suddenly become ten places available for Year 8. This had never happened before. All the panel members were amazed, saying they had never known this to happen, and they'd all been sitting on the panel for years! Six places had been offered already to families. However, they hadn't approached any further families with the other four places. That evening, I had an email offering Olivia a place at the school! The odds were totally stacked against her ever getting a place, being seventeenth on the list, but this is the magic of the Diamond Light Grid, and placing your complete trust in working with the Beings and the Universe as you follow their guidance. Olivia has flourished with her school work ever since and her dyslexia has dramatically reduced. Truly amazing!

Moving on to the Ascended Masters Diamond Light Healing Treatment, this is the most simplistic, pure, high-vibrational healing system and includes some of the Ascended Masters, Archangels and our majestic Unicorns.

I would love to share with you some of my experiences during developing this beautiful healing.

I didn't choose who was going to be part of this healing treatment. They came forward through meditation. They are 12 of the Beings from the Diamond Light Grid. Throughout this whole process, I was making notes of my experiences, writing about the Beings who came forward to work through me for the healing treatment, and also researching about the crystals I had been guided to choose.

I came to the realisation that the qualities the Beings have to offer, their attributes and purpose, actually fit in with what the treatment is about and what it's achieving for the individual, and also on a planetary level. It was through my weekly sessions of completing healing case studies and working daily with the Diamond Light Grid that I was guided through thoughts and visions.

After receiving confirmation that 'this wasn't me making it up', it really was Melchior and Joseph of Arimathea being the main guides throughout, it became so exciting and fascinating to connect with the Beings and complete the research. I also learnt that the crystals I was guided to use for the treatment had all the qualities and purpose of what the treatment was about; the crystals are used to enhance the treatment only – this is not a crystal healing. It's the work of the Archangels, Ascended Masters and of course the Unicorns, which is the main essence of this healing modality.

During one healing session, a Being appeared in my room. I described him to Dianne immediately afterwards and we realised it was Maitraya. I had a strong sense that he wanted to be included on the Diamond Light Grid. On further investigation, this was confirmed, as he helps with personal and global peace, love, joy and laughter. All the attributes the Diamond Light Grid works with.

On another occasion, I was given a new chakra to work with. Again, me being me, I questioned this: did I just think this? Surely there can't be more chakras? This was truly exciting as Dianne felt the name may be connected to the Zoro Astrian religion. On research, we found out it was! This is one of the oldest religions, a pre-Islamic religion of Iran, and it is also connected with Balthazar, one of The Magi. What great confirmation!

As I practised on Dianne and other volunteers to complete the case studies, for the treatment to be insured, it became apparent what a sacred treatment this truly is. When I invoke the Higher Beings that are part of the treatment, I become transfixed in their energy that comes through me. There are no words to describe how magical it feels. I just want to remain in the energy as long as possible, as it's so mesmerising, radiant and delicious.

I mentioned sacred treatment. This is because of the Beings that work with the method of the treatment. It's methodical. However, it has to be this way, as that's how it has been channelled, and is a likening to the methodical way in which The Magi walked the Diamond Light Grid all those thousands of years ago.

Dianne shared her experience of a reading she'd received. All the Higher Beings came through that we're working with. Melchior described the Ascended Masters Diamond Light Treatment and confirmed the importance of the methodical routine, due to the sacredness of this treatment and the crystals used. Joseph of Arimathea is particularly happy with this, as he has a huge love of crystals. How magical and what great confirmation.

Ascended Masters Diamond Light was launched in Peterborough. I had booked to work at an MBS event, which I don't normally do these days, where I was intending to promote my other healing and massage treatments, as I'd booked this six months prior to meeting Dianne. As the date drew closer, I received guidance that The Ascended Masters was to be launched there. I was to solely promote this treatment. I'm still not sure why it was Peterborough, as the obvious choice would have been locally where I live in Essex, but I trusted what I was given. It was an amazing day. Dianne was with me, promoting her book, *The Sacred Order of The Magi*, and we had a lot of fun.

The Ascended Masters Diamond Light was received with excitement from the public. It was wonderful to work with people I'd never met before and to hear about their experiences from having this healing treatment. This was concrete evidence, if ever I needed any, of its purity, elegance, simplicity, and how powerful it really is.

I became in awe of this whole experience of developing The Ascended Masters Diamond Light, as I realised that all the Beings, crystals and the guidance I had received about the purpose of the healing treatment, fitted together like a jigsaw. It has been a totally mind-blowing experience for me and confirmation of how important it is to simply trust what is given to you, whether it be a thought, vision, feeling, message, or simply a knowing. The learning curve has been great and I now just simply trust and go with it. It's still so much fun sometimes researching what you are given. For example, only yesterday during my lunchbreak at work, I was on the Diamond Light Grid when a dinosaur appeared and walked towards me. I'm not an expert on names for these creatures so I decided to google. As I was visualising the image again, the name triceratops came to me. I typed this in and it was the dinosaur. Working in the current climate of a hospital ward is stressful right now, so the message was reassuring for me.

So this is how Ascended Masters Diamond Light was formed. Eleven months and 64,000 words later, I was able to finally send my work to the underwriters to hopefully be insured. This was passed, and I continued to write a training programme to be able to teach this healing treatment to current healing practitioners, or to people who feel drawn to becoming healing practitioners. I now run a two-day Certified Ascended Masters Diamond Light Healing Practitioners course, for this healing treatment to be taken out there to help as many people as possible and to raise the vibration of our planet.

This is the most exciting journey of my spiritual path so far and I still pinch myself at times! It's been a great honour to have been given the opportunity to develop this and take it forward.

I will now continue to explain about Ascended Masters Diamond Light Healing.

As I've said, this is a sacred treatment and you'll receive a wonderful experience on a personal and universal level by being aligned to your own Diamond Light Grid. By doing so, great changes will occur within you, as well as your own light being placed on Planet Earth, which in turn raises the planet's vibrational level, aiding the ascension process.

Before the treatment commences, you will be aligned to your own Diamond

Light Grid, as explained by Melchior of The Magi to Dianne Pegler in *The Sacred Order of The Magi* book.

The treatment itself is about helping you to find your own personal power. You experience a deep cleansing of all fear-based energies, past lives, worn-out thought patterns, habits and behaviours. You will have the realisation of your full potential and an expanded awareness, as you'll be free from limitations that hold you back. This expanded awareness will also give you a greater connection to the Cosmos. You will receive the wondrous energies of The Magi, Ascended Masters, Unicorns and Archangels. The desired outcome is the realisation of your own soul purpose and journey for this lifetime.

The Diamond Light Grid is already part of you, just like your DNA. It's a geometrical shape, similar to a spider's web, swirling and spinning faster than the speed of sound, vibrating with a tone inaudible to the human ear, and ever shape-shifting. It's full of diamond sparkles and your own wisdom, as it is your own unique creation.

The Universal Diamond Light Grid is etheric and made up of millions of geometrical shapes, spanning the whole universe. There is no beginning and no end. It is the highest vibrational energy I have ever worked with.

By activating these grids, you are helping to make a difference to the world, assisting in bringing the world back to love, in people being there for each other, in bringing unity, peace, joy and compassion to create a feminine/masculine balance, and helping our planet's energy to become harmonised. Working on the chakras of the body is the main focus of this treatment. Extra chakras were channelled, which play a major part in this beautiful transformation and connection. As a result, your sacred mission and purpose in this lifetime will become clear. This is where you align to your soul's purpose; you are connecting by stepping into your own light. Doing this on a subconscious and conscious level will awaken your own inner power and you, in turn, will be helping to create our world as we wish it to be. By placing your own bright light on Mother Earth, you are raising the Earth's energy and vibrations and, in doing so, helping with the ascension process.

I cannot stress enough how powerful this is. The more 'lights' that are switched on and shining bright, the more miracles will begin, and our planet and all that is will be transformed to how they should always have been. This is our opportunity to make a huge difference and play a paramount role in our lifetime for future generations to benefit from, as well as ourselves.

All of my incredible journey with The Magi, the Diamond Light Grid, The Ascended Masters Diamond Light and Magi Sistas Group would not have been made possible without Dianne. I am so thankful that The Magi guided her to contact me and we rekindled our bond from thousands of years ago. This has given me this amazing opportunity to find my lifepath and fulfil my mission, which I'm still working on. I feel so very blessed to have her friendship and guidance. We have both shared such an exciting journey together so far, an amazing rollercoaster, with lots of fun and incredible spiritual experiences along the way. Di, you are an absolute legend and I love you.

I am going to rewind back to the beginning.

I first became aware of Spirit at an early age when I felt someone pinch my back when I was in bed. My back was against the wall and it really frightened me.

The house I lived in was three storeys, the top floor being an attic room. It had a long landing and at the end of the landing was the staircase leading up to the attic room. I always felt someone was standing by the staircase watching me, so much so that, when I went to the bathroom, I always left the door wide open and would sit on the toilet looking down the landing! I was frightened and fascinated at the same time.

As years past, I experienced the feeling of someone being behind me, and I'd look around but no one would be there. Years later after my son was born, there was a 'knocking' noise on my two steel laundry bins in the bathroom. There was no other explanation than Morgan's grandmother was making her presence known while I was bathing him.

When I felt drawn to, I would visit spiritual fayres and have a reading. I was told on numerous occasions that I could develop and connect with Spirit and that I had healing hands. It was then suggested that I develop this. The thought of working with Spirit petrified me and I didn't really understand the concept of healing as I hadn't heard about this back then.

Moving forward to 2011, this was when I finally began to embrace my spiritual path. Up to this point it had been a one-way thing for me. I was happy to contact Spirit through readings but I wasn't happy for Spirit to make the connection with me on a normal daily basis as this scared me.

My close friend, Isabel, gave me the most beautiful Angel as a birthday gift. It was made from crystals and she had brought it from her home country of Mexico. Isabel suggested I write a note to the Angel of how I wish my life to be, and my wishes would be granted. I did this and placed the piece of paper under the Angel. My wishes took a few years to manifest but they were granted. I've always believed in Angels but this is where I really began to connect and work with them.

I was drawn to reading Dianna Cooper and Doreen Virtue books. It was a friend of mine, Hazel, who recommended these books to me. A few months later, she said to me that I was going to be an Angel intuitive. I'd never heard of one so I thought I'd better investigate! Divine timing happened for me to train with Doreen Virtue as an Angel intuitive two years later in 2014. It was a magical four days. On my return journey from the event, I arrived at the train station so elated, I realised there was something missing: I had left my suitcase at the hotel! By this point, I was used to giving healing but had little experience of working with Angel cards, so I felt totally out of my comfort zone. I was there for four days with 600 others. It also became a healing process for me, and a realisation of my life and how I needed to change it.

Back in 2012, as I hadn't been able to book onto the Doreen Virtue training course because it was fully booked, Isabel and I booked onto a local course. It was a certified healing practitioner's course called Reikara, run by a lovely lady, Claire Mission.

It was an amazing day as it was my very first experience of healing. I also met my first Unicorn guide during my attunement, so it really was a very special moment for me.

Isabel and I had also attended our first 'Mind Body Spirit' at Earl's Court. We'd booked to see Dianna Cooper and it was going to be a four-hour session. I fully expected to be bored after an hour. However, within ten minutes of sitting in her presence, we looked at each other and smiled! Four hours felt like forty minutes. It was one of the most profound workshops I've attended. I finally felt I'd arrived home and I really connected with her. It was amazing to be with so many other like-minded people. The whole event was magical and vibrant.

Once home, I felt drawn to investigate certified healing courses with the Diana Cooper School. I soon realised that her training courses were teaching people to teach, but I wanted to become a certified healing practitioner first, as I felt I needed to experience this before I could teach. I was guided to contact a lady called Margaret Merrison from The Unicorn Centre. On speaking with her, I found out that she was the principal teacher of the Diana Cooper School and wrote all the training courses, but she also ran her own certified healing courses for people to be healing practitioners in Angel Healing, Unicorn Healing and Reiki. So I trained with Margaret for all three over a period of time.

This really was the most amazing beginning to my spiritual journey. I had finally found what I'd been searching for. Margaret was an amazing teacher and throughout that first week of training with her, I began to make sense of everything on a personal level for the first time. I'd been feeling isolated from some of my friends and family as I felt I didn't have anything in common with them. We were no longer on the same wave length. Margaret reassured me this was normal. Being on the spiritual path can be a very lonely and isolating journey at times. However, you do find that you attract people who are on their own spiritual journey, and you support each other, forming new friendships along the way. I also realised during the time spent with Margaret how to deal with people I found difficult, but had no choice but to be around, because I still had to see them or work with them. I've always been a 'yes' person, a people-pleaser. I was reassured that its ok to say 'no'. Saying 'no' has taken many years of practice to master, but I'm finally beginning to feel empowered!

I will always be so grateful to Margaret for the invaluable training I received to be a certified healing practitioner. I also learnt so much about myself and how I could change the things I was unhappy about as part of my progression with my spiritual path.

I was excited but also very nervous and questioned on a daily basis if I could really do this. During the training, we went into meditation to meet our Guardian Angel and ask their name. My Guardian Angel came back with 'Bartholomew'. I realised later that night that I'd asked my Guardian Angel his name several months earlier during a meditation on my own, and this same name had come to me. However, I'd thought to myself, 'I've made this up; it's me thinking this.' And I dismissed the name. When I saw Margaret the next day, I shared this with her and she said that was why I must always trust what was given to me. A very valuable lesson learnt. It was so exciting and reassuring that I actually had communication with my Guardian Angel!

As my experience of completing healing treatments progressed, I began to work with different senses. Because I'm the channel, I have no control over this. I began by seeing colours, which were beautiful. Then I started feeling the emotions and physical sensations of the recipient. For example, I would experience palpations or my stomach felt churned and sickly. I then began to see locations, places, people, animals, flowers. This progressed to hearing words or just knowing information. I found all of this fascinating but to begin with, again I questioned if it was just me or was I really receiving guidance? If I had a strong sense that I needed to share the experience with the recipient after the treatment was completed, I would do so, and am still to this day excited by the fact that the information they receive is always relevant and they can relate to what has been channelled through me. In the beginning, I was very nervous about sharing any of the information with them, as sometimes it was quite random things I was given. But they would turn out to be very meaningful to that person, so it was a great learning curve again to simply trust what you are given, because it gives comfort, reassurance and confirmation that there is a genuine connection with the Beings above.

I connect and work with Angels, Unicorns and, in the last four years, Ascended Masters. I have in the past attended mediumship workshops and I also did some amazing training with Chris Gill, an incredible medium and a great teacher. I never believed in myself that I would be able to connect with deceased loved ones for people, but through training with Chris and what I experienced during the workshop a few years before, I began to realise that I could. Unfortunately, while training with Chris, I was also extremely busy with my work and still in the process of writing the Ascended Masters Diamond Light manual, so I wasn't able to give my full commitment to this. I felt it wasn't the right time for me to develop mediumship. I feel very grateful and honoured to have been able to learn from and be trained by Chris. She is a fantastic mentor and a truly beautiful soul. As my path has progressed, working with The Diamond Light Grid and Ascended Masters Diamond Light training course and healing, I feel that mediumship isn't part of my path that they have planned for me. However, I do feel very blessed that I was given the opportunity to experience this in a safe environment.

So, this is my journey so far. I would like to thank Alison for giving me the opportunity to be part of this wonderful collaboration. Without her invitation, I wouldn't have thought of putting pen to paper to share my experiences.

Thank you for taking the time to read my journey. I hope some of it may resonate with you. My message to you is simply to trust what you are given; it truly is guidance from above.

I've recently been guided to create posts about the Diamond Light Grid on YouTube and Facebook, where I take you through a series of meditations to help you create your own Diamond Light Grid, and will be continuing to complete Universal Diamond Light Grid work.

www.diamondlight.co.uk
diamondlight3333@gmail.com
INSTAGRAM: @diamondlight3333
YOUTUBE: Diamond Light Part 1

A beautiful lady who decided she no longer wanted the long working hours of the corporate world, Karen left for a new life as a foster carer. Completing a spiritual course and working with a mentor has kept Karen going in a world that has a different source of stress. I have so much respect for foster carers.

A FOSTER CARER'S JOURNEY

Karen Manton-Prosser

My name is Karen and I'm a 56-year-old foster carer of two special needs boys. I've been fostering now for 18 years and I began this journey when my now 24-year-old birth son was six years old and I was a struggling single mum looking for a job that I could do from home. Here I am, 18 years later, still doing fostering, albeit with special needs children, after my two previous foster children, who came to me when they were three and five, grew up. I'm proud to say that they still call me Mum and it's as if they are my own birth children. I definitely feel as if we knew each other before because there's such a strong bond.

I left a mentally abusive marriage after my then-husband raised his fist to me one night. He never actually hit me but him raising that fist was enough for me to let go of my old-fashioned ideas that, because I'd had a son with him, I should ignore his numerous affairs and remain faithful to the marriage, both for the sake of my son and because I'd be the first divorce within the family. Years of believing that all that had happened to me within that marriage was my fault and that I didn't deserve what little love or attention was given to me, followed. I didn't love myself and I had no self-esteem with regard to myself or my appearance, although funnily enough within my career, I was confident and progressed to finally, many years later, becoming a Client Director within the finance industry. I was at the top of my profession, with clients naming me as the best female account manager they had worked with and being headhunted back into the industry (I left briefly when I divorced but then went back into it and did this alongside the fostering) a few years later.

So, how did I have this confidence within my work but not in myself, you might ask? Throughout my life, I was always able to read situations and people instinctively. By this, I mean that when things happened to me, I would always be given guidance as to how to manage the situation, even if I chose to totally ignore it. I bet that sounds familiar to a lot of people. I didn't know at that time that this was my Guardian Angel speaking to me. I didn't understand any of this. All I knew was that throughout my life, at different times, solutions to my problems were always given. I would drop right into the drama, right into the despair, but always, without fail, the solution would be given to me. I would be guided to do what I needed to do. I now know that meeting my second husband wasn't by chance. I was guided to meet a man who had been treated the same as I was in his first marriage. He was a male version of me and, in fact, I had a son and he had a daughter, same age, just months apart, and he was to start me on the healing process towards love and self-acceptance. I will always be eternally grateful to my Angels for bringing him and my stepdaughter into my and my son's life. We are what we are now to a large extent because of them. Like I say, many episodes throughout my life should have made me open up to my gifts, but I was so engrossed in just 'living' and taking care of everyone but myself, I never opened up to what was being shown to me. That is, until a few years ago when I happened to take a course in Reiki with a then friend of mine.

Healing had always interested me and we found a beautiful Reiki Master who gave us the wonderful gift of being able to enter this world. It was strange, though, that even though I used Reiki in my everyday life for myself, family and friends, I decided that I didn't want to make it into my chosen line of work. I thought at the time it was because I didn't want to spoil my friend's chances of making a success of her Reiki business and, in part, I think it was. However, I feel in the main I was being held back: this was not what was being chosen for me.

Through meeting the Reiki Master, I was invited sometime later to her 60th birthday meal at a lovely restaurant not far from where I lived. I was so surprised to receive the invitation through the post because, although we were Facebook friends, I'd not really kept in touch with her that much after I'd completed my two courses with her. My friend had, though, so there I was thinking I'd really been invited because she had. You see, that was typically me back then! Anyway, to cut a long story short, I went to the meal not knowing anyone other than my friend. I was placed on a table with others, who all seemed very friendly, but I did feel a little strange, to be honest.

As the evening progressed, I naturally started to talk to the lady sitting next to me and she seemed very interesting and sweet. I started to open up to her about my life as a foster carer of then just one special needs boy, and how demanding it was with working full-time within client services. We talked about how physical he could be and how this was affecting me mentally; how indeed my husband was recovering from a mental breakdown caused in part from the stress of caring for this boy. The lady told me things about my situation that were so spot on, I was like, 'Who is this woman?' At the end of the evening, she gave me her business card and when I got home, I looked her up. I found she'd written many books all around her own life experiences and how to basically have a happy life following the tools given in her second book, *Bringing You Back to YOU!*. I was tempted to book some sessions with her but the old me was saying, 'It's too expensive, you can't afford it etc.'

Then one day, I was having a heart-to-heart with my birth son and he said to me, 'You know, Mum, I've always thought you should write a "Dear Deidre" column. Don't you see how people come to you for advice? How you're always there for people? We can be anywhere – the park, the shops, anywhere – and all of a sudden, a complete stranger will be telling you their life story or their worries, and you're there listening and giving advice.'

It was like a light bulb moment when I thought back over my life and I realised that this was true. Even in my job within the client services, what made me so popular was my ability to put people at ease so they felt they could confide in me. I remember one colleague saying, years before, that I could meet a brand new client and within half an hour, they'd be telling me about their medical problems. She meant it as a joke but I realised now that she was right and that it had always been that way. I did have the 'gift' of making people feel as if they could trust me and that I was their friend. This is what had made me good at what I did – not because I was good at the basics of the job overall (which to be frank were not that exciting), but the fact that I could build relationships with people; complete strangers. From my chat with my son, I realised that I needed to put myself first, as I had been the rock holding my husband and my family together, without thinking about what it was doing to me and what *my* needs were.

So, I invested in me and booked six sessions with Alison Ward, the lady I'd met at the birthday meal. Those six sessions became 12 sessions, as I learnt to love myself, acknowledge my gifts, and work through the blocks in my life preventing me from fully understanding what I had to offer. By the end of the 12 sessions, I was living my life using the tools Alison had taught me on a daily basis, and I was so excited by how this had changed my life that I wanted to share it with anyone who would listen to me. I bought a box-full of her book, *Bringing You Back to YOU!*, which describes her life journey and the tools she teaches to live a more fulfilled and happy life. I found myself giving these books to my family and friends and even, on occasions, to strangers when I was guided to do so. I also made the biggest decision and that was to become a Life Fulfilment Trainer for Alison Ward Training Limited. This has meant that I can work with others to improve not only their mental health but their physical lives too. I am passionate about helping foster carers who suffer greatly with self-esteem issues, because managing the behaviours of seriously challenging children who are not your birth children, however rewarding, can be quite damaging to both yourself and your relationships with others. For me, this is the life-long mission, or should I say passion, that my Guardian Angel has in store for me, not the Reiki road as I first thought. I am now able to open my heart and my ears to what is said to me, and to fully appreciate that I am not alone on my life journey but am guided and supported throughout. My faith and my belief in my own abilities are strong, and I no longer ignore what is being said to me but embrace it and want to share my gifts with those who need my help. Never ever doubt that you have a Guardian Angel and that there are Earth Angels too. For me, my Earth Angel was a woman called Alison Ward – and she quite simply changed my life.

www.alisonwardtraining.com
Karen.manton03@gmail.com

You're never too old to find your soul purpose. It took Bev guts to leave her long marriage and lots of inner journeying and reflection to eventually find her passion – being a trauma therapist. What a wonderful therapist she is; all that experience and empathy.

A SURPRISED TRAUMA THERAPIST

Bev Taylor

psychic*

[sahy-kik]

---

adjective Also **psy·chi·cal.**

Of or relating to the human soul or mind; mental (opposed to physical).

Psychology. pertaining to or noting mental phenomena.

Outside of natural or scientific knowledge; spiritual.

*https://www.dictionary.com/browse/psychic

I'm not a psychic in the traditional sense, yet I do seem to have always been interested in the 'human soul or mind' and I've always been drawn to the 'mental phenomena outside natural or scientific knowledge'. I've had my life guided by a still, small voice and there have been a few times when I've 'just known' something is right, or that a certain something needs to be done, or the person sitting in front of me in my therapy room was meant to find me, not another therapist.

I do understand the irony of my story being in this book. However, over the years, I have come to realise that, just because I don't quite fit a category, doesn't mean I'm not in it. It's been the story of my life. I don't quite fit anywhere. Therefore, I've chosen to contribute in the hopes that you might recognise the still, small voices speaking to you, the gentle, but certain 'knowing' that rises within, and the nudges that direct us into action when we miss something ourselves.

As I've already said, I don't see or hear messages from folk in the spirit world and I generally don't 'know' things before they happen, yet I certainly have been guided by a voice or two. I've had nudges and I've 'known some things without knowing them'. Nowadays, I recognise that my gifts come to me in a quiet whisper or a sensing or a nudge by others, and I'm thankful, but I've often been frustrated that I couldn't 'hear' or 'see' like others seemed to. My gifts were initially so quiet that I've spent most of my life claiming that I have none. I just couldn't figure it out. Yet, I had a compulsion to understand my purpose in this life, to understand how I was to be guided by my inner voice and God's voice inside me. So, I started with what I did know. I did know that I wanted to be useful to people on this planet. And that need eventually made me listen hard to my inner world and force myself to take myself seriously. That has always been an issue for me: taking myself and my needs seriously.

I'm one of those people who needs a structure to make sense of things that come to me. My training as a therapist was the structure. I needed to be able to identify how I'm guided. Until I began my therapeutic training, I had no idea that I was intuitive. Nowadays, as a trauma therapist who listens to her clients with a therapeutic structure embedded within, I often get a sense of hidden information that the person in confusion or pain cannot see, and I can then work alongside my client, helping them gain their own awareness, which results in so much better mental health, and that's healing in my book. But I'm getting ahead of myself, for although I'm comfortable with this now, it has been a real challenge for me to accept my skills and intuition, chiefly because of my background.

I'm a farm girl, born and bred, yet I never quite felt like I belonged to that world. I didn't know you could have a really useful job working with people. I'm from a farming community in the United States, to be more specific. In communities such as this, you learn quickly that if your job is not somehow physical then it's not really useful work at all. That message has burned deep within me. So, when all I wanted to do was read – specifically a twice-weekly, home-delivered newspaper called the *Decatur Herald* (Decatur was a large city nearly two hours away) and books posted on a regular basis from the Illinois State Library – they saw me as lazy and disinterested, and a little strange! They weren't wrong about the disinterested and I know now that if they had taken the time to talk to me, they would have discovered what a wonderful world I had found. I often wish I had been encouraged to develop academically, but they were the kind of farmers who needed hard, physical work, not book learning. I mean no disrespect to my family but, no one cared about reading and knowledge. I didn't feel loved, not because of any overt cruelty, but I think because my mum and dad were so busy working their farm that they didn't understand the emotional needs of their children. I find it a sad irony that they were so devoted to each other that they missed out on their children's emotional needs, for my sister felt the same. I didn't feel a part of that life; I felt claustrophobic and I knew that I couldn't find a life there. The 'still, small voice', the 'knowing' and the 'nudges' were strong, but I didn't realise their full nature. Nor did I realise that it would take me years to understand the nature of my instincts because I had no role models aside from my very busy farming family. No one, least of all me, would ever have imagined that my small voices, nudges, and knowing were meant to teach me my own sense of self-worth and were for my role as a therapist. It was a world away.

My journey into therapy and my developing intuition started around the age of 16 when I became interested in God. I found that he loved me and cared and accepted me for who I was. The message for that first year was, you can do anything you dream. And somehow, I knew that the 'anything' would not be found in my small Midwestern community. Like many teens, I had dreams of far-off lands. When I was 17, I very clearly heard God say to me to 'go to Bible College', and he led me directly to the two universities that I later attended. Unusually for me, this voice and knowing was very loud. At that point I had no idea that I would end up being a therapist in England. I just knew that I had turned up at the right places at the right times. For instance, I just 'knew' that after two years at an amazing university in Tennessee, I needed to move to one closer to home. There was no external reason that I should change universities, but I knew I had to move from my beloved college to one in my home state.

Once I'd moved to the Illinois university, and midway through my four-year degree, I remember thinking that I would really like to work in Europe. An opportunity came up for me to join a group of students who were going to England for a summer work project. After the project had been launched and they were asking for volunteers, initially I rejected it because England wasn't Europe. But when three people came up to me within ten minutes of the launch, saying, 'I thought about you', I gave in and gave up, and decided the summer project was for me. And I was nudged directly into the most life-changing experience of my life. If I hadn't moved universities, followed the nudge, I would never have had this opportunity. What an important 'nudge and knowing' that was.

In May 1971, I boarded a Laker Airline plane that was so narrow it looked more like a cigar than a plane. I was so excited and full of wonder that I had this opportunity. As I stepped off the cramped plane, walked down the stairs and put one foot on Gatwick's tarmac, I knew somehow that I would live in England; that it would be my home. I spent the summer in England, falling deeper and deeper in love with this country. It's a love affair that has never waned. When the project was finished, I immediately began making plans to return on a permanent basis.

I came back to England two years later, knowing that this was the country that would allow me to discover who I was. I was home – truly home. Eventually, I married and had children. All during this time I was deeply involved in church. I'd moved from the traditional churches to house churches. The house churches were the kind of churches where, every so often, someone would stand up in a meeting and say, 'I've got a picture' or a 'word'. I often marvelled at this, for I never had 'pictures' or 'words' from God, I just had quiet knowings, or a still, small voice guiding me, if that. I'm a quiet person and yet I do love grand gestures and I always felt a bit 'less than', especially as I had no idea that I had any gifts. Imagine my surprise when I learnt the reason people often have pictures or words is that the majority of humans do much of their thinking and processing in pictures. So it was natural to tell everyone their thoughts and inspirations the way they thought: in pictures. Before I discovered this wonderful thing, I just felt inadequate. I had no idea that what I did was valid, as words or pictures were seen by me as being so much more valid and public.

Take it from one who senses rather than sees, this is quite an alluring and desired gift. And so, I missed my own gifts because they weren't as public.

I realise now that this was because my gifts lay with one-to-one chats with people and not the public words that went with the church services. It meant that I always doubted myself and my validity. The irony of this is that during that time in my life, I was often a part of a leadership team, so it seemed that others could recognise qualities in me that I couldn't see. There's the theme again: I don't quite fit in, even when I'm a part of leadership.

Along the way as a first-time mother, I began to think about what I really wanted to do with my life. Even though I didn't really 'know', I followed my internal nudges and found myself at the beginning of my counselling career. I remember taking the risk and going on an introduction to counselling course. I attended and simply felt that I had come home. I was so excited. Once I had decided this was the right direction, it continued to feel 'just right'. I read every moment of my free time. I couldn't stop. I remember attending football matches (we had season tickets that year) and being desperate to get back to my books. I remember taking my daughter to her end-of-year dance and I sat on the edge of the room, devouring a book about Freud. I also remember not understanding many of the tomes that I was being asked to read, as I had never seen most of the words and didn't understand their context. Then, slowly but surely, everything came alive and I found myself understanding these mysterious concepts and theories. If it had been anything else, I believe I would have given up as I felt very stupid at the beginning and lacking in confidence. That's the power of knowing what you should be doing. It was wonderful.

And then, along the way, I stopped paying attention to an important message that my still, small voice was telling me. My marriage was failing but I couldn't bring myself to believe it. I believed instead that if I understood myself and my husband, eventually it would all work out. It was wrongheaded, but that was the counsellor in me. I also couldn't hear the voice because of my pride and a lack of belief in myself. I spent 17 years ignoring that part of my internal voice. I was a full-time therapist and loving it, feeling fulfilled in my career and from time to time crying my eyes out, trying to get away from my perpetual sadness. When I look back at this time, I realise I was fulfilling an age-old message that I'd taken on: that being 'your needs come second'.

I wanted my marriage to work. It was the most important thing in my life and I was blinded and deaf to the nudges and small voices within me. I held on because I still loved my husband; because I liked being married; because not fitting in was a feeling I was used to; because my needs should come second; because not feeling loved was a theme in my life I was used to and because I couldn't bring myself to admit that I had failed. A failing marriage and being in a situation where love was no longer a part of my married life was something I couldn't come to terms with for many years. For all of those reasons, I found myself being very single-minded when it came to my marriage. I became fixated on staying married. Most crucially, I wouldn't listen to this voice because all the other voices I've just mentioned were so powerful that I chose to ignore the voice in me that was gently saying, 'It'll be ok – it'll be tough, but it'll be ok.' The voices of fear and not quite fitting in and I'm used to it, were many times louder than the persistent gentle voice that arose from time to time. We often choose safety and what we know, even if it's painful, over listening to our small voice.

Counterintuitively, whilst ignoring the 'my marriage is over' voice, I began to get used to the world of the psychic. I started listening to Hay House Radio. Hay House Radio is a station based in the US, whose strapline is 'radio for the soul'. The station taught me to not fear the spirit world, to listen to the small voice inside me and to start trusting myself again. I still ignored the voice for five or more years. Eventually, I recognised that nothing would heal my marriage. I took a giant step and I left it in 2016.

I spent a year in Jordan with my daughter and her family, running a bed and breakfast and healing my heart. In 2017, I came back to the UK and spent another year being severely depressed. I found that, because I had listened to the voices of fear and not fitting in, it had shut down all the 'you are valuable' voices that I had. For the first two years after I left, I gave myself time and threw everything up in the air. I had no intention of ever going back to being a counsellor. During the second year of my separation, I was sure that I would never work as a therapist again. Although it wasn't true, when my marriage ended, I felt I had failed at everything. I was exhausted emotionally and completely rudderless.

The only thing I knew to do was to let my grief and rudderlessness play itself out. When I doubted this, a lovely colleague and friend reminded me to 'stop' and not try to do anything other than to feel what I was feeling. During that year, I learnt first-hand that you can't hurry grief. I knew I could slow it down; I'd seen that in my therapy room. I knew that I couldn't ignore my feelings but I was often afraid that it wouldn't end. That was my truth but not the whole truth. I was learning at a deeper level to trust the process I was in and to trust that I was a valuable human being. I remembered what I'd told so many of my clients: know that what you feel is your truth because it's what you feel, and that makes it valid and a truth in a way because it is what you feel. I always told people that it was important to not believe all the negative feelings, as inevitably we were always too hard on ourselves and they would never be the whole truth. In other words, just because I felt a total failure because my marriage ended didn't mean it was the whole truth. Yes, I felt a total failure and it was important to recognise those feelings, but it wasn't the whole truth for I had been very successful in my business and in so many other relationships. I had to really work hard on that one. When you're finding your way out, you experience feelings as being far more powerful than words or logic!

There were a few positive small voices in my heart during that time, but I kept on not believing everything that I felt as full truth. Eventually, I could hesitantly start acting on some of the good voices and nudges. Virtually one year after I came back to England, when a colleague and friend asked me if I was interested in doing a bit of work for her at her therapy clinic, I hesitantly said yes as I felt the stirrings of better mental health and hope. She didn't ask me to do counselling, because she knew that was an ask too far. For that I am so deeply thankful, as I don't think I could have made that leap. But as I got back into the world of supporting people, I heard this little voice say, 'Go on – do it – go back to counselling.' And I did. Within one week of being back in the therapist's chair, I knew I had made the right decision. My energy levels were back, my mind was sharper and I realised that I had rediscovered my purpose.

There was just one catch. I had been out of the world of therapy for just over two years. I realised that I needed to get some good professional development under my belt. So, I spoke to this same friend and colleague and she suggested Eye Movement Desensitisation Reprocessing (EMDR). We spoke about it at some length. She had discovered it some years ago and had found it had revolutionised her practice. There were a couple of issues for me: it wasn't cheap and the best place to study would mean I would end up doing an MSc. Both daunted me as I was still stuck in the belief that I 'couldn't possibly spend money on myself, nor could I possibly achieve that level of academia'. Eventually, I realised that not only was this course important for my professional development but that it would be a part of my own healing. I was beginning to believe in myself and my place in the world.

I began that course in September 2019 at age sixty-nine. I was beyond terrified. I was afraid of the academic rigour; I was afraid of joining a group of no doubt very intelligent people; I was afraid I would make a fool of myself, and so much more. No one around me had any doubts about my ability to achieve academically or to fit in, yet the doubts were deeply powerful. But just as I knew that counselling was my career back in the mid 80s, I knew somehow that this was the right path as well. It was a quieter voice nowadays, and it only barely dampened down my terror, but the voice was there nevertheless and I trusted it and, nine months on, I realise anew that I have truly re-engaged with my profession and my life's purpose.

The therapy I do is deeply powerful. I have been looking for this type of therapy for many years. In fact, it is a combination of most of the effective theories that I have used over the years. It has helped heal my heart from past traumas and it enables me to do the same for others. It enables that still, small voice, my knowings and my nudges to gain clarity and power.

It's been a long journey and a painful one, and it seems to have come rather late in life, but it has arrived. I have no idea where a lot of my life will lead but I do know that to ignore still, small voices and those nudges is to live a very unhappy life. I have learnt that I am much more than I ever could have imagined. I have learnt that fear as a survival mode is a strong urge but that it can stop us growing and listening.

Whilst I'm not a psychic in the traditional sense, I have learnt that my voice, my knowing and my nudges are just as valid and just as immense. I still look at those of you who have traditional psychic abilities in awe, but the biggest lesson is that I have been given a gift: a gift of healing that I did not know how to value. I still feel a bit of an outsider and feeling love is a challenge for me, in spite of the fact that I have so many lovely friends and family surrounding me. Our early-years experiences leave deep imprints on our souls, but I am so much closer to acknowledging the love that is given to me now and I do feel I fit into the world I inhabit. I actually see being a little bit different is a blessing. I am blessed.

Bevtaylor188@gmail.com
FACEBOOK: @bevtaylortherapy

We move to our final male author who, due to his global corporate lawyer status, has to remain anonymous. Sahara was born in South Africa and was moved to the UK without any notice. His story of growth and acceptance is a lesson to us all.

A MALE CORPORATE LAWYER'S STORY

Sahara Dessert

As I begin writing this, I wonder why I'm so reluctant to be a proud psychic after all these years. Then I do what many lawyers do and check the meaning of the words I'm considering. In this case, I focus on the word 'reluctant'. You see, I am a 40-year-old and a very good lawyer at a top international law firm. Currently, I'm at home at my desk with much more time than usual. Anyone who knows a top city lawyer, knows we just don't have time - we work a lot. I mean that, we work a great deal of the day. Our days are dedicated to the practice of law and keeping our clients, managers and law firm partners happy. It's expected for the coin (or maybe one day bitcoin) we receive in return for our hard labour.

But this is the time of COVID-19; a time without underground travel to convey me to work. I really don't miss standing under some man's armpit as he hangs on for dear life while the carriage shunts along the old tunnels of London or (when the mood takes me to use the bus) sitting near to a vastly overweight and rather smelly lady on my route from Blackfriars to my home in South West London. It's not that I don't like this large lady, but she does undoubtedly pong. You see, she gets on after my stop in the evening and seems to like how I acknowledge her presence when we've unwittingly caught each other's eye. I see softness in her eyes when she gets on the bus; I believe, as a consequence, she settles not far from me and I don't move, even though I know what's wafting my way. I do however quietly open the bus window with all in mind and acknowledge that I'm very far from perfect myself.

Taking you back to my desk at home where I'm sitting, I was explaining that I also have more time because there's less work going around as the economies of the world wait on a semi-pause during COVID-19. It strikes me... where do I start my contribution to this book? I mean the obvious place to start is – when did I know I had psychic abilities? Just so you know, I've been psychic since I was 11 years old, although granted not particularly accurate at it then. For example, I knew I was soon to leave Johannesburg for a new life in London as I sat in my bath one cold Johannesburg winter night; it just occurred to me as I soaked that I was leaving, no doubt about it. This was months before the idea had even occurred to my mother, who lived in London at the time.

With this knowledge in my head and soul, I pondered how it was that I would get to London. After all, my mother had sent me to school in Johannesburg some years ago because my stepfather and I couldn't find a way to co-exist very well; boarding would do me good was their thinking. So, I thought, for sure I wasn't going to London on their ticket! As I sat in the ever-chillier bath in Johannesburg as an 11-year-old living in my father's house on the weekends, I thought somehow my journey to London would be playing some part in the *Teenage Mutant Ninja Turtle* craze at the time. I liked their reptilian do-good-pizza-eating-kick-ass attitude.

Far less grandly, it turns out, there was no world tour on the cards for me with the shelled ninjas. Completely unexpected by my school, my father, or even my mother, a few months before my departure for London, my mother stood outside the headmaster's office a day before term ended and asked for the headmaster's help to write me references and send my grades etc. to a school in England, a school which my mother was applying to for me. I went on school holidays to my mother's house in Cape Town two days later and never returned to my life in Johannesburg as it was. Even she'd had no idea that she and my stepfather would discover through another parent at my school that I was pretty miserable, so he and my mother had quickly decided to bring me to England. It was the most unlikely occurrence, but I knew it was imminent that one evening sitting in a bath past its best warmth.

But that's not quite where I want to start my contribution to you and this book, because I'd like to use some of my deductive reasoning learnt from the practice of law. 'Reluctant Psychic' – I look at those words and I decide 'reluctant' is a good word to describe how I feel about being open as a psychic, even at 40 years old. I've felt reluctant to pursue my psychic abilities for most of my life; up to this point when COVID-19 has come along and changed things.

Sitting at my desk, I continue in my lawyerly habits and look up the meaning of 'psychic', which is defined in my dictionary as 'relating to or denoting faculties or phenomena that are *apparently* inexplicable by natural laws, especially involving telepathy or clairvoyance'. Not that encouraging, I think, upon reading that definition. I mean, what's with 'apparently', I wonder? Then I look up 'clairvoyant', which is defined as a person who '*claims* to have a supernatural ability to perceive events in the future or beyond normal sensory contact'. I note the word 'claims' with a tutt in my mind. These are not emphatic definitions that speak with confidence, are they?

I then turn to the word 'lawyer' in my dictionary and, without yet seeing the definition, I know it will not be tainted with doubt like the last two words I looked up. Indeed, I'm right on that one, as my dictionary provides that 'a lawyer practises law or works as a lawyer', noting 'lawyering is a craft that takes a long time to become proficient at'. I start laughing, and say to myself, 'It takes years to become a proficient psychic *by the way* and there are no "claims" or "apparently" about a lawyer being a lawyer in that definition.' Whilst I note there are well recognised qualifications for categories of lawyers – 'lawyers' and 'the practice of law' is a very broad category of definition for the language found in a dictionary to be so confident, unlike the rather more doubtful description of a clairvoyant or psychic.

There is obviously an imbalance in the modern western world that shows itself clearly in the language we use; if we can't prove something, then we make that abundantly evident in the very meaning of the word we assign to describe it. So, working it out logically as I sit at my desk (after years of legal practice), I can very much see where my reticence as an 11-year-old came from. That, and that the adults of the time strongly believed that 11-year-olds can't tell the future, and should stick to their maths, which they need to catch up on because in South Africa, they're behind the English curriculum! I say imbalance because where is the faith? I'm not talking about only religious faith, although I note that, even with the efforts of established religion, with its vast networks and wealth, the church is struggling to keep its congregations faithful and present to its messages, and its religious messages call upon people to believe without much empirical evidence.

But, I ask myself, 'Do I think the world treats what it can't prove unfairly by dismissing it with language like "apparently" or "claims"?' I will answer this in two ways. The first is that the empirical world is the one we have increasingly lived in for hundreds of years now. There is every place and need for it. After all, it's brought us excellence in science, it's brought us medicine, it's brought us some laws that are really effective at making the world a better place, and it's taken us from some of the past tyranny of certain groups of religion (in very different times); so I believe we are heavily conditioned by the world around us to mistrust that which cannot be calculated. Secondly, in western societies we are coming out of hundreds of years of ideas and rules heavily enforced and ingrained in our culture and practices. So, I don't think it's surprising that we use language to describe psychic abilities with such caution, but I do believe it's time to embrace more of what we can't prove empirically, both for our own wellbeing and certainly for that of the natural world around us. Empirical evidence drives us to focus on numbers, finance and economic growth, whilst hiding our instincts about the direction of humanity and the planet as we know it.

So why do this now? Why would I decide at 40 years old to jump head first into the spiritual world? Well, I tell myself I'm not jumping in. I don't think city law practice and being a psychic fit very well together, and I'm writing under a pseudonym to keep my professional life separate. However, the chances of me remaining a 'normal' corporate city lawyer are as high as me doing a world tour at 11 years old with the *Teenage Mutant Ninja Turtles*. Yet here I sit, knowing my life will never be the same now that I've started writing this contribution, and hanging on for dear life to the career I know, love at times and have nurtured.

To answer the question above, why now? – well, my Angels have broken into such a loud chorus that I can't ignore their calls to get out into the world with a positive message about people needing to embrace more of the world, more of the love, more of the family time and more of trusting the fabric of the physical world as it interlinks with the spiritual world. Their calls are so loud, I feel compelled to write and, as I knew in the bath in Johannesburg that I was leaving for London, I sit at my desk and know my life will be transformed as I speak out, even under a pseudonym.

The very fact that my Angels can tell me to ask someone I'm invited to channel, 'What is it with the word "blueberry"?!' is so random to my logic, and it's so improbable to be on-point, and that person responds giving me a long story about the relevance of blueberries to them, still blows my mind. How is that possible? Yet it is, because that's my experience as a psychic that I know it to be true and possible. There's so much to the world that modern humans have forgotten, and I believe 'that forgetting' is a detriment to them personally and certainly to the planet, which collectively (by our overall behaviour) we are destroying with our numbers games and strictly empirical views.

I sit here and I've come to a stop. So I've decided to open channels of communication with my Angels. I was intending on doing this privately, but I'll share this message with you as I say to my Angels, 'Please open channels to me, my Angels. May I receive your messages with love.'

The message I receive is, 'The less you burn without thought, the less you procreate without plan or care for the world around you, the less you don't bother to pass learning and care along, the less you practise self-care and love, the less you plot, the less you micromanage, the less you remain comatosed by the patterns of the modern western world, the less there will be to be sad about when you realise that the result of having less, taking less, making a better place for each soul bred into human form, means the better parent, partner, child or companion you will be. Be a light rather than a biological robot. Feel pain, feel joy, feel brave, feel remorse. Don't be afraid to learn and to be human.'

I feel utterly inspired, so I begin writing again.

What does this small body of words and message mean for the individual reading this? I suggest that if you're reading this now then you have some interest in the paranormal and some degree of faith in it. By the way, upon checking, the word 'paranormal' has quite a pleasant definition in my opinion, meaning 'denoting events or phenomena such as telekinesis or clairvoyance that are beyond the scope of normal scientific understanding'. I rather like the 'beyond the normal scientific understanding'.

'So what is beyond the scope of normal scientific understanding?' I ask myself. Maybe someday we could measure psychic ability, but for now, what a boon in your life to harness another sense (above sight, smell, taste, hearing and touch) that's beyond scientific understanding. What a hoot that would be to begin to work on a sixth sense; and it would make you appear as wise as an owl. Poor quality jokes aside, my message to you as a reader with an interest in the paranormal is, try to discover if you have some psychic ability. It takes years to decipher the differences between a guess, logical deduction and true channelling, but by starting with guessing and practising listening to your Angels and to your body and instinct, you may be on the road to something new and brilliant. Even if you don't master the gift of channelling, your Angels will guide you if you talk to them and work with them. Most people buy insurance; many make pacts with a religious god or gods; most make political affiliations with other humans, and some form gangs in order to create a sense of safeguarding. Why on earth would you go to these lengths and ignore the help of the Angels?

If you happen to be reading this and you have no faith in the paranormal, or you don't believe it's possible for a psychic to channel advice or a future prediction, or a past event, then that's ok. But surely you could afford to start some form of spiritual journey, even if that is to practise simple forms of kindness to other people and yourself. As the practice of love grows, you're bound to become more aware of events and happenings that you never expected, and you'll find life giving back to you in ways you never believed possible.

There is simply no better time than now for us all to plan to embrace some lessons that COVID-19 should have taught us. These may possibly include:

- You don't miss working in an office every day.
- You enjoy some extra time with your partner, family or friends.
- You've noticed the sky is clearer.
- You've seen pictures of nature recovering and taken delight in it.
- You've realised just how unpleasant aspects of public transport are.
- You've rediscovered an old passion.
- You've developed a new skill.
- You've felt pain and love and it's reminded you that life is real; it is not a conveyor belt of work, sleep and consumerism.
- Your children do not raise themselves and having you around improves their chances in life.

- You can't function perfectly without social networks and there is nothing like meeting someone in person.
- You feel good about being helpful to others.
- You realise there is only so much governments can do without our engagement in democracy and us taking part.
- You realise governments will need to act quickly enough to avert mass extinction on the planet, before it's out time for severely curbed freedoms and loss.
- You realise small personal actions, when done in informal collaborations, can make a big difference.
- You realise companies function for their survival, not yours.
- You realise that, while international trade is important and no one wants to be financially poorer, having some stuff made and grown in your home country might be quite a good idea.
- You've begun to experience child-like dreams or dreams of faith as your daily conditioning of repeated patterns starts to wane.
- You've seen those who are lazy and not careful enough with their lives come to you for help.
- You've seen those who are careful and responsible fall and you've been happy to rush to collect them.
- You've begun feeling it's easier to pick out the bull-shitters now that life has slowed slightly.
- You've realised that being away from your homeland (if you've migrated) has reminded you in some ways of what it was to be you, fully immersed in your own heritage.
- You feel strangely scared and challenged and excited all at once.
- You've considered your value.
- You've considered someone else's value.
- You've heard your Angels sing and you can't turn away.
- You don't hurt or suffer that much when changing things.

I have specifically repeated the word 'you'. Whether you believe it or not, your experience, your life, your ability to breathe and function are such rare gifts.

This human life is difficult and extreme, but being robotic in repetitive work patterns and chores and enjoying the same repeated forms of pleasure, mostly geared to the spending of money, is to be missing out. There are so many gifts and pleasures and ways of growing, which we've been missing in modern western life.

It's one thing to grow into the modern western world and not be able to recognise the difference as the days or work repeat themselves, but it's another – it's a sin and it's a damn fucking shame – to realise it when life takes a pause and then blindly go back to the rush hour of modern life without any real changes. Fuck it, you need to take some stand for yourself and do that with love and the practice of kindness: smell the flowers, cuddle your partner, look up at the sky and remember – in mid 2020 it was free of vapour trails; look up at the sky and think, I'm going to take that trip overseas, but I'm going to make it a journey, a privilege, not my right to have a holiday. You won't need so much distance and distraction if you practise self-care and love and get involved in your community, and for Pete's sake, if you don't like your community, find one you do. Find your tribe and make it better for your presence and care and diligence.

I have more to say but, bar what I say in my final paragraph below, I would rather you read this contribution over a couple of times; a bit like watching a film more than once, you always notice something you didn't the first time. Take a look at decisions already made and see if you see things differently; look at someone kindly who you'd written off – if they remain an arsehole, at least you took another look. Stop being afraid to question, to relook, to reread, to rewatch, to talk to Angels, to forgive, to be strong, to kick someone out of your life who doesn't serve your wellbeing or safeguarding. Making tiny changes can sometimes require the most boldness in your heart and courage from your tummy.

It's not morbid to talk about death as something that is a part of our human lifecycle. I had a Near Death Experience some years ago from a car accident. From my experience, I got an overwhelming sense of the meaning of life as I began the departure mode, or got close to it; I clearly survived in human form, and yes, I did have an inkling, a feeling in the pit of my stomach that something was coming before the accident – like I really couldn't picture arriving at the intended destination during that journey. That foreseeing aside, I believe by divine intervention I survived, given the state of the vehicle I was driving and the impossibly small space left in the interior for my body to be wrapped up in. I tell you this, not because I like sharing the story – it fills me with true horror – but because that day I saw good and I saw evil, I saw death and I saw life, I saw theft and I saw immense kindness and bravery. Most importantly, I knew nothing mattered except that I could live the love I had in my life, i.e. love is the core of all that is good. 'Love' – look it up (to me our linguistic description of love is very good) and ask yourself if the various relationships in your life, including your own relationship with yourself, really have the hallmarks of love.

Finally, despite not relishing sharing this personal experience with the world, I had a chance to embrace love in my life, and I took it; and I failed many times; I made mistakes, I got side-tracked, I got confused. I experienced the extremes of life, the brief period of relative poverty, the need to get away from dangerous, unhealthy relationships; it was a real mixed bag, changing my path towards a kinder life, but I'm delighted I kept at my core that glimpse of how important love is. Please use your experience of COVID, this period of relative quiet, and make changes. Don't expect to be perfect but be steady and repeat acts of love and faith. Your world will be a better place and you will find it harder to ignore the natural world around you. I believe my Angels when I hear that this time is a chance; this time is a lesson that if you can suddenly be on lockdown from a virus, then a turbulent planet with drought, tornados, starvation and toxic air can lock you down too and rob your children of the gifts we currently experience in many parts of the world, like food security, clean air and order; the experience of a sick Earth really will be like the nightmare contemplated by some religious scriptures. Take this chance and make the changes.

We close our stories with an account from a dear friend and soul sister of mine, Karen Ward. Karen is a wise, gentle soul who worked with deaf people then moved to a hospice where she provided bereavement support for children and families. I will never forget the laughter we enjoyed during our two-year crystal course. We were often told off for giggling.

LIFE, DEATH AND BEYOND

Karen Ward

'This existence of ours is as transient as autumn clouds,
To watch the birth and death of beings is like looking at the
Movements of a dance.
A lifetime is like a flash of lightning in the sky,
Rushing by like a torrent down a steep mountain.'
Gautama Buddha

Life is precious. Throughout history, people have gone to extraordinary lengths to survive even the most horrendous situations. Equally, people have taken great risks to save the lives of others. We are currently living through a global pandemic. Many people have died around the world. Here in Britain there is considerable fear, not only for our own lives but also for the lives of those we love. Life has become uncertain in so many ways. There are significant changes affecting our day-to-day existence, with the potential loss of employment, financial security and freedom. Our children are unable to go to school, see grandparents or friends. People are adapting to survive. Others are risking their own lives to care and provide services. It's often at these times, when we're facing the possibility of our own death, or the death of someone we love, that we really focus on what's important in life.

I have over 20 years' experience of supporting bereaved people, both adults and children. I also had the privilege of working in a hospice for over 18 years as a palliative care social worker and bereavement lead. I have witnessed, on a daily basis, the importance of life and death and the question of what comes next. We are all just a ripple in the fabric of time, but it's *our* time that we are experiencing. We connect with each other not just in a physical way but with our minds, hearts and, I believe, our souls.

In considering 'life, death and beyond', I want to first explore my own life and some of the experiences that have influenced me and how I view life. I believe we are all shaped by our experiences, both worldly and spiritually, and by the many interactions we have with others we connect with throughout our lives. My experience of death and dying has had a huge impact on me and I've been honoured to provide support and walk alongside people at the end of their days. It has also been a privilege to support so many bereaved adults and children. They have all taught me so much about life and death, and have given me insight into the strength of the human spirit. It's important to raise awareness of death and grief because they are inextricably a part of all our lives. And what is beyond death is unknown. My exploration of 'beyond' is just that: an exploration. Everyone has the right to their own individual belief.

When asked to write a chapter for this book, my first thought was, am I psychic? I've considered myself to be intuitive, but psychic? So I googled the meaning and it gave the Oxford definition as:

'Relating to or denoting faculties or phenomena that are apparently inexplicable by natural laws especially involving telepathy. Greek: Psychikos meaning of the mind, mental and soul.'

Well, given that definition, I can safely consider myself to be psychic to some degree in view of my personal and professional experiences; yet reluctant, in as much as I've become more discerning as to whom I discuss my experiences and beliefs with, because sometimes you can just see that people think you're a little strange, even if they're too polite to say!

I have definitely thought about things and then they've happened. I think of people and they appear or contact me out of the blue. I've seen clairvoyants, who have given me messages I knew were true from people who have died. I have heard many inexplicable deathbed phenomena and the experiences shared with me by bereaved people.

One of my own personal experiences was around the death of my lovely dad. He was in hospital. He'd been told earlier that day he had cancer. I arrived at the hospital in the evening and my mom handed me a piece of paper with it written on. I was cross as I'd told the ward sister that Mom and Dad had difficulty hearing and that I should be present for any discussions. She apologised and said she was off the ward at the time. I spoke to Dad, reassuring him that it would be all right; it meant he could come home and we would get the hospice involved. Very suddenly, he became agitated and weak. I'll never forget the frightened look in his eyes.

A doctor eventually came and said he thought Dad was dying. By now he was unconscious. My brothers both came to the hospital but were too upset to stay. Mom and I sat by Dad's bedside, talking to him and holding his hand. In the early hours of the morning, we both fell asleep. I felt a tap on my shoulder and looked around, thinking it must be the nurse, but there was no one there. As I looked back at my dad, I saw a change come over his body, and his essence or soul seemed to leave him. I have no idea who tapped me on my shoulder. I now believe it was an Angel or maybe Dad, who made sure I was awake to witness his transition.

There are many twists and turns in life and often, when we look back, we can see defining moments, where we have either chosen a particular path or been presented with a situation that has made our choice for us. It is these moments of bliss and times of challenge that shape us into who we are, providing us with the opportunity to continually adapt and change. Life shapes us and we gather knowledge and experience along the way.

When I think about my own life and experiences, I can identify those magical and challenging moments that have shaped the person I am. Like many, I have had the moments of pure bliss, such as when my own two wonderful daughters were born and then being at the births of their daughters. There have also been times of difficulties and challenges that have tested me greatly. There are special people who come into our lives. Some stay forever and others seem to bring just what you need at the time and then leave. Reading a book, watching a film, talking to a friend can all change our thinking and enhance our awareness and sense of who we are as we develop our mind and soul.

Reflecting this journey that is my life, I've considered how my childhood has influenced the person I am today. I was a quiet, reserved child often given to imaginings and fears. I was very frightened of the dark and for years believed a monster lived in our loft. (We had a very small loft – it would have needed to be a very small monster!) Of course, I never told anyone this. I'm aware, from my years of supporting children before and after someone important to them dies, that children often have lots of worries that they never share with anyone. Sometimes it's because they're unsure how people will react; other times it's because they're concerned for others.

My brother told me when I was quite small, probably about four or five years of age, that I'd been adopted by Mom and Dad and I wasn't really their daughter. We laugh about it now but for all the years I thought this to be true, it had a profound effect on me. I was too frightened to ask my parents. My brother was just teasing me and quickly forgot what he'd said but it worried me for years. I think I was about eight when, for some reason, I saw my birth certificate. Phew! But even now, so many years later, I can remember that awful anxiety in the pit of my stomach. There is a saying, 'sticks and stones may break my bones, but words will never hurt me'. This is so untrue. Words are very powerful. They can cause terrible hurt but can also heal. I think this experience highlights too how important it is for us to feel securely connected to others.

I am the youngest child and only daughter with two older brothers. Our parents were very kind, loving people. They worked hard to give us the things we had. Our home was just an ordinary terraced house, made extraordinary by the loving attention given to it by my parents. My dad was always decorating, especially at Christmas. The smell of paint still brings back memories of Christmastime for me. Despite the earlier worry that I might be adopted, I always felt loved and cherished by my parents. I had a very happy childhood in many ways but, thinking back, I remember being anxious about so many things.

I think that I was a little odd as a child and quite serious. I had a strong sense of right and wrong and disliked conflict or injustice. I can recognise that, even as a child, I cared deeply for people and my ability to empathise was already well developed.

My belief in the power of the mind over the body started from quite a young age. When I was about 14 years old, I suffered from very painful menstruation.

I used to concentrate on the pain and then visualise it as a dark cloud, which I could then move to my toe and then out of my body. Although I could still feel some pain, it was more bearable. I have no idea where I got the notion to do this. I know for certain it would not have been suggested to me by my mom. It was many years later I shared that I did this, as I was worried I'd be considered strange.

I hadn't realised just how bad the pain had been back then, until I was in labour with my first child. Using a similar technique along with some yoga breathing, I managed the contractions quietly on my own. I expected the pain to get worse. After all, this was child birth! I didn't alert the staff and, because I appeared to just be lying quietly, the midwives didn't check on me. My first indication that I was ready to give birth was when I started to want to push and I nearly gave birth to her in the toilet!

Over the years, I've been amazed at the power of the mind over matter. At the hospice, we observed mothers who survived way past their prognosis because they didn't want to leave their children.

As a child, I attended Sunday School, Brownies, which was connected to our local church. If I stayed at my friend's house at the weekend, I would attend the Roman Catholic church with her. I found the Catholic priest rather scary. He talked of a vengeful God and said we were all sinners. Even in my own church, I quietly questioned in my head the point of all the pomp and ceremony. I didn't believe that I needed to go to church to talk to God, or that not going made me a bad person. It was very confusing in one sense, but in my simple, childish brain it was so clear to me. Even then, I felt I had a strong link to something. I didn't even necessarily call it God, but it was higher energy and power that responded in a benevolent way, full of love and understanding.

When I was in my twenties, I really questioned the whole God and Jesus story. I considered Jesus to be a good person but not necessarily sent from a greater power. It was around this time I found quite randomly, on the floor in my home, a small plastic crucifix. It was slightly mangled as if it had been trodden on and it had the body of Christ on it. I couldn't quite bring myself to put it in the bin despite disliking it intensely. However, it didn't matter where I put it, I kept finding it on the floor when I was cleaning. Eventually, I decided it was sent to make me revise my thinking on Jesus, and I still have it now.

Over the years, from reading, research and life experiences, I have come to believe that Jesus was sent from a higher power; an angelic Being sent to shine a light into the world and give meaning and purpose to our lives. I believe there have been others such as Gandhi and Mother Teresa. I think we all have a part to play in bringing light to the world, although this can feel too overwhelming when we witness so much injustice and violence. When faced with a mountain to climb, all we can do is move each little rock and do the best we can. Small acts of kindness can make a huge difference.

My experiences of working in a hospice and speaking to patients and their families, including children, have considerably enhanced my knowledge and experience of life, and my view of it. When talking with people who are facing their death, the subject of religious and other beliefs is often explored. I've been privileged to have very profound conversations with people as they try to find some meaning and purpose to their life and impending death.

I recall a long conversation with a Muslim gentleman. I was enquiring if he needed any assistance to ensure he could manage his religious observances. He took my hand and said, 'My dear, I have my heart and my God. That is all I need.' We talked at length about his religion and what it meant to him. Together, we reflected that most religions fundamentally provide messages that are very similar: to love each other, to be kind and care for those less fortunate, and to live a good life. He died peacefully the next day. I have never forgotten that conversation as it made me aware of the need not to make assumptions about people's beliefs based on their religion, but to always explore what is important to them.

A young man I'd been asked to support appeared very depressed, despondent and uncommunicative. I had tried a few times to talk to him, but he'd just nod or shake his head non-committedly. I was aware from his family that he had wanted to travel to Switzerland to end his life earlier in his illness. But his love for his family had prevented this. However, his death was now very near and he had emotionally shut down. I felt quite hopeless and helpless that I couldn't connect with him. So, before I went to see him one time, I asked for angelic assistance to say or do whatever would help him at this moment. Initially it was just the same, with him barely acknowledging me, but within five minutes I was amazed. He was talking to me! He shared many difficult and painful thoughts and feelings about his life, and his reflections about death and what comes after. Whilst he was talking to me, I looked down and, lying on the floor between us, was a beautiful white feather. Thank you, Angels!

Another life-changing experience for me was walking the Inca trail to Machu Picchu in Peru in 2005 with my daughter, Danielle. It was to raise money for the hospice where I worked and was in memory of my dad, who had died the year before. I hadn't really trained, so my fitness level was poor; I was overweight and one of the oldest in the group. To say it was a struggle is to put it mildly. My daughter said afterwards she'd worried she was going to come back an orphan.

There's a point on the trek where, if they don't think you're fit enough to complete it, they ask you to return to base camp. I was dreading this happening to me. I'd been the last one in the group all day. My daughter must have walked twice the distance required by repeatedly walking back to encourage me. There was a moment when I thought I couldn't go on. I was slumped over my walking sticks, breathing heavily. And I asked for angelic intervention to help me. My daughter recalls looking back at me at this moment. What she witnessed was me suddenly standing up straight. It was as if I'd been hauled up by some invisible force and it certainly felt that way. I started to walk with renewed energy. I'd asked for angelic intervention and it was given to me. On that day, I wasn't the last one into camp! I managed to complete the trek, despite a stomach bug and the nails of both big toes hanging off.

The final assent to the Sun Gate is achieved by scrambling on your hands and knees up a steep incline. Ouch! But it was worth every painful step to be gifted with a stunning view of Machu Picchu, with the sunshine streaming down and a magnificent blue sky above. Machu Picchu is a magical place and the energy is incredible. Surviving that trek and completing it despite everything gave me great confidence that I'm much stronger than I think and can do anything I set my mind to.

In Deepak Chopra's book, *Synchro Destiny,* there is an exercise where you ask yourself the question: 'Why am I here?' It's an interesting exercise as often we travel through life simply reacting and responding to demands and challenges. Considering this question gives an opportunity to identify what is important and give some structure to life. My own experience of this exercise was how many of my reasons were about helping others. I'm not sharing this to try to say how good I am. For me, it highlighted that, whilst I believe very strongly that it's important to care for others, I must recognise the need to live my life and care for myself as well.

One of the books that's been influential in both my personal and professional life is *Man's Search for Meaning* written by Viktor Frankl. He was a psychiatrist who was incarcerated in concentration camps during the Second World War. His story is one of survival in one the most hideous of situations. For me, three main messages come out from his reflections. Firstly, no matter our circumstances, we have a choice about how we think and behave. Frankl describes how, once inside the camp, they were stripped of everything, even their bodily hair. Everyone was equal in their misery and fear. Yet choices were made. There were those who turned to the wall and just let themselves die. There were some prisoners who became Capos and assisted the soldiers in punishing the other prisoners, and they were often crueller. There were soldiers who showed kindness. There were those prisoners who stole bread from others and those who gave their last piece of bread to someone they felt needed it more.

Secondly, he talks about incidents where destiny appeared to save him; just little twists of fate. He simply trusted his gut feeling or intuition. Or maybe he influenced it by his positive mindset and belief that he would survive.

Thirdly, we all need meaning and purpose in our lives. Frankl kept his belief that he would survive by using his time to observe camp behaviour, and visualised himself giving a lecture on his experience. Each of us needs meaning and purpose in our lives, particularly when trying to reconstruct our life after a loss.

'Man can reserve a vestige of spiritual freedom, of independence of mind, even in such terrible conditions of psychic and physical stress.' Frankl (2004)

We don't choose our family. However, I'm very fortunate to be able to say that I would choose all of mine, and I feel lucky to have them in my life. My family give me a sense of love and connection. There are also those special people who are called 'friends' but are as much part of my family as anyone. I've been blessed with some special friendships that have enriched my life greatly.

I want to mention one particular occasion, when an act of kindness from my friend caused a ripple effect. My partner had recently left me. I was in the final months of my Social Work qualification. I had no money, and no way of earning any as I was on my final placement. I had two children. My eldest was approaching her 18th birthday and had a part-time job and was buying food for us. I was so sad that I would be unable to give her the birthday celebration I knew she wanted. I couldn't even afford to buy her a gift.

One day, an envelope was pushed through my door with £50.00 in it. This was a lot of money at that time. I knew it was from my friend. It made such a difference. And she refused to let me pay her back. So, I passed it on to someone else who was in need. When they paid it back, I passed it to someone else. It has come to be known to me as magic money. It's these random acts of kindness that are like dropping a pebble in a pool, and the ripple keeps going and giving to others in need.

The Gentle Art of Blessing by Pierre Pradervand is another book that influenced and awakened me to the power of blessings. I had the honour of attending a weekend workshop he facilitated in 2010. Blessings and prayers have the potential to change so much. They're a simple but effective way of giving to others. Bless situations, bless people who challenge you, bless everyone you meet. This not only benefits those you are blessing, but you gain from it too. I've been blessing people and situations for many years now. One of the benefits of blessing is that you are giving without any expectation of reward, other than the lovely feeling you get from giving unconditionally.

'To bless means to wish, unconditionally and from the deepest chambers of your heart, unrestricted good for others and events.' Pradervand (2005)

I'm a member of a blessing circle that meets every four to six weeks. It's a beautiful group where we can share in sacred confidence our thoughts and feelings. Normally, there is a group meditation, then we share poems or extracts from books that have resonated with us. We then bless people in our lives; those we love and those who challenge us. Finally, we send healing and love in the form of a blessing to the Earth and all its inhabitants. I feel that meeting with like-minded people is vital when we talk about being psychic. The situation is improving and more people are now open to what they consider to be 'New Age' thinking, when it is in fact 'old age' thinking. But it can be lonely and easy to become disconnected from the energies if you don't have contact with like-minded souls.

My life, so far, has shaped me into the person I am today. I am reminded of the words of a wise 13-year-old, who I met through my work. She'd not had an easy life, made worse by the recent death of her beloved grandmother and her own chronic illness. I asked her, if she could change anything in her life, what would it be? She thought for a moment and then replied, 'Nothing.' I invited her to expand on this reply and she said, 'I am who I am because of all the things that have happened to me. And I like me!'

'The most beautiful people I've known are those that have known trials, have known struggles, have known loss, and have found their ways out of the depths. These persons have an appreciation, a sensitivity, and an understanding of life that fills them with compassion, gentleness and a deep loving concern.' Elisabeth Kubler Ross (1975)

Grief is such a little word for what is often described as the worst experience in life, causing great pain and upheaval. Grief can wrap you up in a dark cloud that makes seeing a future difficult and separates you from the rest of the world. The pain of grief is not just emotional and mental but affects you physically as well. Feelings of exhaustion, headaches, body aches and stomach pains are frequently experienced.

People are often shocked by their experience of grief and feel there must be something wrong with them. I believe this is partly because people rarely share with others how awful they're feeling when they're grieving and often, if people do enquire, they respond with, 'I am fine'. My experience of supporting people through grief is that, for some, the experience is so profound in the way it affects them that it's more akin to Post Traumatic Stress reaction.

Grief is a life-changer. You cannot go back to how you were before the experience. I liken it to a vase that's been thrown on the floor. The shattered bits can be fitted and glued back together but there are cracks and maybe some bits missing. Sometimes, however, the vase is improved by its reshaping. Having supported many adults and children over the years, I've also witnessed great positive changes that loss and grief can bring to life. For some, it can be a catalyst for significant changes and renewed focus on the future. Whilst it's not an experience you would want a child to have, when supported, children can grow through their grief and are more understanding of others who may be suffering in some way.

People who are grieving have psychic experiences, but are often reluctant to repeat them to others, fearful of the response they may receive. Grieving people have shared these experiences with me over the years and I'm often struck by how similar their experiences are. When sharing them with me in their support sessions, they often stated that they hadn't told anyone else.

The experiences are as follows: hearing the voice of the person who has died or seeing them. Electrical equipment breaking; lights coming on and going off unexpectedly; radios working that are not plugged in and without batteries. Clocks stopping or alarms going off at the time the person died. Songs being played on the radio or television or other places when talking about the person or on a particular anniversary. White feathers in places they would not be expected to be. Messages to prevent accidents in the form of butterflies or birds. Animals appearing to 'see' something or someone when nothing is visible.

It may be possible to prove that some of these experiences are connected to the workings of our minds to imagine and create. But the fact remains that some of these continue to be inexplicable.

Grief is individual and can be exacerbated by other factors. Health, financial security, support networks, loving relationships and environmental issues can affect how a bereaved person is able to survive their grief.

People facing death also grieve. They grieve for a future they can no longer have; many regrets and unfulfilled dreams they had planned for later in their life. We think there is always time, but the reality is we can never know when our life may change or end. Always follow your dreams; go to that place you've always wanted to visit; heal those relationships that have become estranged. Use each day wisely and with joy.

When I'm facilitating training in grief, many of the participants have an awareness of the stage theory of grief proposed by Dr Elisabeth Kubler Ross. Interestingly, this theory came from her work with dying patients as she tried to understand their emotional processes as they approached death. Her theory was highjacked and used by others to explain grief responses in bereaved people. In her later career, she became interested in research into Near Death

Experiences and trying to find out what happens after death. She had many psychic experiences in her life, and had no doubt from her research that there is an existence of life after death. The analogy of an emerging butterfly explains this very well. Elisabeth also states that we all have a Guardian Angel and that our loved ones wait for us.

'We are created for a very simple, beautiful and wonderful life. My greatest wish is that you will start looking at life differently.' Kubler Ross (2008)

Beyond Death

One of the fundamental mysteries of life is what comes after death. We know that our bodies cease to operate, but then what? Is there nothingness, or is there a heaven or wherever you believe we might go after death? Is there a form of life after death?

My dad didn't believe there was anything after death. We had many discussions about what happens after you die and he promised that, if he had 'a happy surprise' and went to heaven or some beautiful place when he died, he would get a message back to me. He had a dream a few days before he died that he was in a beautiful garden where he felt really happy, and he hadn't wanted to come back from it. About five months after Dad died, I saw a clairvoyant. She said Dad was there and he wanted to tell me he had had a 'happy surprise'.

There's a lovely book I have used in helping children understand the permanence of death when they ask why their loved one hasn't come back yet. It's called *Water Bugs and Dragonflies*, written by Doris Stickney (1982). It describes how a group of water bugs at the bottom of a pool observe other bugs sometimes climb up a reed at the side of the pond, but never come back. A small group of bugs make a pact that if it happens to one of them, they will come back and tell each other what happens next. One day, one of these bugs finds himself climbing up the reed. He comes out on top of the pond and settles on a lily pad and falls asleep. During this time, he is in a cocoon, until he metamorphoses into a dragonfly. At first, he is excited by his wonderful new wings, but then he remembers his promise.

He can see his friends at the bottom of the pond but, try as he might, he cannot now break through the water to get to them because of the changes in his body. This vision of death as a transition to another form of life is evident in other accounts that seek to explain life after death.

Elisabeth Kubler Ross gives an account of her visit to Majdanek concentration camp in Poland after the war, in her book, *The Wheel of Life*. She found that in the children's barracks, there were hundreds of pictures of butterflies carved into the walls. After many years of working with terminally ill people and studying death, she realised that those children knew they were going to die, and the butterfly represented the transition from life to death and beyond.

Maybe death is just that: a transition. We become something else. Water can be liquid, snow, ice, steam or a beautiful cloud in the sky, but it is the same element. Coincidently, human bodies are approximately 70 per cent water. Research by Masuru Emoto (2001) discovered that water is affected by emotions, words, music and other vibrations. Interestingly, water also makes up around 70 per cent of Earth. Perhaps, in our search for what is next, we are forgetting our connection to the rest of our planet and Universe.

When I studied Reiki and Crystal Therapy, I learnt to feel energies and channel them. At that time there was no proof and even some scepticism as to the validity of energy therapies. Now science has caught up and they can measure electromagnetic energies and changing brain patterns in meditators. Studies into the power of prayer and blessings have also demonstrated the connections we have with each other and the power of our intentions. There is a mystery as to certain energy and matter that exists on Earth and throughout the Universe. Scientists refer to it as Dark Matter and Dark Energy. The term 'dark' is used because it is unknown. Basically, scientists are unable to identify exactly what it is. What they do know is that Dark Energy is found in humans, all living things, everywhere on this planet and out into the Universe and the stars. The future is exciting; there is so much that is revealing itself to us and the possibilities are endless. Maybe the answer to what happens after death is not that far from being revealed to us.

When this pandemic is over, we will all be relieved but also grieving. Grieving for those people who have died; grieving for the changes that are inevitable. As with individual grief, we cannot as a planet return to the lives we had. Globally, nationally and individually there will be a paradigm shift that will give new meaning and purpose, both negative and positive, to all our lives.

Each one of us will be faced with a choice about how we manage these changes. As Frankl said, we can choose how we respond, how we survive and find a way to thrive in these challenging times.

Life is precious. We are just passing through this earthly existence. Fill your life with love. Stay connected to family, friends and others. Fill your life with laughter. Fill each day with making yourself happy and those around you happy too. Be kind. Question and challenge injustice. Make each day count. Death is not to be feared. Life is full of endings and beginnings, a multitude of transitions. Death is just another transition to the next phase of our eternal existence.

'We have stopped for a moment to encounter each other, to meet, to love, to share. This is a precious moment, but it is transient. It is a little parenthesis in eternity. If we share with caring, light heartedness and love, we will create abundance and joy for each other. And then this moment will have been worthwhile.'

Chopra (1996)

karen.wardcc2@gmail.com

Final Word

Dear reader,

It's time to say 'farewell'. We do hope these stories have inspired you and awakened you to your innate psychic gifts. Aren't the authors amazing? They have been so open and honest about their psychic journeys in order to comfort and reassure you.

If you are still unsure or you need some further help moving forward, follow us on our Facebook page www.facebook.com/Reluctantly-Psychic and/or visit the website www.reluctantlypsychic.co.uk where you will be given further inspirations and information about forthcoming events, courses and workshops.

If you would like your story to feature in our second book of *Reluctantly Psychic*, please email me at alison@reluctantlypsychic.com

Remember, dear reader, you are here at the time of the Great Awakening. It is time to shine your light like a beacon on the Earth and be the person you were meant to be; reach out to any of the authors that you resonate with and start your onward journey of being psychic and proud.

Bless you,

Alison Ward, concept creator of *Reluctantly Psychic,* author and visionary

Glossary

Ascension – the process of evolving as a human Being, moving from the denser 3D living to a higher frequency where you hold more love and release lower vibrational energies such as hate, jealousy, gossip etc. As you release more, you hold more light, love and truth. You move away from negative people, find your tribe and your soul purpose.

Awakening – a sudden or gradual event where you start to look at life differently and realise you are here to make a difference to the world by being you; fucking amazing YOU!

Chakra – the seven chakras are the main energy centres of the body. There have been a further five identified over the years as humans evolve.

Clairaudient – the ability to clearly hear. It may be guidance from your spirit guides, Angels or simply from hearing a conversation or piece of music, to give you clarity, guidance or even comfort from a deceased loved one letting you know 'all is well.'

Claircognizance (clear knowing) – when you simply 'know' something. You feel it as truth deep in your soul.

Clairsentience (clear feeling) – when you sense how someone is feeling. You may pick up their feelings, pain and be able to describe it clearly as if you are truly experiencing it.

Clairvoyant – the ability to clearly 'see' the future, maybe in a vision or a dream.

Crystal, Indigo, Rainbow, Starseed – all names given to people in a collective group, believed to be new souls born into this world, with no or very few past lives and with profound psychic abilities and a specific role in shifting the world into a new evolutionary way through love.

Empath – highly sensitive individuals who have a keen sense of people around them and what they are feeling and thinking. Empaths have deep empathy and often feel what a person is feeling.

HSP (Highly Sensitive Person) – this is described as a 'personality trait' in the dictionary but we contest this and state it's a natural born gift where HSPs and Empaths feel and sense things deeply.

Indigo – *see Crystal etc.*

Karuna Reiki – a powerful form of Reiki that will be conducted by a Karuna practitioner and taught by a Karuna Reiki Master/teacher – an ancient healing art rediscovered in Japan, this treatment harnesses the life force energy in us to aid healing. You can learn to self-heal from a Reiki Master teacher as well as helping to facilitate healing in others, animals and sending distant healing. There are many different forms of Reiki, Usui Reiki being the original.

Medium – someone who connects with deceased loves one and the spirit world and conveys messages to the living.

OBE – Out of Body Experience – to leave your body when you are in a deep sleep. A sensation of being outside one's own body, typically of floating and being able to observe oneself from a distance.

Psychic – having natural abilities as above. 'Faculties or phenomena that are apparently inexplicable by natural laws, especially involving telepathy or clairvoyance.'

Reiki Attunement – a sacred ceremony performed by a Reiki Master/teacher to attune the student with the Reiki symbols and therefore further enhance their psychic gifts, awareness, and ability to heal and self-heal. There follows a 21-day post-attunement cleansing, where the student is required to self-heal every day and continue the cleanse so their vibration evolves and increases with light and life force energy. This ancient art was practised by the Buddhist monks in the temples and that is where the sacred ceremony of attunements originates from.

Sirian Starchild – a Sirian Starchild or Starseed (see *Crystal etc.*) believes they originate from the star, Siria.

Soul Purpose – awakening to what you came to Earth to do. Before you came to live this life, your soul chose to learn certain lessons, then evolve as they were learnt and accepted. The soul's purpose is to discover its natural, innate gifts and share them with the world to make a difference. The soul is here to be creative in a human form and will feel free, alive and very happy when it is awakened to such gifts and purpose.

Source, The – described as the energy centre of existence. Imagine that your soul is like a lit candle. When we behave and live as ONE, in the ONENESS we join our candlelight to the great flame from Source. The Source is infinite and all accepting and loving.

Spirit Guide – a person who has lived on Earth and has now passed on but has a role to support and encourage you as you live your earthly life. You can connect with your spirit guides by meditation. They take the form of animal spirit guides too.

Starseed – *see Crystal* etc.